W9-BIS-685

An Archaeology of Manners

The Polite World of the Merchant Elite
of Colonial Massachusetts

CONTRIBUTIONS TO GLOBAL HISTORICAL ARCHAEOLOGY

Series Editor:
Charles E. Orser, Jr., *Illinois State University, Normal, Illinois*

A Continuation Order Plan is available for this series. A continuation order will bring delivery of each new volume immediately upon publication. Volumes are billed only upon actual shipment. For further information please contact the publisher.

An Archaeology of Manners

The Polite World of the Merchant Elite of Colonial Massachusetts

Lorinda B. R. Goodwin

Peabody Essex Museum
Salem, Massachusetts, and
Boston University
Boston, Massachusetts

Kluwer Academic/Plenum Publishers

New York, Boston, Dordrecht, London, Moscow

F
67
. G646
1999

ISBN: 0-306-46156-0

©1999 Kluwer Academic/Plenum Publishers
233 Spring Street, New York, N.Y. 10013

10 9 8 7 6 5 4 3 2 1

A C.I.P. record for this book is available from the Library of Congress

Printed in the United States of America

Dancing [women]. From F. Nivelon's *The Rudiments of Genteel Behavior* (1737). Courtesy, The Winterthur Library: Printed Book and Periodical Collection.

To James, who dares me ...

Foreword

A glance at the title of this book might well beg the question "What in heaven's name does archaeology have to do with manners? We cannot dig up manners or mannerly behavior—or can we?" One might also ask "Why is mannerly behavior important?" and "What can archaeology contribute to our understanding of the role of manners in the development of social relations and cultural identity in early America?"

English colonists in America and elsewhere sought to replicate English notions of gentility and social structure, but of necessity diverged from the English model. The first generation of elites in colonial America did not spring from the landed gentry of old England. Rather, they were self-made, newly rich, and newly possessed of land and other trappings of England's genteel classes. The result was a new model of gentry culture that overcame the contradiction between a value system in which gentility was conferred by birth, and the new values of bourgeois materialism and commercialism among the emerging colonial elites.

Manners played a critical role in the struggle for the cultural legitimacy of gentility; mannerly behavior—along with exhibition of refined taste in architecture, fashionable clothing, elegant furnishings, and literature—provided the means through which the new-sprung colonial elites defined themselves and validated their claims on power and prestige to accompany their newfound wealth.

In his book *The Complete Colonial Gentleman: Cultural Legitimacy in Plantation America* (University Press of Virginia, 1998), cultural historian Michal J. Rozbicki probes the determined quest for gentility by members of America's emerging planter elite. The colonials equated gentility with cultural legitimacy, the achievement of which Rozbicki saw as a "constant struggle, a dynamic that cuts across the network of cultural, political, and social relationships." Rozbicki's study is one of several recent works by historians that underscores the timeliness and importance of Lorinda Goodwin's work *An Archaeology of Manners: The Polite World of the Merchant Elite of Colonial Massachusetts*.

Goodwin's examination of mannerly behavior as part of New England merchants' struggle to attain cultural legitimacy has many parallels with Rozbicki's study of the plantation elites of the Chesapeake and the Caribbean. The cultural dynamic that arose from the quest for gentility fostered the development of a highly demarcated subculture among New England merchants, with its own rules for inclusion and exclusion, supported by a densely interrelated network of kinship. Goodwin takes a fresh look at the subculture of the New England merchant elite. She draws on social history and anthropology to establish the historical and cultural context for examining the transnational development of cultural identity among merchant elites in England, Europe, and British America, and scrutinizes evidence derived from material culture studies and historical archaeology to explore ways of reading artifacts as active elements in the pursuit of gentility by New England's nouveaux riches. Mannerly behavior involved not just the ephemeral media of speech and gesture, but was inscribed in symbolic ways through material culture, via artifacts that bespoke education, style, and taste—all important elements of gentility.

Goodwin utilizes manuals of etiquette and manners to demonstrate two important criteria of mannerly behavior. To be authentic and reputable, manners must be dictated by an authoritative source; for this reason it is no surprise that etiquette books and manuals of advice proliferated and enjoyed wide distribution and use during this period. At the same time, the dynamic of the pursuit of cultural legitimacy among elites requires that specific forms and props of mannerly behavior change just enough over time to ensure that manners continue to set elites apart from nonelites. Hence, as Goodwin demonstrates, mannerly behavior has a strong expression through material culture and is ripe for archaeological study. Indeed, an archaeology of manners is not only possible but essential; by recognizing the ways that material culture was mobilized as a symbolic medium through which to convey the appropriate values, taste, manners, and style that were part of the pursuit of gentility, historical archaeologists can make important contributions to our understanding of the formation of American culture and identity.

In her concluding chapter, Goodwin, quoting Miss Manners, makes the important point that "etiquette is the greatest friend of the powerless." For the merchants of colonial New England, mastery of manners paid dividends in cultural capital, a far from inconsequential form of power. In *An Archaeology of Manners*, Lorinda Goodwin demonstrates that the interdisciplinary field of historical archaeology offers a stimulating medium for exploring the ways that the merchant elite of New England—as citizens of British America—pursued cultural legitimacy by employing mannerly behavior and its material symbols to meld their wealth and power with the values of English gentry culture into a distinctively American ethos of gentility.

Mary C. Beaudry
Boston University
Boston, Massachusetts

Preface

The subject of the present study has its origins in a long-distance correspondence. While trying to decide how best to incorporate the data from my dissertation into a book, I described the Turner family as "the makers of manners" to Chuck Orser, who encouraged me to explore mannerly behavior. As I researched I found, as others have done, that manners provide a superlative opportunity to study a range of anthropological and historical archaeological topics, including the history of New England merchants, social behavior, material culture, period literature, and the changes that culture undergoes when it is moved from one place to another distant place.

As engaging as all those topics are, I soon found, to nobody's surprise, that I would need to focus very narrowly in order to keep the project from ballooning out of all compass. Even when part of a culture appears to be neatly packaged and prescribed, as it is in courtesy literature, it is subject to selective application in the past, and to any number of interpretations in the present. I focus on the way one aspect of life (mannerly behavior) was used by a small group (Massachusetts merchants) during one century (about 1660–1760), informed by my training in archaeology at Boston University and in American civilization at the University of Pennsylvania. The present work therefore synthesizes research from historical archaeology, social history, material culture, and anthropology. Perhaps by drawing from so many fields, I shall satisfy no one completely, but it is my hope that this work will encourage others to explore related disciplines further, stimulating collaboration between these fields, as well as between American and British scholars.

Because of the dual nature of manners, which are both the means by which hierarchies are reinforced, as well as the marker that distinguishes a virtuous individual regardless of birth, I also found that two key, interrelated ideas repeatedly surfaced in the course of this study. The first corresponded with my interest in studying the archaeological manifestations of personal identity. The roles one played as an individual, family member, and citizen might be carefully delineated as never before, even agreed upon by contemporary observers in print in the

early modern period, but the proof of the genuinely successful commun-
ciation of one's identity was to be found in the material pudding. Dress or
other possessions and novel or exotic artifacts confirmed or belied the
status that one claimed or to which one pretended; birth was no longer
the single concluding factor in determining social aspirations. It was
knowledge, first of one's own identity, second of one's place in society, and
finally, of appropriate material display, that was critical to maintaining
one's identity and successfully playing a particular role in society.

The other concept that appeared involved another sort of identity:
the way that communities, of different sorts and sizes, are formed and
maintained. The newly powerful merchant community generated controversy as well as commerce in the early modern period because of its
lack of easy identification within an antiquated hierarchy. Although the
social identity and relevance of the merchant and his family varied over
time, no one (including the merchants) seemed to have any trouble in
identifying them, or in precisely where they seemed to challenge accepted social norms. This was particularly clear in the British American
colonies, where merchants rose, in many instances, to social heights
that were not attainable in England. Within the changing shape of the
merchant class, there were certain consistent, approved values that also
were revered outside that community—it was the embrace of these that
helped to define the merchant class and to ease its assimilation and the
subtle redefinition of their roles in a wider society. Although group
identity was largely based on one's individual identity, once accepted
into a powerful group, that association frequently proved to be the more
powerful identity.

The final discovery that I made was one of the relevance of mannerly behavior in the past to present life, linked by issues of identification. In conversational discussions of my research, many people suggested connections with Jane Austen (several of her novels had been
made into films just as I started this work), Judith Martin (who writes
as "Miss Manners"), or Martha Stewart's advice on entertaining. Certainly communication, etiquette, and celebrative display are all elements in this work, but I believe the strongest connection between
mannerly behavior in the past and in the present can be seen in the
"civility movement" that is slowly gaining currency in the United States,
which in my opinion is significantly involved with the reconciliation of
individual and group identity with that of the wider community. Throughout history, the value of manners has been rediscovered periodically,
when the restraint of personal passions and egos was necessary for the
good of a changing society. The Turners and their associates were as

beneficent or greedy, as stupid or clever, as other people in the past or since; the practice of mannerly behavior did not automatically cure their social shortcomings. What participation in civil life did (and does) allow is communication between individuals that might not otherwise be possible, something that never goes out of style.

Acknowledgments

One of the very great pleasures of research is the exchanges with other scholars and other interested individuals. Sometimes these can take place over many years of acquaintance; sometimes a chance meeting can uncover a wealth of ideas and resources. To all those who helped me on this journey, my most profound thanks (and my sincere apologies to anyone I inadvertently forgot to thank individually below).

The Peabody Essex Museum has helped support my work since I started research on my dissertation. My thanks to Frederick H. West, Jeffrey P. Brain, and John Grimes; Dean Lahikainen, Paula B. Richter, and Joan Whitlow; William R. Sargent and Eric Wolkin; William T. La Moy, MaryAnn T. Campbell, Kathy M. Flynn, John Koza, Nicole Rioles, and Jane E. Ward; and Daniel R. Finamore and Lyle Forbes. Jeff Brain's editorial advice has been of particular help to me and I am especially grateful for the excellent (and exacting) work of the Photography Department—Mark Sexton, Jeffrey R. Dykes, Jean R. Rees, and Kathy M. Flynn.

My colleagues in the Department of Archaeology at Boston University have always been supportive and I would like especially to thank Mary C. Beaudry for her advice, guidance, and generosity in sharing her unpublished research on the Tracys of Newbury.

I undertook a significant part of this work with the generous support of a Winterthur Research Fellowship at the Henry Francis du Pont Winterthur Museum, Gardens, and Library. My very great thanks to Gary Kulik and to Neville Thompson, who directed me to many of the treasures in the library. Thanks also to Pat Elliott for her unstinting assistance. I am also immensely obliged to the staff of the Maritime Archives and Library at the National Museums & Galleries on Merseyside. Tony Tibbles and Dawn Littler graciously gave me access to (and permission to copy) the Earle-Denham letters during a busy stay in Liverpool.

The staff at the House of the Seven Gables Historic Site in Salem allowed me to begin my explorations by conducting excavations at the Turner house. Thanks to David Goss and to the present Director of Education and Public Programming, David Olson. I would be remiss if I did not thank again the crew who helped me excavate at the Turner house in 1991: Christy Vogt Dolan; Linda Ammons; Monique Bussell; Patty Craig; Jean, Amy, and Andrew Dabbs; James Goodwin; Beth Krueger; Nancy Ortins; Joyce Rodenhiser; Jason Strepzek; Carolyn White; and John Worrell. Similarly, I thank my dissertation readers: Karin Calvert, Henry M. Miller, and Robert Schuyler.

My thanks to Richard Bushman, Abbott Lowell Cummings, and John Styles for their advice and encouragement, and to Cary Carson who kindly allowed me to use his excellent drawings of the Turner house. Two fellow Penn alumni, Lu Ann De Cunzo of the University of Delaware and Shirley Wajda of Kent State, also shared their expertise and enthusiasm.

I would like to thank Charles E. Orser of Illinois State University, Normal, for his support of this project, and Eliot Werner of Kluwer Academic/Plenum Publishers for his patience and good advice. I could not have undertaken this work without the unstinting help of readers whose helpful criticism and encouragement gave me the confidence to keep writing. My deepest gratitude to Mary Beaudry, James Goodwin, Edward L. Bell (of the Massachusetts Historical Commission), Lu Ann De Cunzo, Dan Finamore, Ruth Greene (of Boston University), and Silas D. Hurry (of Historic St. Mary's City). Any errors are, of course, my own.

My family, especially my parents Joyce and Al Rodenhiser, and friends (especially Beth Krueger and Jessika Bella Mura) gave me all the support I could have asked for and I thank them for it. Katie and Increase once again attempted to refile my notes according to feline notions of orderliness and I appreciate their disinterested affection.

My husband, James Goodwin, is the best thing since sliced bread. In addition to doing more than his share of the domestic maintenance (again), he dug, read, criticized, and handled an unprecedented number of computer-related crises. Asking the very best questions, he also sustained me in every way imaginable. My love, respect, and appreciation to him most of all.

Contents

Introduction

The Polite World of the Merchant Elite of Colonial Massachusetts

There will be a connection with the long past—a reference to forgotten events and personages, and to manners, feelings, and opinions, almost or wholly obsolete—which, if adequately translated to the reader, would serve to illustrate how much of old material goes to make up the freshest novelty of human life. Hence, too, might be drawn a weighty lesson from the little-regarded truth that the act of the passing generation is the germ which may and must produce good or evil fruit in a far-distant time.
—*Nathaniel Hawthorne, The House of the Seven Gables*

Traveling from Boston to New York in 1704, Madam Sarah Kemble Knight recorded her acute observations of the people she met on her journey. Perhaps it was because she was well educated (she had been a teacher and also was familiar with handling court records), or maybe it was because she kept a shop and was the wife of an American factor for a London merchant, or it simply may have been native curiosity, but she paid close attention to the interactions of those she met, particularly in relation to their material world. Her entry written in New Haven, Connecticut, on October 7 is evidence of this. She watched with discernment as a tobacco-chewing farmer entered the shop of a local merchant, and, somewhat timorously, waited:

He advanc't to the middle of the Room, makes an Awkward Nodd, and spitting a Large deal of Aromatick Tincture, he gave a scrape with his shovel like shoo, leaving a small shovel full of dirt on the florr, made a full stop, Hugging his own pretty Body with his hands under his arms, [he] Stood staring rown'd him, like a Catt let out of a Baskett. At last, like the creature Balaam Rode on, he opened his mouth and said: have You any Ribinen for Hatbands to sell I pray? The Questions and Answers about the pay being past, the Ribin is bro't and opened. Bumpkin Simpers, cryes its confounded Gay I vow; and beckoning to the door, in comes Jone Tawdry, dropping about 50 Curtsees, and stands by him: hee shows her the Ribin. *Law You*, sais shee, *its right Gent ... tis dreadfull pretty.* Then she enquires, *have You any hood silk I pray?* wch being brought and bought, Have You *any thred silk to sew it wth* says shee, wch being accomodated wth they Departed. They [country folk] Generaly stand after they come in a great while speachless, and sometimes dont say a

word till they are askt what they want, which I Impute to the Awe they stand
in of the merchants, who they are constantly almost Indebted too; and must
take what they bring without Liberty to choose for themselves; but they
serve them as well, making the merchants stay long enough for their pay.
(Knight 1970: 42–44)

In this book, I will examine courtesy literature to understand better
the relationship between manners, material culture, and social institutions in the merchant community of seventeenth- and eighteenth-
century Massachusetts. Their use of mannerly behavior allowed the
merchant elite to form a recognizable and powerful social identity, with
flexible mechanisms for inclusion and exclusion, which was manifested
through different gender roles and the use of material culture in ritualized social occasions. The manners that informed this conduct had a
long and lively line of descent. Derived from elite British practices that
were appropriated from the courtly literature of the continental Renaissance, these British-American manners were again adapted to serve
the new intellectual, physical, and commercial environment of the
New England provinces. But even through transoceanic transport
and cultural filtration, this polite behavior retained a recognizable core
of polished values—nonchalance, graciousness, honesty, and modest
restraint—that were as valued by the New England merchants as they
were by sixteenth-century Italian courtiers.

Social change promotes the use of manners both to reinforce existing social structures and to accommodate new additions to them. The
role of merchants in early modern England was the subject of heated
debate. Since merchants' arrival to prominence on the social scene with
the advent of capitalism, they traditionally were accused of having more
money and political interest than was generally considered safe for
those who were not born to the landed elite. That social flux provided the
medium necessary for a renewed interest in mannerly behavior on both
sides of the Atlantic. By selecting elements from the existing universe of
polite conduct, New England merchants were able to appropriate the
aspect of the English landed elite, to establish their own social and civic
authority, and to form a formidable social entity. To maintain their
positions in a rapidly evolving society, these merchants integrated the
costly and exotic goods that they imported into their interpretation of
Renaissance European traditions of courtesy.

Madam Knight's journal entry rather succinctly (and conveniently)
includes many of the elements that I discuss in this book. There is the
shadowy image of the merchant, who, although only seen peripherally,
controls this situation, the buyer's desire for the goods the merchant

sells, and the economic (and social) peril that supposedly threatened those who eagerly sought these new goods. Although she draws a rather severe picture of "Bumpkin Simpers" and "Jone Tawdry" (her choice of appellations is very informative), Madam Knight notes, however, that although mixed with awe, there is a balance of power existing between the customer and the merchant. The merchant has social stature and access to the desired manufactured goods, but the country fellow has the means to purchase the goods, whether in the form of "pay" (commodities), "mony" (cash money), or "trusting" (credit). The overstated courtesy of "Jone" and the reticence and lack of confidence showed by "Bumpkin" were at contemporary, conventional odds with the couple's desire for (and, more importantly, their ability to purchase) silk and manufactured notions, goods that were once the best indicator of polite, elite society.

Madam Knight's later observation about the distinction between city and country life also suggests what importance cities had in polite training: "We may Observe here the great necessity and bennifitt both of Education and Conversation; for these people have as Large a portion of mother witt, and sometimes a Larger, than those who have bin brought up in Cities; But for want of emprovements, Render themselves almost Ridculos, as above" (Knight 1970: 44). Even her deprecatory statement about their lack of tutelage and, therefore, lack of polish, is telling: she espouses the rather revolutionary idea that education, rather than family descent, can confer gentility. Personal improvement, in tandem with the improvement of the home and community, was the hallmark of the gentleman in the early modern period.

But these early British Americans—the crudest of hicks from the provincial sticks—*were* already aware of polite behavior and had a rudimentary idea of manners. Their language, especially the use of *I pray,* reflects a distant kinship to courtly speech. Although "Bumpkin Simpers" lacks that *je ne sais quoi*, the perfect nonchalance and restraint of body and character that characterized the most polished of mannerly behavior, he carefully covered his spit with his foot, something recommended by courtesy writers even before the influential Erasmus did in 1530. And although she does so too enthusiastically, "Jone Tawdry" knows it is polite to curtsy and deems the ribbon "right Gent."

If we were to observe "Jone" distantly, on the arm of her beau "Bumpkin," brave in her newly trimmed silk hood, there would be little to distinguish them from some other middling English consumers— save for their manners. And polite behavior *was* carefully observed and criticized; it had to be to succeed. The power of social sanction, seen in frequent comments on impoliteness in journals and diaries, is a clear indication of how important manners were to social life. This should inform how we approach other aspects of material life or power structures in the past.

HISTORICAL ARCHAEOLOGY, MERCHANTS, AND MANNERS

No one has ever excavated a curtsy. No field archaeologist has recovered and catalogued a wine health toast, a proposal of marriage, or a gracious nod of recognition in church. Yet all of these activities have their material components, and archaeologists have written extensively about these through research on consumer behavior, dominance, public display, and elite allegiance-building, to name just a few. These recent studies emphasize the ways in which historical archaeology can demonstrate the cultural meanings of portable material culture and architecture; both types of artifacts embodied forms of nonverbal communication and were also used as props and stage settings for expressions of mannerly behavior.

The present work is derived from my dissertation research on the excavations at the Turner house in Salem, Massachusetts. Although the house is more frequently associated with Nathaniel Hawthorne (the house is better known as his "House of the Seven Gables"), it was constructed in 1668 by Captain John and Elizabeth Turner, the first of three generations of the Turner family to live there. In addition to being extremely wealthy merchants in the Atlantic trade, the Turners were also very active in Salem politics and social life.

In the course of my research on the Turners, I encountered frequent references to the second John Turner, Colonel Turner, treating political cronies and friends to food and drink at ordinaries and at his home. Most of these friends were related to him (and each other) by marriage; all were connected with trade in some significant way, most went to the same church, most were also in the militia together, sat on the bench together, and undertook public improvements together. I have also incorporated documentary data from the Mascarene family of Cambridge and Salem, and the Earles, a Liverpudlian merchant family living in Italy, to add other perspectives to this research (Figure 1).

At first, manners might seem an unusual avenue by which to approach the archaeological record. After all, one cannot actually observe a courteous gesture in the stratigraphic record, any more than one

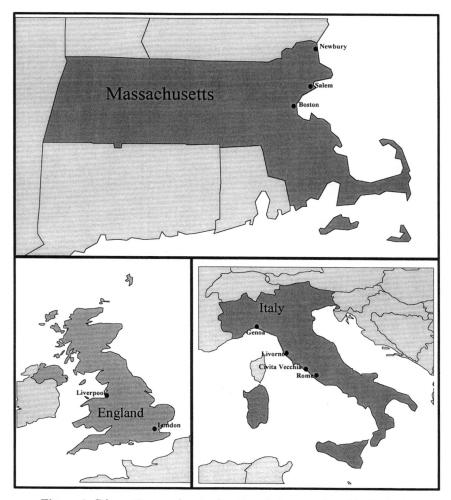

Figure 1. Schematic map showing location of sites mentioned in the text.

would find a "please" or "thank-you" in the bottom of one's sifting screen. A historical archaeologist, however, may read about such interactions and the proper study of artifacts necessarily incorporates the contemporary knowledge of the full range of their uses, both practical and symbolic. We find the material remains of polite ritual events while working on sites that were also settings for some of these displays or interactions.

In discussing the 1991 Winterthur Conference on Historical Archaeology and the Study of American Culture, Mary C. Beaudry posed the question, "Does use of artifacts and material culture to construct context or to elucidate the archaeological record mean that you are doing something other than archaeology? Is archaeology only dirt, only excavation?" In her essay, "Reinventing Historical Archaeology," she proposes that:

> Our goal is to study culture, American culture writ large, the culture of slaves and free blacks, of immigrants and working people, of colonial elites and industrial capitalists. Archaeology is an approach to this study, and we all know that an archaeological approach can be applied as readily to documents, landscapes, and aboveground material culture as it can to things buried in the ground. (Beaudry 1995: 480).

Historical archaeology is not limited solely to the study of written records or excavated material culture but has the whole of culture as its purview, and the study of mannerly behavior, starting with artifacts and documents, is but one viable approach to this.

The methods of historical archaeology can, in fact, be tremendously useful in the study of manners. Historical archaeology provides the tools to examine both the documentary data and the material data within an anthropological framework. Letters and diaries, contemporary fiction and prescriptive literature, probate inventories, and paintings or other illustrations are just a few of these documents. In terms of material culture, there are the archaeologically recovered data, such as small finds, as well as the domestic and landscape architecture to inform the researcher. Another particular benefit in examining this through archaeological research is the differing scales at which one can address the issue of manners, revealing much about the individuals involved, the regional or even national differences, or the elements of a philosophical framework.

Historical archaeology is also a way to look beyond the explicit statements of etiquette books and diary accounts to the underlying actions that actually took place in the community theater. Historian Richard Bushman noted that "courtesy books remain the essential guides to the principles of genteel behavior in the eighteenth century because they codified the ideals of polite society" (1993: 38). By examining what was not meant to be seen (archaeologically deposited artifacts) and the materials that were inherently, explicitly a formal part of the display of mannerly behavior (curated artifacts, architecture, and landscape), historical archaeology also has the potential to integrate these apparently disparate realms into a whole context.

THEORETICAL ORIENTATION

My approach to this book is shaped by several sources. These influences are not all rooted in archaeological research, but all are anthropologically informed. It was virtually impossible for me to visualize this work in any but dramaturgical terms. The structure of the following chapters should suggest the ideas of premise, character motivation, props (including costume and settings), scripts, and roles.

While I find the use of dramaturgy a useful way to discuss formal (or formalized) behavior in the past, particularly with respect to the more public displays and interactions, I am cautious in employing the terms *prop*, *script*, *costume*, or *setting* in any more than a passing sense. These words are tidy but deceptive descriptors, ultimately robbing the objects of the personal investment of meaning with which its owner or user imbues them. I use them occasionally strictly because I am looking at the most public, most general meaning of each of the artifact categories, in relation to the merchant class. A prop is taken up in a play as a blatant symbol (perhaps of many things), whereas an artifact may be used as a symbol, but also has more subtle, personal meanings for the individual employing it. Personal choice, no matter how rationalized, reflects unknown ideals that may have nothing to do with overtly stated principles, and I do not pretend to have uncovered all of them. Hence, the carefully considered title of this book; mine is just one way to approach this topic.

With this in mind, it will come as no surprise that much of my inspiration for this work has come from other studies that incorporate the metaphor of theater. Rhys Isaac's (1982) excellent work on elite life in colonial Virginia, Peter Borsay's (1984 and 1989) studies of public, urban rituals, and Pierre Bourdieu's (1996) examination of taste and social distinction have contributed to my approach here. Recent research on manners also has strong connections with dramaturgy. Richard Bushman (1993) occasionally employs the metaphor, while Christina Hemphill (1988) has explicitly used the idea in describing face-to-face encounters and embodied behavior. Joan Wildeblood and Peter Brinson's (1965) book was written specifically to inform stage actors about the deportment and social and physical context, including portable material culture, costume, architecture, and landscape, of the characters they might play.

Much of my approach was inspired by Erving Goffman's work examining the sociology of social behavior, especially *The Presentation of Self in Everyday Life* (1959) and *Behavior in Public Places* (1963). These studies are particularly significant because Goffman directly explores the role of etiquette in Anglo-American society. While it initially might seem that his observations of middle-class American society in the 1950s do not have any direct bearing on elite merchant life in the seventeenth and eighteenth centuries, Goffman particularly examines etiquette, the roots of which can be traced at least as far back as the English settlement of this country. The unspoken, culturally accepted contracts involved in social engagement, its regulation, and the dangers of unwanted social obligation or embarrassment are as clearly visible in a crowded elevator as in an eighteenth-century counting house on Salem harbor.

Understanding the expression of text and subtext, both in verbal conversation or through the deployment of props (such as clothing, entertaining, or architecture), is similarly in large part the goal of the present work. Goffman wrote:

> When an individual enters the presence of others, they commonly seek to acquire information about him or to bring into play information about him already possessed. They will be interested in his general socio-economic status, his conception of self, his attitude toward them, his competence, his trustworthiness, etc.... Information about the individual helps to define the situation, enabling others to know in advance what he will expect of them and what they may expect of him. Informed in these ways, the others will know how best to act in order to call forth a desired response from him. (1959: 1)

Over and over in the letters and diaries I examined, the writer described what he or she did and why. There is a palpable anxiety over appearance—even the justification of actions taken—on the written page. These are the dangers described by Goffman; the broken rules of engagement, inappropriate conduct, and denial of subsequent engagement for failing to adhere to the mutually agreed upon script of social intercourse all conspire to undermine the individual's intentions and aspirations.

SCOPE OF THIS BOOK

While other works have studied either merchants *or* manners in depth, this book is focused principally on the social realm of the merchant community, how it was created, expressed, sustained, and reproduced through mannerly behavior. Although this is a very narrow aspect of the intersection of several wider topics, it is nonetheless complex and diverse.

In recent years work in history and historical archaeology that has focused on merchants has informed my work on the relationship between merchants and manners. Archaeological work by Mary C. Beaudry (1995; n.d.), Lu Ann De Cunzo (1995a), and Paul Shackel (1993), historical research on merchants by David Hancock (1995), and the research on manners and material culture by Richard Bushman (1993) have all contributed to my thinking and the directions of this book.

I have used the presence of material culture carefully, trying to make connections when supported by primary sources that state preference, action, or intent. Rather than focusing on the more personal expressions of meaning of artifacts, I have addressed the most public expressions of polite behavior and issues of group identity. Starting with the base of my own archaeological data on the Turners and their contemporaries in Salem and elsewhere in Massachusetts, I have added the documentary data from the Mascarene and Earle families for comparative purposes and supportive evidence. I have used data from sites associated with merchants (especially those excavated by Beaudry and De Cunzo) and other related archaeological data. To these, I have added secondary historical research on merchants or on mannerly behavior.

I synthesize many of the connections between what I perceive in the documentary and archaeological evidence and what exists in contemporary prescriptive literature. Besides those media, I have drawn information from plays, novels, and other period fiction. Novels like *Clarissa* or *Pamela* or *Roxana* are just as useful as the prescriptive literature when they show the consequences of breaking the social code, which was recognized by readers. Characters like those in *Tom Jones* or *Joseph Andrews* betray their social status, their pretensions, and their good or bad intentions through their actions in social situations. Social commentary, letters, newspapers, and journals, both from American and British sources, have also been very helpful. Illustrative art work has also informed my perspective, combining the material world of the setting with the social expression of behavior.

The time period for this study is roughly from 1660 to 1760, a date range that is significant for several reasons. In terms of the history of manners, this century is significant because at this time manners had made the complete shift away from the mentality of the Renaissance courts and was being expressed in terms of *polite* rather than *courtly* behavior, but had not yet made the transition to the more rigidly codified *etiquette*, which emerged at the end of the eighteenth century.

In England, despite a number of wars with the Netherlands and France as well as internal rebellions, this period was considered a remarkably peaceful one. From the Restoration of Charles II in 1660 and through the accession of George III in 1760, London still held sway in taste-making, but provincial capitals like York and Bristol were also starting to flourish, and Bath gained favor as a fashionable spa resort. The emergence of the novel brought to the fore writers like Richardson, Fielding, Defoe, and Swift and papers like *The Tatler* and, later, *The Spectator* became sources of information and opinion in coffeehouses and in homes.

It was a time of advances in many fields. Boyle had formulated his theory of gases in 1660, the same time that Pepys began his diary. Christopher Wren designed St. Paul's Cathedral in 1670, and Hogarth painted *A Harlot's Progress* about 1731, Johnson's *Dictionary* was published in 1755, and Wedgwood built his first factory by 1759.

Almost 50 years after settlement by Roger Conant in 1626, Salem was one of the communities affected by King Philip's war, followed by the witchcraft trials in 1692 and the Great Awakening between 1720 and 1750. Elsewhere in Massachusetts, the paintings of the Freake family were executed in 1674. Cotton Mather published his *Magnalia Christi Americana* in 1702 and Samuel Sewall wrote his diary between 1674 and 1729.

This period also reflects the time during which the Turner family held sway in Salem, an era of increasing influence and power of British-American merchants in the Atlantic trade, but is concluded before the emergence of those merchants in the Pacific trade in the late eighteenth and early nineteenth centuries. Social mobility in the Massachusetts merchant community had decreased considerably by that time and merchant power was fully consolidated. The role merchants played in social as well as commercial spheres was being debated in England and America at this time and was tied to debates of class (particularly in the redefinition of the "gentleman"), luxury, and morality.

SUMMARY OF CHAPTERS

I begin in Chapter 2 with a brief overview of the history of manners and how they were transformed at certain points of history to survive social change through the preservation of old ideas and the integration of new ones. Mannerly behavior was codified in the *courtly* literature of Renaissance in the sixteenth century, rearticulated in the early modern period as *polite* or *civil behavior*, and, later, stripped of its moral content and reformulated to deal exclusively with social situations as *etiquette* at the end of the eighteenth century.

Even as the English adopted and adapted courtesy literature from the Italians and French, so did British-Americans create their own idea of mannerly behavior. The exclusive connection between high status and polite conduct persisted but was diminished, and had profound ramifications for the merchant elite who emerged in seventeenth- and eighteenth-century Massachusetts.

In Chapter 3 I delineate what characterized the ruling elite in England and Massachusetts based on emic and etic terms and show how the Massachusetts merchants manipulated those ideas in order to consolidate their place in power. At the same time that merchants were making vast fortunes and challenging what was essentially a medieval class structure, the notion of the "gentleman" was undergoing significant restatement and moving away from the old, restrictive notion of land and title to an emphasis on deportment or manner. I believe that the two developments were integrally linked and that the merchant elite in Massachusetts incorporated both the new ideas of the importance of behavior and the old icons of high social station to "historicize" their place in leading colonial communities. The relationship between merchants and their communities is a particularly important one, because at the same time that mercantile capitalism was reshaping and enlarging provincial capitals in England, the urban "renaissance" was concentrating taste and consumers in a ready-made market audience for goods and manners. Merchants in England and America physically shaped their urban environments as they themselves benefited from this new urbane life.

I introduce the families who provided the principal background for this study: the Turner family of Salem, Massachusetts; the Mascarene family of Cambridge (Massachusetts) and Salem; and the Earle family, an English merchant family who occasionally lived and conducted business in Italy. The data on the Turner family are a result of my own archaeological exploration of their home, constructed by Captain John Turner in 1668 and eventually sold by his grandson, the Honorable John Turner, Esquire, in 1782. The letters written by John Mascarene to his wife Margaret Holyoke Mascarene between 1761 and 1764 describe a colonial merchant's life in London during an exceptionally vibrant time in that city's history. The Earles of Liverpool were a successful merchant family who established trading houses in Livorno (Leghorn), Genoa, and Civita Vecchia. A series of letters exchanged by Mary Earle and her husband's business associate Joseph Denham between 1763 and 1781 reflect the social mores in the English expatriate community as well as the relationship between men and women in merchant life.

In Chapter 4 I examine some of the connections between material culture, social status, and identity. As both the consumers of newly available manufactured goods as well as the agents in providing these things to the general public, merchants were at the center of controversy about the relationship between material goods and morality. After examining some of the recent discussions on the study of historical consumption, I describe how items of clothing, foodways, and architecture and landscape were consciously used to shape and express cultural (oftentimes, polite) ideals. In some cases, artifacts literally shaped or embodied qualities like "luxury," "novelty," and "patina" at the same time that they were valued for their ability to provide a means of display *and* restraint. Connections between elite social rituals (both private and public) and their mercantile business were found in the home, which was used both as a place to conduct business and a genteel setting for subtle, inclusive, and exclusive rituals of polite behavior.

In Chapter 5 I demonstrate how women, often barred from working outside the home, both produced and reproduced elite merchant life. Courtesy literature provides an intriguing paradox, underscoring the difference between the expectations that the writers (frequently male) had for women's physical and mental capacities while expressing what they feared women were capable of. These proscriptions were expressed in legal form and, locally, in informal community regulations.

Although there were women who participated in the mechanics of mercantile trade in limited ways, more frequently the work that women were legally (or socially) permitted to do was significantly circumscribed. I argue, however, that in addition to contributing to the family business as "deputy husbands," women also acted as "social gatekeepers" and as "informal advocates," active conduits in transmitting information through informal channels for business deals (similar to Goffman's notion of a "bridging device" [1963: 126]).

Intimate teas and private dinners at which both sexes were present were used to cement alliances through marriage, and these alliances were, in turn, crucial in the negotiation of business and political alliances in Salem and elsewhere. Similarly, there were exclusively male ritualized gatherings that were enacted by the merchant class as well as the larger community to reinforce ties as well as social boundaries between groups. The prescribed roles and scripted situations provided a chance to observe the formal social qualities of the actors, for entrance into or exclusion from the elite group, as well as opportunities to consolidate existing bonds through marriage and further business connections.

In Chapter 6 I discuss how manners were used, not only by the merchant class in Massachusetts and England, but also how they serve generally as cultural boundaries at which negotiations of many sorts can take place. Manners are simultaneously barriers and bridges. As constraining as mannerly behavior was often described to be, participation in the carefully created and maintained polite world conferred tremendous power, even freedoms, on its successful practitioners.

Not only useful as social filters at the group level, manners also had significant ramifications for the individual. As seen in several instances in the three historical family groups represented in this book, individuals broke the social rules in some serious ways. Yet, because of their participation and acceptance by others of the elite, they were saved from outright expulsion from that group. Polite behavior bestowed immunities along with social power.

Mannerly behavior was used not only to exclude, that is, mark the rustic from the urbane and the untutored from the sophisticated, but also was employed as a bridge in times of social confusion. It is only half the story to look at the conservative, exclusionary side of polite behavior, that element that preserves old power hierarchies. At important historical moments, a gateway was opened for social commingling of a sort not previously permitted, and each time, manners were used to re-create a hierarchy that was similar to the old one, but refitted to accommodate new social changes. I believe that at the heart of mannerly behavior is communication: manners are best understood as an opportunity for agency and action. At the same time that the individual as a social construct was emerging, manners allowed the expression of individuality while preserving the means of communication between individuals and groups. The merchant elite of Salem and elsewhere understood this and exploited it successfully.

CONCLUSION

In the introduction to *Learning How to Behave: A Historical Study of American Etiquette Books*, Arthur Schlesinger wrote:

> The rise and progress of courtesy would, if for no other reason, merit interest as a sort of barometer of changing attitudes toward greater affairs, but it also deserves attention for its own sake as a functional trait of civilization. Manners, far from being apart from life, are veritably a part of life, revealing men's hopes, standards and strivings. (1968: vii)

Manners are reflective of more than superficially polite encounters, but even though the "standards" Schlesinger mentions are written down in the form of courtesy works, without live informants, it becomes difficult to understand how manners shaped a distinctly American merchant elite. These rules were flexibly applied and subject to cultural interpretations. The present work demonstrates this fact: although examining a very small area of a much larger, very complex picture, the cultural canvas was repainted many times. The same subject was used but approached from a slightly different perspective each time.

As Lawrence Klein put it: "At its most aggressively synthetic, the language of politeness sought to impose general order over large tracts of human experience, bringing its various referents into one interpretive scheme. The premises, criteria and standards of that scheme can be most easily grasped as expressions of an idealized vision of human intercourse" (1989: 587). In this way, mannerly behavior has provided a framework—an "idealized vision" or script, if you will—and merchants provided the cast, props, and settings. Like Madam Knight's pronouncements and observations, manners provides the opportunity to observe a group and place their lives and actions within a specific frame of reference.

History, Archaeology, and the Ideal World of Manners

*I should swear she had been bred in a court; for besides
her beauty, I never saw anything so genteel, so sensible, so
polite.*
—Henry Fielding, *Tom Jones*

*What accords with nature and reason is a ready guide to
decency; the taste of fools is not.*
—Desiderius Erasmus, *De civilitate morum puerilium*

INTRODUCTION

Sophia Western, the object of Lord Fellamar's praise in *Tom Jones*, has
qualities that were formerly associated only with court life, although
she herself was "bred" in the country. Like many of her nonfictional contemporaries in the eighteenth century, Sophia learned her becomingly
polite ways from her family (in her case, her well-trained, "citified" aunt)
and from novels rather than courtesy literature (Barker-Benfield 1992:
295). But mannerly works—like Erasmus's *De civilitate*—that crystal-
lized during the Renaissance and continued to permeate society in the
early modern period were certainly the most important form of courtesy
instruction, selected and edited to suit the current practitioners. Directly or indirectly, prescriptive literature had a wide influence that
created and continued to shape society, especially the growing middle
class.

This chapter focuses on the historical definition (and modern study)
of manners, particularly for the early modern period. Although what
might be described as the earliest work on manners was recorded in
Egypt more than 4,500 years ago (in *The Instructions of Ptahhotep*), and
comments on manners abound in classical Greek and Roman texts,
there is a specific core of courtesy books from the time of the Renaissance
that directly informed the manners that were practiced in England and
New England in the seventeenth and eighteenth centuries (Aresty 1970:
12). A summary and description of these guides is necessary to understand the importance of their transportation and adaptation to the
colonial Massachusetts setting.

Of course, many of the rules for polite behavior practiced by the colonists may not have been acquired directly from a treatise, but like Sophia Western, Massachusetts colonists "read" and learned from other media and the formal behavior of others around them. While the mannerly behavior that was designed specifically for court life was modified in degree for less exalted settings and selectively edited to suit the needs of different social situations, it is surprising how much of that courtly core survives intact, indeed, nearly verbatim, two or three centuries after the Renaissance. Even the spirit of morality that characterized the courtesy literature until the end of the eighteenth century, including the way that manners were supposed to be practiced, was retained.

"Changes in ideals of behaviour thus reflected, as always, a shift of economic power in society and the revolution in thought which that shift brought about" (Wildeblood and Brinson 1965: 33–34). Changes in manners appear when tremendous social changes, particularly political or economic, occur. In this respect, manners are an admirable cultural barometer, capable not only of marking the refinement, but also indicating the importance of civil behavior. It is possible to observe the effects of diachronic change through the study of their use. After the Renaissance, modern scholars have observed another increased interest in manners in the late seventeenth and early eighteenth centuries, which I attribute to the increasingly large middle class, the debated issue of rank, and the changing definition of a "gentleman."

In recent decades, historians, anthropologists, material culture scholars, and historical archaeologists have dealt specifically with manners in order to understand "the human side of the courtesy books" (Mason 1971: 298–299). It is within the context of these studies that I set this present work and establish the parameters of the polite world of the Massachusetts merchants. I begin with a brief overview of the Renaissance courtesy works and describe the relationship between them and the later, English and American treatises.

THE EVOLUTION OF COURTESY LITERATURE

Modern mannerly behavior stems from the need or desire to organize, ritualize, and heighten the experience of communal eating. Although it is now common to equate polite behavior with table manners, the historical reality was actually much more complicated. The transition of courtesy literature from its origins in court life before and during the Renaissance to the civility revolution of the early modern period to etiquette in the late eighteenth and nineteenth centuries is well documented.[1]

What has been called courtesy or conduct literature is a diverse genre. Prescriptions for good behavior can be found in contemporary social commentary, educational treatises, satire, novels and other fiction, and sermons as well as in mannerly works. Those works devoted to courtesy covered a wide range of topics, including religion, the nature and origin of nobility, public service professions, advice for princes and other heads of state, domestic duties, education and the care of children, travel, friendship, details of personal behavior minutely considered, and discussions of appropriate dress, conversation, and recreation (Mason 1971: 293–329).

John E. Mason divided courtesy literature into four groups in his survey work *Gentlefolk in the Making* (1971). *Parental advice* books are the oldest form that originated with kings writing advice for their heirs. One example of this would be Sir Walter Ralegh's *Instructions to His Son*. *Policy works* also deal with polite conduct, but with special emphasis on statecraft and public affairs, as in Lord Chesterfield's *Letters*.[2] *Polite conduct* treatises were general, more impersonal works on the logical theory of behavior and were particularly prevalent in the mid-seventeenth century. By the eighteenth century, these works became entirely moral and didactic. This form included Erasmus's *De civilitate*, Baldesar Castiglione's *The Book of the Courtier* (*Il Cortegiano*), Giovanni della Casa's *Il Galateo*, and Peacham's *The Compleat Gentleman*. *Civility* texts were books of maxims including more general discussions,

---

[1]This work does not pretend to be a definitive study of the history of manners. Several excellent surveys have been written and should be the starting point for anyone who is interested in the topic. These include Aresty (1970), Benson (1935), Carson (1966), Hemphill (1988), Mason (1971), Schlesinger (1968), and Wildeblood and Brinson (1965). Readers who are interested in the American world of polite behavior in relation to material culture should not overlook the concise summary in Bushman (1993).

[2]A brief word on Chesterfield. Philip Dormer Stanhope (1694–1773), 4th Earl of Chesterfield, wrote his *Letters* to his illegitimate son Stanhope between 1737 and 1768. Although it was never originally intended, the *Letters* were published a year after Chesterfield's death. I use his writings here to describe one contemporary view of manners, as they were not used as prescriptive work until after 1774. The *Letters* were heavily edited for the American audience who reacted strongly to what they perceived as his lack of morality: Abigail Adams, although forbidden to read Chesterfield by John Adams, did so anyway and pronounced him a "mere Lovelace" (Carson 1966: 31). Adams further castigated him for "inculcating the most immoral, pernicious and Libertine principals into the mind of a youth" (Schlesinger 1968: 12). In the bowdlerized form, however, Chesterfield was lauded as the arbiter of elegance, and Carson claims that Chesterfield was second only to Franklin in popularity (1966: 31).

first intended for noble pages, but later reduced to servants' guides. Eventually these were replaced by etiquette books for the middle class in the late eighteenth century. Mason includes works by Bacon and Joseph Addison in this category (Mason 1971: 292–299; Wildeblood and Brinson 1965: 51–53).

These divisions are problematic because they overlap too often; Chesterfield's *Letters*, for example, could be described as parental advice, a policy work, or a civility text. I prefer a division of courtesy works roughly based on chronological appearance. What can be called *courtly literature* appears up to nearly the middle of the seventeenth century, after which *polite* or *civil behavior* distinguished the form until about 1770, when *etiquette* began to take its modern form. Courtly literature stressed precedence, the qualities of the true nobleman, and the communal meals associated with court life. Polite behavior came to the fore with the removal of widespread social influence from courts to major urban centers. It emphasized gracious bearing rather than true rank, though the literature still contained a highly moral and hierarchical content. Etiquette focused on specific social situations without the moral overtones, when the rise of Romanticism stressed merits of individuality rather than the uniformity of court life (Curtin 1985: 408–409).

"As kings suppressed independent armies and conducted wars themselves, the European aristocracies of necessity gravitated to the royal courts, where power was henceforth won and lost. There the practice of the courtly virtues became as essential to success as valor in battle had once been" (Bushman 1993: 34). By conspicuous and competitive displays of clothing, horses, equipment, and servants, resources and intentions were diverted from the more dangerous political and military intrigues against the central throne. The behavior that governed the displays became codified in practice and in the material accoutrements used by the practitioners.

Until they were replaced in the late seventeenth and eighteenth centuries by growing towns as the arbiters of taste and polite society, courts were the centers from which innovation diffused. As innovations or alterations in ceremonial, celebrative, or communal eating were introduced to the courts, they found their ways into courtesy literature as well.

Courtesy works from this period stemmed from experiences of court life and addressed and reflected the increasing interaction between members of the elite classes. Apart from the clergy, virtually all the audience for these written works would have been found in the nobility or other landed elite. They too would have been exposed to the new life at court and the novel material culture, which included napkins and forks.

Literacy, material culture, and polite behavior, originally restricted to the elite, eventually became more widely (not to say popularly) used, as access to goods and education were increasingly available after the Renaissance with its attendant changes to commerce and public works. These early texts were designed to reinforce hierarchy and were intended for an audience that was elite and male. At the same time, they were also used to promote the sense of community necessary to the centralized state. Prescriptive literature continued to educate the children of the elite in the appreciation of precedence and deportment, emphasizing the roles accorded to rank in communal behavior and the paternalistic duty to those in the lower classes.

As the Renaissance courts provided the ideals of behavior, it is no surprise that they also supplied the words to describe them. *Courtesy* and *courteous* are derived from *court*, referring to behavior that is appropriate to that in a prince's court, "graciously polite and respectful of position and feelings of others; kind and complaisant in conduct" (*Oxford English Dictionary*, 584: *s.v. courtesy, courteous, court*).

The word *manners* is simply the plural of *manner*, the inherent character of something or the way something is done. But as early as 1225, manners also referred to personal conduct or behavior, particularly their moral connotation (*Oxford English Dictionary*, 1717: *s.v. manner*).

Etiquette is a much later addition, being introduced into English by Lord Chesterfield in 1750 (*Oxford English Dictionary*, 901. *s.v. etiquette*). It is derived from the French *"l'estiquette"* referring to a "ticket," or instructions that were posted on a castle wall. It refers to the prescribed ceremony of court and precedence or the conventional rules of personal behavior.

For the purposes of this study, I define *manners* or *mannerly behavior* as the embrace and practice of prescribed, formalized behavior (in everyday life as well as in special, ritualized events) with the intent of promoting a particular sort of society. This behavior is reflected in both physical and moral deportment, readily identifiable within a group, but perhaps not easily described, even by its practitioners. It includes more than merely that behavior that does not disgust; it is a sensibility and awareness of *why* one wants to behave politely.

Italian Renaissance Courtesy

Courtly literature was formulated in Italy in the fifteenth and sixteenth centuries, emerging with new Renaissance ideals of style and beauty (later to be matched by the ideal of the "gentleman" in sixteenth-century England). Besides instructing in the arts of eating at the table, these early courtesy works discussed personal deportment and were concerned with "universally" recognized notions of good taste that included simplicity of demeanor, consideration for others, personal honor, restraint, and freedom from affectation. The most notable of these books included *The Book of the Courtier* (*Il Cortegiano*) by Baldesar Castiglione (1528), *Il Galateo* by Giovanni della Casa (1550), and *The Civile Conversation* (*La Civile Conversazione*) of Stefano Guazzo (1579) (Carson 1966: 17–19).

William Michael Rossetti, brother to the painter Dante Gabriel Rossetti and the poet Christina Rossetti, points out that, apart from archaic rules that govern the use of a shared cup or utensil, the manners in thirteenth-century Italy were not so different from those of nineteenth-century England (1869: 34). There seems to be very little change in the courtesy or demeanor aspect of these books from the early Renaissance through the first half of the eighteenth century, and in fact, many of the later works (Italian, French, or English) cribbed unabashedly from those written earlier. Emphasizing moral and civil behavior, these guides examined personal space and the behavior of the individual with the intent to ease society through the restraint of passions and persons. Writing in 1528, Castiglione defined the real function of the courtier's good manners:

> I consider that just as music, festivities, games and other agreeable accomplishments are, so to speak, the flower of courtiership, so its real fruit is to encourage and help his prince to be virtuous and to deter him from evil. Then we must consider that the merit of good deeds consists in two principal things: to choose a truly virtuous end for our intentions, and to know how to find convenient and suitable means for its attainment. (1976 [1528]: 285)

Although Castiglione's dialogue on the perfect courtier remained popular for centuries, Giovanni della Casa's work of 1550 was one of the two principal influences on virtually all subsequent courtesy works (Mason 1971: 253). In the *Galateo* della Casa warned specifically against brutish behavior. "Some monsters thrust their snouts, like pigs, into their broth, and never raise their eyes or hands from the victuals, and gorge rather than eat with swollen cheeks, as if they were blowing at a trumpet or a fire.... You must not so soil your fingers as to make the napkin nasty in wiping them: neither clean them upon the bread which you are to eat" (della Casa 1869: 68).

The body and its functions provided infinite topics for discussion. "You should not scratch yourself at table, nor spit; or, if spit you must, do it in a seemly way. Some nations have been so self-controlling as not to spit at all." Washing was not to be done in public except before going to table "so that he who dips with you into the same platter may know that for certain" (della Casa 1869: 69, 70). Della Casa described not only personal behavior but also how behavior in company must be regulated.

> You must not smell at the wine-cup or the platter of any one, not even at your own; nor hand the wine which you have tasted to another, unless your very intimate friend.... In company, and most especially at table, you should not bully nor beat any servants; nor must you express anger, whatever may occur to excite it; nor talk of any distressful matters—wounds, illnesses, deaths, or pestilence. (della Casa 1869: 68–69)

Guests were not to be pressed to take food they did not want and especially not drink. As will be seen ever after, bad behavior was not only compared to bumpkins and animals but blamed on foreign traditions: "Thank God, among the many pests which have come to us from beyond the mountains, this vilest one has not yet reached us, of regarding drunkenness as not merely a laughing-matter, but even a merit" (della Casa 1869: 70).

Most of the books that addressed women (more frequently as a topic than an audience) spoke more of how to regulate their "animal natures" than to prescribe social graces. In the last decade of the thirteenth century, Francesco Da Barberino wrote of this in his *Document d'Amore*:

> A woman should never go out alone. An unmarried young lady had better wear a topaz, which is proved by experience to be an antidote to carnal desire.... A Lady's-maid should not tell tales to her mistress of any peccadilloes of the husband; still less should she report to the husband anything against his wife, unless it be a grave and open misdoing. (Da Barberino 1869: 49)

Castiglione devotes a small portion of his work to women but is comparatively generous in his estimation of their worth and potentials; he even submits that they have the same intellectual capacities as men (1976: 218). His character, the Magnifico Guiliano, describes the perfect woman at court:

> Leaving aside, therefore, those virtues of the mind which she must have in common with the courtier, such as prudence, magnanimity, continence and many others besides, and also the qualities that are common to all kinds of women, such as goodness and discretion, the ability to take good care, if she is married, of her husband's belongings and house and children, and the virtues belonging to a good mother, I say the lady who is at Court should properly have, before all else, a certain pleasing affability whereby she will know how to entertain graciously every kind of man with charming and honest conversation, suited to the time and the place and the rank of the person with whom she is talking. (Castiglione 1976: 212)

There was, of course, a balance to be maintained between winning ways and decorous behavior:

> Her serene and modest behaviour, and the candour that ought to inform all
> her actions, should be accompanied by a quick and vivacious spirit by which
> she shows her freedom from boorishness; but with such a virtuous manner
> that she makes herself thought no less chaste, prudent and benign than she
> is pleasing, witty and discreet. Thus she must observe a certain difficult
> mean, composed as it were of contrasting qualities, and take care not to stray
> beyond certain fixed limits (Castiglione 1976: 212).

Along with della Casa, another writer, not Italian, was the other
major influence on writers of courtesy literature. The great humanist
writer Desiderius Erasmus of Rotterdam (1466?–1536) traveled and
taught throughout Europe at the time of the breakdown of the feudal
system. Although he argued with Luther, his works were attractive to
Reformers and churchmen alike. His *De civilitate morum puerilium* (On
Good Manners for Boys) was written in 1530 and dedicated to Henry of
Burgundy in the hopes that it would be of service to boys of all classes:

> My purpose is rather to encourage all boys to learn these rules more willingly
> because they have been dedicated to a boy of such momentous destiny and of
> such outstanding promise. For it will be a considerable additional spur to all
> the young to observe that children of illustrious descent are dedicated to
> learning right from their earliest years, and are competing in the same race
> as themselves. (Erasmus 1985: 273)

Erasmus wrote about the body, including cleanliness, personal habits,
and posture, dress ("clothing is in a way the body's body, and from this
too one may infer the state of a man's character" [1985: 278]), behavior in
church, banquets ("it is boorish to plunge your hands into sauced dishes"
[1985: 282]; "Do not throw bones or similar left-overs under the table to
litter the floor" [1985: 283]), meeting people ("By no means should he
think along these lines: what have I do with a stranger …? This mark of
respect is being bestowed not on a mere man … but on God" [1985: 286]),
on play ("He who yields in a contest achieves a nobler victory than he
who grasps victory at any cost" [1985: 288]), and on sharing a bedroom
("Silence and modesty are laudable qualities" [1985: 289]).

While *De civilitate* was ostensibly addressed to boys of all stations,
status and hierarchy remained at the heart of Erasmus's work. Indeed
they formed the structure of the work and its principal topic, respect for
rank. As with other courtesy works, knowing one's own place, and its
relation to others—both greater and lesser—was key. "It is degrading
for people of good family not to observe the manners of their position.
Those for whom destiny has decreed an ordinary, humble, or even rustic
lot should strive all the more keenly to compensate for the malignity of
fate with the elegance of good manners" (Erasmus 1985: 289). And
knowing this place, a person should be able to moderate taste between

gaudiness and carelessness, to give an indication not only of station, but of personality:

> Style of dress should be in accordance with one's means and station, one's locality and its standards, neither conspicuous by its shabbiness nor indicative of opulence, loose living, or arrogance. A degree of negligence in dress suits young men provided it does not lapse into slovenliness.... The greater a man's wealth, the more agreeable is his modesty. (Erasmus 1985: 279)

Erasmus stressed the virtues of respect, moderation, complaisance, imitation (the better to learn), and self-restraint. While modesty was very important, it too was nothing without attendant humility: "Modesty should be displayed, but modesty of the becoming sort, not that which attracts attention" (Erasmus 1985: 286).

English Manners

When the Renaissance brought increasing change west to England, it brought the manners necessary for coping with that change as well: "The language of classical and Italian citizenship was applied to the English landed elite at a moment of constitutional chaos in the mid-seventeenth century and remained thereafter a standing possibility for conceptualizing the relations of English gentlemen to their political world" (Klein 1989: 585). Most of the courtesy books were translated into Latin or English (particularly in later reprintings), but frequently the ability to read them in their original languages was considered a further mark of education and good breeding.

Soon thereafter, the rise of capitalism and the "urban renaissance" of the late seventeenth and early eighteenth centuries escalated the need for manners at the same time that they were the source of those manners. Capitalism expanded ways of getting wealth for many and provided the goods to display that wealth; Braudel remarked on the coincidence of capitalist wealth and table manners to organize table luxury (1981: 203–207). As wealthy artisans and merchants now materially resembled the landed elite in England, manners became increasingly important to distinguish old rank from new riches.

Towns grew with capitalism, increased concentrations of wealth in specific areas, and spread new ideas and goods to the countryside. The increasing populations and close living in towns also made manners imperative. As Klein states:

> The language of courtly behaviour and refinement, though initially applied merely to the English court, was transferred in the later seventeenth century to the English gentleman and his culture as the court diminished in cultural

status and other cultural matrices (most notably, the West End of London) were becoming dominant. (1989: 585)

Urbanization, fueled by commerce, also concentrated the effects of commerce and thus exposed city dwellers to new material culture and ideas; cities became the new centers of polite, that is to say, *urbane*, living. The increase in population and the taste-making capacity of the urban elite had the effect of spreading the vector of manners from cities into the hinterlands. Manners, combined with notions of taste and fashion and the goods that concurrently made the taste and were used in polite rituals, helped further spread mannerly behavior. The court lost power as a social influence. This may be due to what Aresty describes as a succession of "dull" monarchies—neither Anne nor George I was particularly interested in fashionable pursuits—or it may be that after the 1670s, the royal court lost influence to towns, especially London, because of the increase in urban populations and influx of strangers coming to do trade (Aresty 1970: 130; Staves 1989: 120).

Urban improvements tended to have a wide effect even beyond the city limits. In addition to the swelling ranks of the urban middle class, who were avid competitors in material display, their more public entertainments also spread the mannerly ideal. Richard "Beau" Nash tried to "rescue" the rural gentry from uncouthness by publishing the informal rules or "honorary laws" for the entertainments at the Pump Room at Bath (Borsay 1989: 261). Nash announced that "gentlemen crowding before the ladies at the ball show ill-manners, and that no do so for the future—except such as respect nobody but themselves." He further dictated that "no gentlemen or lady take it ill that another dances before them—except such as have no pretence to dance at all" (Turberville 1926: 117). At these public entertainments social distinctions posed a serious barrier to free intercourse, and the upper classes were criticized when they did not join the general assembly. Polite restraint encouraged control of the dress of guests, curbing excessive behavior and promoting good manners and sociability. This had the effect of developing "a wide penumbra" around polite elite society and introduced the paradox of manners that promoted general intermingling while still attempting to maintain class lines (Borsay 1989: 275–276).

There was an overt public discussion of manners in reaction to riotous city life in the late seventeenth century. Urban places, as well as being centers of polite life, were thought to be crime-ridden and viceful. The question of morality in towns led to the formation of the Society for the Reformation of Manners in London, Bristol, and smaller provincial cities in 1699. They were intended to be a "Check to the *Open Lewdness* that was acted out in many of our Streets" (Corfield 1982: 144). National campaigns attempted to regulate uproarious Restoration manners, "to exert tight control over the unruly forces of the market" unleashed by the very forces that created that market (Barker-Benfield 1992: 57). These attacks on taverns, bear-baitings, prostitutes, obscene ballads, and fairs were very much an attempt to curb the lower classes, however. Societies for the Reformation of Manners were reestablished in 1738 and 1757, but were most effective in the 1770s.

English courtesy works devoted themselves to defining the sober moral virtues of a responsible ruler rather than describing the decorative courtiers of Italy (Bushman 1993: 35). It was principally the Italian works and Erasmus, as well as the Bible and classical writers, that seem to have directly inspired the later English writers, including Henry Peacham (*The Compleat Gentleman* [1622]), Richard Allestree (*The Gentleman's Calling* [1682], *The Ladies Calling* [1673], *The Whole Duty of Man* [1694]), and Richard Brathwait (*The English Gentleman* [1630] and *The English Gentlewoman* [1631]).

Henry Peacham stressed "temperance and moderation of the minde, wherewith as a bridle, wee curbe and breake our ranke and unruly Passions." In addition to religion and goodness, he believed that "good learning and the Artes to conferre a great helpe and furtherance hereunto, being a polisher of inbread rudeness" (1968: 185, 186).

Brathwait's *The English Gentlewoman* was extremely popular and went through many reprintings. He promoted homely qualities of industry and economy to women, emphasizing how without these, virtue and modesty were similarly absent:

> Others sleepe out their time in carelesse security: saluting the morning with a sacrifice to their Glasse; the noone with a luscious repast; the afternoone with a Play or Pallet repose; the Evening with a wanton consort ... to belull the abused soule with the sleepe of an incessant surfet. Others have crept into such an Apish formality: as they cannot for a world discourse of ought without some mimicke gesture or other, which, seeme it never so complete to them appears ridiculous to the beholder. (1631: 29)

In addition to disdaining the "Apish formality" of excessive manners, Brathwait also recognized that more than rank was necessary to achieve honor and gentility. "Gentility consists not so much in a lineall deblazon of Armes, as personall expression of vertues. Yea, there is no Ornament-like Vertue, to give true beauty to descent. Again all this will make gentlewomen objects of imitation both in life and death. Honor does not receive its first life from descent" (1631: 157).

Allestree's works focused on the importance of a calling in life. Since the gentleman was blessed with the "advantages" of education, wealth, time, authority, and reputation, he must use them to better ends than squandering. Even with these advantages, the gentleman must not abuse his position.

> His *Behaviour* will be affable and civil, not insolent and imperious; as one that knows Humanity and gentleness is a common debt to Mankind, and therefore will not think fit to contract or dam up his civility into so narrow a compass, that it shall swell into a compliment, and mean flattery towards those above, and not suffer one drop to descend on those beneath him: but dispense its streams so, that all channels may be filled with it. (Allestree 1682: 24)

It is no mistake that Allestree described many of his ideas about manners under "education." Character was key but it had to be polished into mannerly behavior.

Another significant influence on later English courtesy readers was John Locke (1632–1704). In addition to his important philosophical works, he also published *Some Thoughts Concerning Education* in 1693. His approach to manners was rooted in the training of the character of a child, from which manners would naturally spring. Once that was achieved, dancing masters could embellish the youth with the more ornamental gestures of civility.

> Never trouble your self about those Faults in them, which you know Age will cure. And therefore want of well-fashion'd Civility in the Carriage, whilst *Civility* is not wanting in the Mind (for their you must take care to plant it early) should be the Parent's least care, whilst they are young. If his tender Mind be fill'd with a Veneration for his Parents and Teachers, which consists in Love and Esteem, and a fear to offend them; and with *Respect and Good Will* to all People; that respect will of it self teach those ways of Expressing it, which he observes most acceptable. Be sure to keep up in him the Principles of good Nature and Kindness; make them as habitual as you can, by Credit and Commendation, and the good Things accompanying that State: And when they have taken root in his Mind, and are settle there by a continued Practice, fear not, the Ornaments of Conversation, and the outside of fashionable Manners, will come in their due time. (Locke 1989: 125)

Examples of good behavior—whether from caring adults, decent court life, or books—were always to be sought. Locke and other courtesy writers were keenly aware that imitation was the key to learning how to fit into a society and altering manners to be complaisant with the company there.

> But of all the Ways whereby Children are to be instructed, and their Manners formed, the plainest, easiest and most efficacious, is, to set before their Eyes the Examples of those Things you would have them do, or avoid. Which, when they are pointed out to them, in the Practice of Persons within their Knowledge, with some Reflection on their Beauty or Unbecomingness, are of more force to draw or deterr their Imitation, than any Discourses which can be made to them. (Locke 1989: 143)

In the early part of the eighteenth century, newspapers also became important guides to mannerly behavior as well as opinion and news. Especially influential were Steele's *The Tatler* (started 1709), Steele and Addison's *The Spectator* (begun 1711), and Johnson's *The Rambler* (1750). The influence of these papers must not be underestimated; they were enormously popular and enjoyed a wide circulation. Joseph Addison boasted that each copy of *The Spectator* could be passed around to 20 people (Wynne-Davies 1990: 298). Typical of newspaper commentary on manners in London is the following excerpt from a July 1711 issue of *The Spectator*:

> Whereas, originally, the growth of good manners had arisen from the desire to mingle amicably with one's fellow men, the seeming difficulty mankind experiences in avoiding exaggeration and extremes led to an absurd excess of "civilities." Throughout the previous era these had become so burdensome that in desperation "the Modish World," said the Spectator, had "thrown most of them aside." "At present ... an unconstrained Carriage, and a certain Openness of Behaviours are the height of Good Breeding. The Fashionable World is grown free and easie; our Manners sit more loose upon us. Nothing is so modish as an agreeable Negligence.... Good Breeding shows itself most where ... it appears the least." (quoted in Wildeblood and Brinson 1965: 209)

Not only did the newspapers comment on observed behavior but they also provided moral lessons that were attractive to upwardly mobile middle-class Whigs, who were largely proponents of trade. As the manners of this class were intimately tied to establishing and maintaining social networks to foster commerce, the lessons were eagerly absorbed.

Women often owned and read works intended for men, but there were also courtesy books written specifically for the female audience. Works intended specifically for women tended to be conservative, emphasizing the perceived weaknesses of women's minds and bodies. In addition to Brathwait's *The English Gentlewoman*, three very popular books addressed women's roles: *The Ladies Calling* (1673) (probably written by Richard Allestree), *The Lady's New Year's Gift: or, Advice to a Daughter* (1688) by the Marquis of Halifax (George Savile, 1633–1695), and *Instruction for the Education of a Daughter (L'Éducation des Filles)* (1687) by the archbishop of Cambrai, François de Salinac de la Mothe Fenelon (Benson 1935: 16).

None of these authors was willing to put women on the same par as men. *The Ladies Calling* divided the life of women into virginity, wifehood, and widowhood, as opposed to the "advantages" of wealth or education described for gentlemen. Allestree stressed the virtues of modesty, meekness, compassion, and piety.

Lord Halifax's *Advice to a Daughter* (1688) advised ladies to let Halifax believe that he was the domestic ruler, even though he knew he was ruled by looks and tears (Carson 1966: 61). His work may be understood as a reaction to social life after the Restoration. He dealt with the marital state of women rather than education, and focused on how to deal with faults in a husband, like drunkenness or penuriousness. Like many, he argued that men were more rational, but that women wielded power through their wise influence.

Fenelon, extremely influential in France, was interested in the education of women (Benson 1935: 18). He too emphasized the moral virtues and urged parents to encourage simplicity of nature rather than a too studious niceness of manner:

> Accustom them to a plain, and easily practiced Neatness: Shew them the best way of making things; but shew them rather how to make shift without them: Tell them, that it is a sign of a mean and low Temper, to be grumbling for a Pottage not well season'd, for a Curtain not plaited as it should be, or for a Chair not of the just size. It is doubtless the token of a much better Temper, to be voluntarily and Studiously Gross; than to be Delicate about matters of so small importance. (Fenelon 1707: 222)

The Marquise de Lambert (1647–1733) was the author of *A Mother's Advice to Her Son and Daughter* (reprinted in part in *Angelica's Ladies Library*) and was a friend and contemporary of Fenelon. Although she shared some of his views, Lambert remarked that neglecting the education of daughters was a loss to men (Benson 1935: 23–24). Richard Steele published *The Ladies' Library* in 1714, compiling selections from different writers. The selections tended to be pious and conservative and the volume was one that Benjamin Franklin recommended to his own daughter (Benson 1935: 22–23).

What had its origin in Italy was appropriated, reinterpreted, and reinvigorated for English readers in the seventeenth and eighteenth centuries. Courtesy works from France also found their way to England in translation and in the original. A selective process that had begun with the influence of della Casa and Erasmus was continued, with English readers and translators choosing what suited their tastes and society. This was continued in America, and particularly in New England, where the Puritan influence added another filter to the selection process.

Manners in America

In *Learning How to Behave: A Historical Study of American Etiquette Books* (1968: viii), Arthur M. Schlesinger determined that the rise of American manners was hampered by five factors: the immigrant population was not drawn from the "best part" of the Old World; there was an absence of a "native aristocracy" to set standards; the real necessity of taming the wilderness took precedence over exploring the "graces of living"; many immigrants were not familiar with English standards of manners; and there was a comparatively small number of women for whom men would want to compete in politeness. He determined that what manners did exist were thanks to the upper classes who strove to emulate the English social stratification and were based more on religion and morality than civility, usually to control the lower classes and preserve the hierarchy through sumptuary laws (Schlesinger 1968: 1–2).

Manners both arise from and are sustained by social change. Even if America did not have the "best part" of the Old World population or a "native aristocracy," the increasing gentility of the middle class in England ensured that there were enough well-read immigrants who were familiar with the classics of courtesy literature, and the possibility for social mobility in the first several generations of colonial settlement ensured a lively interest in pursuing the arts of genteel expression.

Books on manners were being read in the first settlements in the New World. Religion and law in New England also regulated and enforced notions of decency, rank, and morality: part of the Puritan tradition involved constant reminders to parents to educate and properly raise their children (Hemphill 1988: 30). Even though English and continental courtesy literature was being imported almost immediately, this selective process made New English manners unique from the start.

Social status was still important, however. Hemphill points out that even though there were no vast differences in wealth in the earliest settlements, there was still considerable social stratification (1988: 18). Manners were employed in tandem with law and religion to continue a "tradition" of an elite into the New World that obscured the shallow roots of that tradition under a genteel cover. It was not a simple matter of emulation, though that was part of the story, for there was a good deal of selection and editing of specific behavioral choices. Mannerly conduct did not serve only to preserve and maintain the social hierarchy. The upper classes, and particularly the merchant elite employed manners in many ways, as I demonstrate in the following chapters.

Courtesy literature was imported with the earliest settlers to America. William Brewster of Plymouth owned Guazzo's *The Civile Conversazione* in translation and Richard Brathwait's *Description of A Good Wife*. Brathwait's sober country conservatism appealed to the Puritan sensibilities. John Winthrop, Jr., owned Castiglione's *The Courtier* in Latin. Other books that appeared in libraries from Massachusetts to

Virginia included Henry Peacham's *The Compleat Gentleman*, Richard Brathwait's *The English Gentleman*, and Richard Allestree's *The Whole Duty of Man*, all of which were still found 200 years later in the libraries of Thomas Jefferson and George Washington (Carson 1966: 20).

Advertisements in Boston show that books by Tillotson, Plutarch, Wollaston, Rollins, Milton, Pope, Hume, Livy, Tacitus, Sallust Cicero, *The Tatler*, *The Rambler*, *The Spectator*, and tracts by Cotton Mather were for sale (Wertenbaker 1949: 27). These works would have appealed both to the Puritan mind and the mercantile ethic, but novels like Richardson's *Pamela* and *Clarissa*, with their bourgeois morality, were also popular. Locke's *Some Thoughts Concerning Education* (1693) was widely circulated in America. He was popular for the same reasons that Steele and Addison were, for his Whiggish views and a concern with the inner moral character.

At least 44 different conduct works were imported or printed in New England between 1620–1738, including Richard Brathwait's *The English Gentleman* and *The English Gentlewoman* and Richard Allestree's *The Ladies Calling*. Both of these authors were royalists, godly, and appealed to the Puritan reader (Hemphill 1988: 18, 572). In addition to his novels, Samuel Richardson also anonymously wrote *Letters Written to and for Particular Friends*, intending it for country readers, and it was also very popular in America (Carson 1966: 38).

Although Fenelon's *Instructions for the Education of a Daughter* was popular in England and France, women in America were probably more familiar with his *Télémaque* (1699) in which the secondary character Antiope was properly devoted to domestic affairs with modesty, reserve, even-temperment, and filial obedience (Benson 1935: 19). Allestree's *The Ladies Calling* was a mainstay, as was Lord Halifax's *Advice to a Daughter* (1688), and the Abbé d'Ancourt's *The Lady's Preceptor* (1743) (Schlesinger 1966: 7).

Before the nineteenth century, most decorum books were imported, but there were also early examples of American writers producing books of American manners or adapting European versions. New York brought out the first books on manners printed in America (a reprint of Richard Lyngard's *Letters of Advice to a Young Gentleman Leaving the University* [1696]). One of the first native American writers on manners was the Boston schoolmaster Eleazar Moody, who in 1715, published *The School of Good Manners*. The first part addressed Puritan morals and virtues, the second listed rules of manners, such as: "Gnaw not bones at the table, but clean them with thy knife" (Bushman 1993: 31). The similarity to Erasmus's admonishment that "to gnaw bones is for a dog; good manners requires them to be picked with a small knife," is unmistakable, indicating the mannerly guides were derivative and, in some ways, conservative (Erasmus 1985: 284). In addition to many sermons and lectures, other American works addressing some aspect of mannerly behavior include Cotton Mather's *Ornaments for the Daughters of Zion*, published in 1692, and Franklin's *Reflections on Courtship and Marriage* (1746) (Schlesinger 1968: 8).

Judging from domestic and foreign diarists, seventeenth- and eighteenth-century Americans were keenly aware of manners. Although he saw a wide range of good and bad social behavior, Alexander Hamilton, visiting Boston on his journey in 1744, was pleased with what he found of the merchant elite there:

> The better sort are polite, mannerly, and hospitable to strangers, such strangers, I mean, as come not to trade among them (for of them they are jealous). There is more hospitality and frankness showed here to strangers than either att York or at Philadelphia. And in the place there is abundance of men of learning and parts; so that one is att no loss for agreeable conversation nor for any sett of company he pleases.... I must take notice that this place abounds with pritty women who appear rather more abroad than they do att York and dress elegantly. They are, for the most part, free and affable as well as pritty. I saw not one prude while I was here. (Bridenbaugh 1948: 146)

Madam Sarah Knight was not so fortunate in one of her encounters on the road in 1704. Not far outside of Dedham, Massachusetts, Madam Knight was troubled with an innkeeper who was more interested in satisfying her own curiosity than in offering the weary traveler a place to rest:

> She then turned agen to mee and fell anew into her silly questions, without asking mee to sitt down. I told her shee treated me very Rudely, and I did not think it my duty to answer her unmannerly Questions. But to get ridd of them, I told her I come there to have the post's company with me to-morrow on my Journey, &c. Miss star'd awhile, drew a chair, bid me sitt, And then run upstairs and putts on two or three Rings, (or else I had not seen them before,) and returning, sett herself just before me ... that I might see her Ornaments, perhaps to gain the more respect. But her Granam's new Rung sow, had it appeared, would affected me as much. (Knight 1970: 6–7)

The connection between manners and social station is clearly seen here. When accused of lacking manners, the public-house keeper donned jewelry—material indications of what she believed to be her own status—the better to impress Madam Knight with her situation. Both of the women in this encounter believed themselves to be the social superior, and when it was seen that the other did not share that opinion, claims to that status were made, with words, manners, and things. David Shields conveyed the significance of material communication in his work on the history of belles lettres in America:

> In the British American colonies, where no long-standing aristocracies com-
> manded automatic deference, social rites (and social games as preparations
> for these rites) to assert status became critical to self-understanding. They
> took on peculiar weight because of the lack of signs that fixed one's place in
> the social hierarchy in the Old World. In Europe titles, blood, offices, and
> good breeding established one in the scheme of things. Merchants and
> talented persons of the middling orders exerted energies to secure offices and
> titles, marry into the blood, and acquire the habiliments of good breeding....
> In the American colonies refinement of manners, graces, polite accomplish-
> ments, and fashionability of dress and equipage were measured against a
> metropolitan standard. The occasions when aspirants to reputation gath-
> ered to assert their quality and undergo judgment had Old World origins.
> (1997: 141–142)

Even when the occasion was a simple encounter at a public house rather
than a ball or private dinner, manners and material culture were used,
even necessary, to express and claim status.

British-Americans did not follow European manuals slavishly, even
when these books were understood to be well received in their land of
origin. The colonists chose carefully of what they read and these selections were further modified by filtering them through the teachings of
church sermons and parental admonitions. However, as researchers, we
must begin with the overt statements that we know many in the past
encountered and that formed the basis for many of the manners in their
society. "To understand the lives of the American gentry, at least in their
parlors and formal rooms, we must make an effort to recover life in this
courtesy-book world" (Bushman 1993: 38). But native reactions to mannerly behavior, however, was split between those who believed that one
could not emulate England enough and those who believed that English
manners were effete and dissolute. This became even more of an issue
with the increase of feeling against England in the latter third of the
eighteenth century, when "English" manners were "more honour'd in
the breach than in the observance."

CONTEMPORARY VIEWS AND THE SEVERAL PARTS OF MANNERLY BEHAVIOR

Because of the common lines of descent and despite national or
regional variations in the form of courtesy, many of the European and
American books shared a core of similarities. Despite little variations
in form, much of the intent of these works survived the centuries and
cultural translation: "The naturally decorous is recognized as such by
everyone. Nevertheless in these matters too it is occasionally appropri-

ate for us to play the polypus and adapt ourselves to the customs of the region" (Erasmus 1985: 274). There are several elements that seem to occur repeatedly, including goodness and moderation of character, polish, and proper behavior with respect to others.

Some authors were more concerned with polish, while others emphasized the goodness of character that was the wellspring of good manners:

> The essence of good manners consists in freely pardoning the shortcomings of others although nowhere falling short of yourself: in holding a companion no less dear because his standards are less exacting. For there are some who compensate with other gifts for their roughness of manner. Nor should what I have said be taken to imply that no one can be a good person without good manners (Erasmus 1985: 289).

Locke wrote that "Young Children should not be much perplexed about it; I mean about putting off their Hats, and making Legs modishly. Teach them Humility, and to be good-natur'd, if you can, and this sort of Manners will not be wanting: Civility being, in truth, nothing but a care not to shew any slighting, or contempt, of any one in Conversation" (Locke 1989: 203).

Chesterfield, although he admired and recommended Locke's treatise on education, would have shuddered at the literal practice of Locke's recommendation that children not be bothered about the niceties of polite movement right off. "By *manières*, I do not mean bare common civility; everybody must have that, who would not be kicked out of company; but I mean engaging, insinuating, shining manners; distinguished politeness, an almost irresistible address; a superior gracefulness in all you say and do" (quoted in Mason 1971: 286). Politeness, by his lights, meant polish, with all traces of the application carefully removed. Some felt it was all; the luster that made gold precious. Some thought this refinement was trickery and false knavery, the gateway to foreign decadence.

Certainly moderation of behavior, between foppishness and crudity, in person and behavior was generally prescribed. Polonius's advice to Laertes might be that of a wily courtier well trained in the politics of court, but it was also the prescription for careful, gentlemanly living and was universally approved: "Give every man thine ear, but few they voice; Take each man's censure, but reserve thy judgment. Costly thy habit as they purse can buy, But not express'd in fancy; rich, not gaudy; For the apparel oft proclaims the man" (*Hamlet*, Act 1 sc. iii 68–72).

Another point that was generally accepted was the internalization of the qualities behind manners, the goodwill that was to prompt the sincere practice of civility. Most writers agreed that there must be a moral heart to polite behavior or else it was meaningless. Ben Franklin, one of the most popular American writers, observed that mere imitation was not enough to learn gentility. Gentility entailed an internalization of manners and taste: "The true Gentleman, who is well known to be such, can take a Walk, or drink a Glass, and converse freely, if their be occasion, with honest Men of any Degree below him, without degrading or fearing to degrade himself in the least" (quoted in Shields 1997: 38). According to Shields, this was to conquer the omnipresent fear of degradation so that one could share public spaces with members of the lower classes (1997: 38). Knowledge of one's rank and internalizing the morals of manners meant not only obliging the powerful and taking care of the poor, but treating people with respect (though not equality).

An excellent example of this successful internalization was described by Dr. Alexander Hamilton in Rhode Island. He wrote about "King George," an "Indian king," who not only possessed large tracts of land and many head of stock, but was also a gentleman with his family similarly gentle in bearing: "His queen goes in a high modish dress in her silks, hoops, stays, and dresses like an English woman. He educates his children to the belles letters and is himself a very complaisant mannerly man. We pay'd him a visit, and he treated us with a glass of good wine" (Bridenbaugh 1948: 98). Not only did George possess the material attributes of a gentleman, but he educated his family in a mannerly fashion and treated strangers with polite courtesy. Hamilton was convinced that George was sincere, as befitted a mannerly person.

Good manners were frequently illustrated by the description of bad manners, and bad manners were always described with vehemence, if not absolute gusto. Negative comparisons with animals, children, country folk, foreigners, or those perceived to be clownish were designed to fix the archetype of the unmannerly lout in the minds of genteel aspirants. Bonvicino da Riva wrote in the thirteenth century: "To snort like a salmon, gobble like a badger, and complain while eating—these three things are quite improper" (quoted in Elias 1978: 69). Another example comes from the same period: "If a man snorts like a seal when he eats, as some people do, and smacks his chops like a Barvarian yokel, he has given up all good breeding" (quoted in Elias 1978: 51). In 1530 Erasmus listed other rude habits to avoid: "It is also unseemly to toss your head and shake your hair, to cough unnecessarily, to clear your throat, likewise also to scratch your head, to pick your ears, to wipe your nose, to stroke your face as if wiping away your shame, to rub the back of your head, [or] to shrug your shoulders (a characteristic of some Italians)" (1985: 287).

About 200 years later Moody, the author of *The School of Good Manners* (1715), warned that "[t]here is scarce a sadder sight, than a clownish and unmannerly Child. Avoid therefore with greatest diligence so vile an Ignominy" (quoted in Bushman 1993: 31). Hamilton also used an animal comparison in describing some shy Rhode Islanders: "They were as simple and awkward as sheep, and so wild that they would not appear in open view but kept peeping att me from behind doors, chests, and benches. The country people in this island, in generall, are very unpolished and rude" (Bridenbaugh 1948: 150).

But at the same time, writers urged that practitioners use common sense in their judicious use of mannerly behavior. There was no reason to suffer for the sake of politeness. "To suppress a sound which is brought on by nature is characteristic of silly people who set more store by 'good manners' than good health" wrote Erasmus (1985: 275). And the French courtesy writer Antoine de Courtin noted in 1672 that "civility requires you to be polite, but it does not expect you to be homicidal toward yourself" (quoted in Elias 1978: 75).

Once the individual had been regulated, the next level of mannerly behavior took place in company. One's attitude toward others had to be careful, thoughtful, generous, and modest. Civility was already rooted in Christian religious teachings, and was a constant refrain in courtesy literature:

> He should not set himself above anyone, or boast of his possessions, or undermine someone's resolution, or mock the character and customs of any people, or divulge a secret entrusted to him, or spread fresh rumours, or damage anyone's reputation, or hold a natural disability as a matter of reproach to anyone. For such behaviour is not only outrageous and uncivil but also foolish, tantamount to someone calling a one-eyed man one-eyed, or a bandy-legged man bandy-legged, or a cross-eyed man cross-eyed, or a bastard a bastard. (Erasmus 1985: 288)

The pitfall of too much politeness was as bad as the use of too little. This flaw was, again, perceived as a lack of schooled restraint: "A polite country Squire shall make you as many Bows in half an hour as would serve a Courtier for a Week" (Wildeblood and Brinson 1965: 210). Overpoliteness was attributed to ignorance, as in what Madam Knight observed in "Jone Tawdry's" overenthusiastic curtseying and what Dr. Alexander Hamilton found in the deference of an old man at a tavern in Ipswich: "He frequently accosted me with please your honour, with which grand title, like some fools whom I know, I seemed highly pleased tho I was conscious it did not belong to me" (Bridenbaugh 1948: 122). At the same time that it marked the old man either as a flatterer or as unschooled and insensitive, it placed the burden on Hamilton of accepting what he could not honorably accept as his due. Locke had remarked on obsequiousness in 1693:

> There is another fault in good Manners, and that is *excess of Ceremony*, and an obstinate persisting to force upon another, what is not his due, and what he cannot take without folly or shame. This seems rather a design to expose than oblige: Or at least looks like a contest for mastery, and at best is but troublesome, and so can be no part of *Good-Breeding*, which has no other use or end, but to make People easie and satisfied in their conversation with us. (Locke 1989: 203)

The error of excessive "delicacy" or the overdevotion to manners was also a fault described in courtesy literature. Readers were taught to be flexible, employing mannerly behavior appropriate to the situation at hand. Fenelon cautioned that an overscrupulous attention to manners would defeat the purpose of social intercourse with worthy people. If loutish behavior could be forgiven, however, politeness could also mask base motivations:

> This evil Delicacy, if not repress'd in Women who have Wit, is still more dangerous in Company, than all the rest: almost all Persons, will be to them insipid, or troublesome. The least defect of Politeness, appears to them a Monster. They are always scornful, and nauseating. You must make them therefore understand betimes, That there is nothing so injudicious or absurd as to judge superficially of a Person by his External Manners: in stead of thorowly examining his Soul, his Notions of things, and his useful Qualifications. Make them see by several Instances, That a Country-Man of a gross, or (if you will have it) of a ridiculous Air, with his unseasonable and course Compliments, if he have a good Heart, and a regular Understanding, is more to be Esteem'd; than a Courtier, who, under an accomplish't Politeness, hides an ungrateful, unjust Heart, and which is capably of all manner of Dissimulations and Basenesses. (1707: 222–223)

In addition to personal restraint, the moral component of manners, and complaisant goodwill toward others, there was also an element of sensibility, of sensitivity to what was properly part of polite discourse. Dr. McGraw trampled all of these norms in an unpleasant encounter with Dr. Hamilton in 1744:

> He [McGraw] and I unhappily engaged in a dispute which I was sorry for, it being dissonant to good manners before company, and what none but rank pedants will be guilty of.... The thing that introduced this was an action of McGraa's [*sic*] which exceeded every thing I had seen for nastiness, impudence, and rusticity. He told us he was troubled with the open piles and with that, from his breeches, pulled out a linnen handkercheff all stained with blood and showed it to the company just after we had eat dinner. After my astonishment att this piece of clownish impudence was over ... He pretended

> to have travelled most countrys in Europe, to have shared favour and ac-
> quaintance of some foreign princes and grandees and to have been att their
> tables, to be master of severall European languages, tho I found he could not
> speak good French and he merely murdered the Latin. (Bridenbaugh 1948:
> 85–87)

McGraw, presumably an educated man, broke every rule of civility and restraint. He was guilty of obstreperousness, indelicacy, and bad taste, but, worse, he lied about the intimate terms on which he was with "princes and grandees" and his mastery of languages.

Lying was the greatest cardinal sin against civil behavior, not only because of its moral transgression, but also because insincerity was antithetical to polite behavior. Because manners required some masking of the unattractive personal truths that were part of human nature, absolute, convincing sincerity was required to abrogate the little white lies that might be required to restrain passion and cloak unpleasant physical characteristics.

But, some argued, the polite lies of manners were bound to lead to worse ones, and so politeness and manners could never be anything but dishonest. Everywhere, but particularly in America, honesty was used as the excuse given for perceived lapses in manners.

> Morison … was a very rough spun, forward, clownish blade, much addicted to
> swearing, att the same time desirous to pass for a gentleman; notwithstand-
> ing which ambition, the conscientiousness of his naturall boorishness
> obliged him frequently to frame ill tim'd apologys for his misbehaviour, which
> he termed frankness and freeness. It was often, "Damn me, gentlemen,
> excuse me; I am a plain honest fellow; all is right down plain dealing, by God."
> (Bridenbaugh 1948: 13–14)

There was a conflict (that has never been resolved) between "honesty" and "politeness," where the two were seen to be in opposition. If manners were seen as an artifice (in the best sense of the word) that subdued the brutish nature of humanity, then it was a short step from masking that truth to outright falsehood. Some saw any mannerly behavior as pretentious, unnatural, and therefore, essentially hypocritical. Some detractors associated politeness with decadent (usually foreign) lifestyles. Others still were angered by the notion that "manners, not solid virtue, made 'friends,' and 'friends,' not able service, made one's career" (Curtin 1985: 401).

The audience needed to be convinced of the knowledge and sincerity of the practitioner. One might own the pretty gestures but lacking a commitment to them was a real and considerable failing. The use of manners without concurrent, internalized goodwill was anathema. In the 1780s, the Marquis de Chastellux complained of Americans: "All their politeness is mere form ... none of it arises from feeling; in a word, politeness here is like religion in Italy" (quoted in Carson 1966: 36).

The key to manners is the perfect practice of a completely artificial set of behaviors with such perfect ease that the observer is convinced of the practitioner's sincerity and the utter naturalness of the behavior. Manners are practiced to become a second, better, nature. Any slip in this reveals the work that has gone into learning them, and thus undermines the entire effect. Castiglione recognized this in *The Book of the Courtier* when he wrote:

> I have discovered a universal rule which seems to apply more than any other in all human actions or words: namely, to steer away from affectation at all costs, as if it were a rough and dangerous reef, and (to use perhaps a novel word for it) to practise in all things a certain nonchalance which conceals all artistry and makes whatever one says or does seem uncontrived and effortless.... So we can truthfully say that true art is what does not seem to be art; and the most important thing is to conceal it, because if it is revealed this discredits a man completely and ruins his reputation. (1976: 67)

Court life was political by nature and manners to some extent were a form of self-interested practice. Honesty and earnestness in learning polite behavior lent grace to the performance. This superb quality of nonchalance, often described as the *je ne sais quoi*, was what most convinced the audience.

It is interesting to note some of the criticism that various of these works drew, both from foreign and local contemporaries. Too much mannerly behavior was deemed effeminate and characteristic of foreigners. For example, Lord Chesterfield was castigated for being a "Frenchified fop" (Chesterfield 1992: xi). His *Letters* were also at one point criticized by Samuel Johnson for teaching "the morals of a whore and the manners of a dancing master" (Boswell 1986: 77). Quite apart from the fact that there was some animosity between the two when the statement was made, at the time, dancing masters were necessary as trainers of the body, but by no means fit to mend the mind or spirit.

Baltazar Gracian y Morales wrote *The Courtiers Manual Oracle, or, The Art of Prudence* (1685). His "Maxime CXCI" described one who "gull'd with excessive Courtesie" as "a kind of Cheat":

> There are some who stand not in need of the herbs of Thessaly to bewitch with, for they charm fools and vain people merely with a low Bow. They make a Traffick of Honour, and pay for it with the wind of some fair words. He that promises all promises nothing, and promises are so many slippery steps for fools. True Courtesie is a debt, that which is affected and uncommon, is a Cheat. It is not a civility but a dependence. (1685: 174)

Gracian y Morales states this sentiment even more plainly: "Punctiliousness is tiresome. There are whole Nations sick of that Nicety" (1685: 168).

The sentiment distinguishing the smothering of some impolitic truth in the name of civility and outright deceit shows up repeatedly throughout the centuries of literature. Even in Richardson's *Clarissa*, Mr. Lovelace, later used as a byword for deceit and violent abuse of manners by Abigail Adams, understood, if he did not practice, the difference: "Pray, sir—Civility is not ceremony" (Richardson 1985a: 761).

RESEARCH ON MANNERS IN ANTHROPOLOGY, HISTORY, AND HISTORICAL ARCHAEOLOGY

There has been a significant body of work by historians on the world of polite behavior, and anthropologists, material culture scholars, and historical archaeologists have made some interesting use of this material. Each field addresses some aspect of social control, the creation of emotion, and the communication of information, but Hemphill notes that while historians focus on collective rituals and study them diachronically, anthropologists tend to examine more intimate rituals in a particular time and place (1988: 3–5). Perhaps too, the timing of these studies reveals something of the time: many of the works I surveyed were published between 1966 and 1970, possibly in consideration of the cataclysmic social changes of the 1960s.

In 1899 Thorstein Veblen wrote *The Theory of the Leisure Class*, in which he associated manners with the conspicuous consumption of leisure and the display thereby of dominant status. "In large part they [manners] are an expression of the relation of status,—a symbolic pantomime of mastery on the one hand and of subservience on the other" (1994: 47). He claims that the use of manners is better understood in terms of the effort that must go into polishing the display than in the goodwill courtesy presumably conveys.

> Their ulterior, economic ground is to be sought in the honorific character of that leisure or non-productive employment of time and effort without which good manners are not acquired.... Refined tastes, manners, and habits of life are a useful evidence of gentility, because good breeding requires time, application, and expense, and can therefore not be compassed by those whose time and energy are taken up with work.... In the last analysis the value of manners lies in the fact that they are the voucher of a life of leisure. (Veblen 1994: 48–49)

Like Veblen, Pierre Bourdieu understood the social function of manner and manners to signify authority and taste-making:

> The embodied cultural capital of the previous generation functions as a sort of advance (both a head-start and a credit) which, by providing from the outset the example of culture incarnated in familiar models, enables the newcomer to start acquiring the basic elements of the legitimate culture, from the beginning, that is, in the most unconscious and impalpable way— and to dispense with the labour of deculturation, correction and retraining that is needed to undo the effects of inappropriate learning. (1996: 70–71)

A very different approach to the study of the meaning of manners is found in *The Civilizing Process* by Norbert Elias (1978). Elias's view of manners is essentially diffusionist, that customs are developed by the upper classes and then travel outward and downward to the lower classes. As these manners were dispersed, the elite reacted by increasing their own level of refinement to distinguish themselves from others who practiced the now "debased" form of manners. Courtesy books, spreading with the increase of literacy, had the effect of speeding this cycle. Elias attributes the potency of manners (not given legal sanction) to the power of shame and public censure. Embarrassment marks a stage in the continuing evolution into civilization from the uncivilized.

Although sociologist Erving Goffman does not describe specific manners, he does discuss the mechanics and functions of mannerly behavior as performed on the social stage. His notion of "performance" is particularly apt to the understanding of manners in a social context: "Once the proper sign-equipment has been obtained and familiarity gained in the management of it, then this equipment can be used to embellish and illumine one's daily performances with a favorable social style" (1959: 36). His relevance in studying manners is also seen when comparing descriptions of what contemporary authors wrote about manners with his own observations: "Performers may even attempt to give the impression that their present poise and proficiency are something they have always had and that they have never had to fumble their way through a learning period." Furthermore, "to be a given kind of person, then is not merely to possess the required attributes, but also to sustain the standards of conduct and appearance that one's social grouping attaches thereto" (Goffman 1959: 47, 75).

Goffman's description of social "engagements," "interactions," and "boundaries" is similarly useful, even if his sociological terminology is somewhat stilted. Consider the following in the context of military training days (discussed in Chapter 4):

> In order for the engagement to maintain its boundaries and integrity, and to avoid being engulfed by the gathering, both the participant and bystander

will have to regulate their conduct appropriately. And yet even while cooperating to maintain the privacy of the given encounter, both participant and bystander will be obligated to protect the gathering at large, demonstrating that in certain ways all those within the situation stand together, undivided by their differentiating participation. (1963: 155)

Those who have surveyed the history of manners as used in the English-speaking world include Benson (1935), Wildeblood and Brinson (1965), Carson (1966), Schlesinger (1968), Aresty (1970), and Mason (1971). In a finely wrought monograph, Benson examines the way women were perceived through history based on the courtesy literature designed to regulate their behavior. Wildeblood and Brinson successfully use an extensive description of manners, including those affecting dress, portable material culture, and architecture, to instruct actors about the social context from the thirteenth to the nineteenth centuries. Carson and Schlesinger both examine the effect manners had (or did not have) on the American colonial scene. Aresty provides a very general but engaging discussion of the history of manners from their earliest appearance. Mason wrote one of the most comprehensive guides to the origins of English courtesy literature from 1531 to 1774.

Other scholars have addressed the topic of polite behavior as part of larger studies. The most significant of these to my mind is Richard Bushman's *The Refinement of America: Persons, Houses, Cities* (1993). Bushman uses the history of manners to initiate a thoughtful discussion of the important notion of gentility in American social history. David Shield's (1997) work on belles lettres in eighteenth-century British America also incorporates the understanding of mannerly behavior to that movement, and G. J. Barker-Benfield (1992) uses manners to explore the culture of sensibility and the literary roots of modern expressions of feminism. Lawrence Klein in several articles (1989; 1995) explores the vocabulary of the renewed interest in civility and manners in the eighteenth century in relation to political philosophy. His work apparently follows in the footsteps of J. G. A. Pocock's work that traces the redefinition of virtue in relation to the "increasingly transactional universe of 'commerce and the arts'" (1985: 48).

Very important to the present study, Christina Hemphill's 1988 dissertation rigorously tackled the direct study of "embodied" manners (those used in "face-to-face" behavior) in colonial America. By comparing what she calls the "big rules" of society, including those dispensed by the law, church, and morality, and the "little rules" of etiquette, Hemphill observed that, in general, manners changed conservatively, and when changes did occur, they were certainly indicative of significant social upheaval in the culture at large (Hemphill 1988: 13).

Behavior of any sort, ritual or everyday, is the meat and drink of anthropologists and therefore is an appropriate focus of historical archaeological investigation. The present study does not represent the first time that historical archaeologists have scrutinized mannerly behavior, but until recently no studies have used manners as part of a larger study. Recently two important studies dealing specifically with different aspects of etiquette have appeared. These include Wall's investigation of domestic and public spheres in New York City (1994) and Shackel's study of personal discipline in Annapolis, Maryland (1993). While these two works approach their topics from radically different perspectives, both emphasize the relationship between the adaptability of manners and social change. My emphasis is similar, incorporating the study of manners in my research on colonial merchants.

In *The Archaeology of Gender: Separating the Spheres in Urban America*, Diana Wall's exploration of domestic sites in New York City at the turn of the nineteenth century reveals the active roles played by men and women in the separation of home and workplace. Wall detected a shift in documents and archaeological assemblages that underscores the relationship between social behavior and material culture, particularly where meals were concerned. The timing and service of meals, and, therefore, the sorts of settings and vessels chosen to facilitate this, changed from 1780 to 1840, at the same time the workplace was removed from the home. The archaeological recovery of different sets of tablewares indicates the increased emphasis on family meals as rituals that established the centrality and sanctity of the family in what was perceived as an increasingly hostile and commercial world. This is compelling because Wall demonstrates the meaning of place settings as more than mere display or acquisition: they represent the conscious adaptation of the family to outside forces and the very localized creation of social order in the domestic space (Wall 1994: 163).

Paul Shackel uses the history of manners as evidence to support his work in *Personal Discipline and Material Culture: An Archaeology of Annapolis, Maryland, 1695–1870*. He examines the probate inventories of Annapolitans for mention of artifacts that were used to practice personal discipline and maintain order in Annapolis society, including toothbrushes, clocks, and matched sets of ceramic tablewares, and attempts to correlate these with concurrent shifts in prescribed behavior.

While I agree with his assessment of the increasing emphasis on the individual over time, I believe he has overstated his case on two points: his understanding of "rigid civility" and his focus only on the conservative aspects of courtesy literature. Shackel's search for the "rigid civility" in the upper classes of colonial Annapolis is problematic, because what he describes is really "etiquette," which does not appear until the 1770s (Shackel 1993: 140). Etiquette, with its explicit delineation of social situations, its promotion of the individual through separate elements of tablewares, and its lack of moral precepts, unlike the courtly and polite literature that anteceded it, arrives with the Industrial Revolution and the Romantic movement. I would argue that elite Annapolitans employed all the civil behavior that was practiced within the colonial social context and likely most of what was being utilized was *directly* derived from London sociability.

Manners do change at times of upheaval, but perhaps as much to embrace new situations as to reaffirm old structures. For example, there was a proliferation of texts on manners in England in the seventeenth century but I believe it was also used to accommodate the most successful and wealthy of the rising middle class, who now could afford the material accoutrements of status but lacked the education that was part of the life-training of the landed elite. The use of the term "gentleman," rather than "prince," "nobleman," or "courtier," in these titles (*The Compleat Gentleman*, *The English Gentleman*, *The Gentleman's Calling*) is an important clue in indicating the target audience of these works. The landed elite stood to gain from alliances (marital or commercial) with the rising merchant elite, and manners gave them the means to reconcile archaic notions of gentle status without the patina of hereditary title.

Additionally, even before literacy became widespread, which might have made courtesy texts widely available, artisans, servants, and merchants all had opportunities in their work capacities to observe the use of artifacts in mannerly situations. The knowledge was available to them even if they lacked the opportunities to practice such behavior. The potential for learning through observation cannot be underestimated: even when courtesy works were available, more often it was the presence of the practitioner in company that provided the best instruction. Chesterfield recognized this fact when he adjured his son to visit courts and well-bred people for "polishing," and Locke recommended a "civil" tutor as the best guide for behavior:

> To form a young Gentleman as he should be, 'tis fit his Governour should himself be well bred, understand the Ways of Carriage, and Measures of Civility in all the Variety of Persons, Times, and Places; and keep his Pupil ... constantly to the Observation of them. This is an Art not to be learnt, nor taught by Books. Nothing can give it but good Company and Observation, joyn'd together. (1989: 150)

I disagree with Shackel's interpretation that manners were created and maintained solely in order to "naturalize" an uneven social order;

this is only half of the story (1993: 152). While the conscious separation of social groups is certainly one effect, and often a goal, of mannerly behavior, the exercise of courtesy described in virtually all the texts examined underscores that manners were also a means by which one could interact politely with members of other social groups while maintaining hierarchical separation. This is particularly important in the early modern period with the rise of capitalism (see Johnson 1996). Certainly the elite were not the only members of a larger society to use a particular, distinguishing behavior (even if they were responsible for the codified, formal written treatises that survive); this occurs in every social group, in occupational groups, religious groups, and gender groups, just to name a few. But all of these groups have mechanisms by which they are allowed to interact with nongroup members as well as the means to distinguish members from nonmembers.

It was the rise of *so many* people who could afford to act and be treated as individuals that accounts for the rise of interest in polite behavior in the seventeenth and eighteenth centuries. With uncertain material cues no longer able to distinguish persons of rank from persons of wealth, polite behavior was a way to ameliorate escalating and widespread demands for respect. By applying rules extracted from notions of noblesse oblige, there is no cause to question rights to respect because, within this system, nearly everyone is accorded a minimum level of respect.

ARCHAEOLOGY, MERCHANTS, AND MANNERS IN COLONIAL MASSACHUSETTS

My interest is in Essex County, Massachusetts merchants who, as economic and social provincial leaders, needed to demonstrate their elite status in a socially acceptable manner. As one of the most explicitly codified and remarked aspects of social life, polite behavior is one means by which it is possible to examine both the processes that adapted British elite culture to this new environment and the material and ideal results of that translation. While the English landed elite did not comprise a significant part of the immigrant population, a new group eventually emerged to fill that role in the northern American colonies. Not only were the merchants who lived and worked on these sites brokers of commodities, but they were also leaders of civic and social activities, bringing what awareness they had of British elite behavior into play in the public sphere. The merchant elite relied on their financial power

for political, social, and military influence. They also acted as the inter-
preters for the behavior that they imported along with the goods. In this
respect they were the "makers of manners."

The probate records for the Turners do not list courtesy literature
explicitly, but we cannot know from an entry like "some Small books"
or "a number Pamphlets" whether they owned these works. Looking
at listings for probate inventories for 200 years in Salem and Essex
County, only one entry exists for a courtesy work: a copy of *The Gentleman Instructed* was listed in the 1771 probate of the Honorable Andrew
Belcher (Cummings 1964: 244; Essex Institute, *The Probate Records of
Essex County, Massachusetts* 1916, 1917, 1920).

This certainly does not imply that the Turners or other Salem
residents were not reading or practicing the material found in courtesy
literature. Based on contemporary accounts of their activities and my
observations of their material life, I believe they were fully invested in
the mannerly culture of the period, acting in accord with prescribed
manners. I have supported this with discussions of the primary courtesy works (and related media) and secondary discussions of how manners were used. We know from Hemphill that these works were popular
in New England and more importantly, we know from the archaeological
and documentary data that the Turners, the Earles, and the Mascarenes were concerned with polite behavior.

Historically there has been a link between merchants and manners
because of that group's exposure to new situations through trade and
because of the role merchants played as part of the expanding middle
class in the early modern period. Again, change is the key. The nature
of mercantile endeavor brought them into contact with a wide population from many traditions, both at home and abroad. "The social psychology of the age declared that encounters with things and persons
evoked passions and refined them into manners; it was preeminently
the function of commerce to refine the passions and polish the manners"
(Pocock 1985: 49).

It was also in their own best interest to be the models in the usage
of the goods and ideas that the merchants imported:

> The contrast with the old style of man put pressure on the new type to
> associate his development with "manners" in a redefinition of virtue: there
> was considerable apprehension that participants in the new economic world
> were inevitably "involved in dependence and corruption." ... Mannerly con-
> duct necessary to business and credit included "courtesy." Such "a [p]resenta-
> tion of self" was "a matter of economic survival," although the prospects of
> "unlimited acquisition and accumulation" also required a "transformation"
> in "the rules of civility, of politeness." (Barker-Benfield 1992: 86, 87)

In the middle ages, merchants were among the better educated and were thus exposed to the rudiments of gentility. "The church schools stressed the teaching of virtue along with that of grammar. To the merchant this was of supreme importance; at a pinch, his children could go through life without much knowledge of Latin, but it was essential that they be brought up virtuously, well instructed in *bonis moribus*" (Thrupp 1992: 164).

The merchant's training prepared him for roles not only in trade but in local government: in English towns, wealthy merchants were frequently part of the town government, and in politics, would have had the further opportunity to observe the practices of other elites. From the start, the notions of this authority and hierarchy were a part of that education and the heart of mannerly training:

> One of the arts he had to acquire in this capacity, the art of good manners, depended primarily upon a sensitivity to differences in status. The code of good behavior was not elaborate; indeed, it could almost be summed up in the necessity of restraining the temper, especially before inferiors or superiors. Being an avoidance of the sin of anger, this restraint had a moral aspect. It had also the value of bestowing a personal dignity that the merchant felt to be peculiarly fitting to his station. (Thrupp 1992: 164–165)

Again, this quote shows the connection between morality, manners, and restraint for merchants as well as everyone one else.

What particular use and meaning would merchants in colonial Massachusetts have found in a code of mannerly behavior? In a situation where there is an abrupt disconnection (and increasingly more distanced relations) between the traditional ruling group and the rest of a society, new actors and rules would have had to fill that void. For a time the leadership was taken on by the Puritan oligarchy, until the distance between the strict interpretation of Puritan philosophy and the realities of a booming sea trade became too great. After that time, the merchants rose in economic and civil power, and, I propose, successfully took the place of the traditional elite, in part because they imitated their mannerly behavior and portrayed themselves as the "natural" inheritors of this role. Although they were not accepted as anything more than rude provincials back in England, the mannerly merchant elite of America used their polish to their great advantage at home. Carson points out they "enjoyed same position of Australians" in London (1966: 23)

These American merchants, conscious of their newly elevated place in a community that was somewhat removed from the established scrutiny of the Old World, were keenly aware of the flexibility that mannerly behavior offered them in communicating with other groups above and below their own social station. They made the most of this at the same time that they sought to secure and solidify their own ranks. So many of them had come from families that were but one or two generations away from humbler artisan or farming origins that they must have been cognizant of the fact that they would be biting their own backs to cast aspersions just for superiority's sake. With the rapid accrual and potential for even quicker dissipation of fortunes based on trade, mannerly behavior would have mitigated sudden social downfalls, providing behavior that could transcend economic status.

"In the seaports a new sophistication appeared. Merchants grown rich in the West India trade were having their portraits painted by Smibert and Blackburn and going to hear Dr. Colman and Dr. Cooper, if not out of piety then to set an example in decorum to the lower classes" (Carson 1966: 25). Besides decorum, mannerly behavior was also useful in inculcating the workforce with the values of modesty, frugality, piety, forthrightness, and restraint.

While indentured servants and slaves were used in the merchant's business activities, the fact was that many free men and women sold their labor to them as well. These situations were frequently exploited, at times horribly so, particularly for the sailors who ventured on merchant ships and their families who waited for them to return. But the relationship was one of mutual reliance, because the shipbuilders, farmers, coopers, tailors, and others were essential to the merchants' production and distribution of goods. It is not to say that the families of the merchant elite were always polite to their subordinates, but the mechanisms certainly existed for them to deal with them safely (in both the cultural and literal senses), carefully, graciously, and perhaps, later on, democratically.

Ultimately, "the refinement of America involved the capture of aristocratic culture for use in republican society" (Bushman 1993: xix), and it was a transformed set of manners, clearly rooted in Europe, but unmistakably American.

CONCLUSION

New manners arise at times of social change. Archaeologists and historians see the material results of broad changes of society that are concurrently visible in courtesy literature. In many ways, manners are what made change possible, used to reaffirm some parts of previous hierarchy while providing some sorts of flexibility to accommodate new situations. Selection and adaptation more so than simple imitation characterized the translation of English and European manners to the

New World. Like Portia's young English suitor, Americans got their behavior everywhere, but this hybrid speaks to the inherent suppleness of manners in being adapted.

Polite behavior can be legally enforced, imparted through religion, or a stipulated secularly through the heavy weight of social censure: "Manners were, literally, the moral equivalent of free institutions, capable of simulating the effects of institutions" (Klein 1989: 591). Merchants were keenly aware of the power of manners and they wielded them, distinguishing their elite group identity from others, but also providing the means for predictable behavioral expectations within their class necessary for their own survival. Manners worked to distinguish the individual, where material culture no longer served as an accurate indicator of rank and as middle-class aspirations blurred formerly rigid social stratifications.

Richard Bushman wrote that "Life in the courtesy books was confined almost entirely to the times and places of formal entertainment.... Judging by their houses and furnishings, the American gentry, despite the long hours they spent in tanyards, cornfields, or countinghouses, took pains to claim a place for themselves in the courtesy-book world" (1993: 46, 47). I see a much closer relationship, however, between the working world of the merchants and the courtesy book rituals of their polite society. There was never a complete separation of one world from the other, because polite behavior and public and private rituals were used to further commercial ends, helping to produce and reproduce the life of the merchant elite.

The Merchant Community in Massachusetts and England

It has been observed, that there is no profession in which more courage is required than in this; for merchants who trade to foreign countries, encounter and strive among men, and sometimes against the four elements together; which is the strongest proof that can be of the resolution of man.
—Rolt, *A New Dictionary of Trade and Commerce*

What is wrong with trade?... Why should men not be merchants? Which is more civilized, a Roman legion, or a caravan of merchandise?
—Margaret Drabble, *The Realms of Gold*

INTRODUCTION

In this chapter I define the terms *merchant* and *elite*, creating a definition based on both emic designations and etic observations, and suggest how this emerging class attempted to consolidate their place in society in England and in Massachusetts (and elsewhere in New England) in the seventeenth and eighteenth centuries. At this time, merchants as a group fit awkwardly in the existing social structure, both in terms of the wealth that they were able to accrue (giving them the appearance that had formerly been associated only with the landed elite) and the effect that their businesses had on national and local economies. There were questions about the damage that expenditures on foreign goods did to the British economy, the metaphysical trauma reputedly suffered by the "lesser sorts" when exposed to cheap finery and goods previously only available to the wealthy, and the threat to a heretofore stable social structure in England, where pedigree and landed status were being challenged by power gained through money and influence, and in Massachusetts, where Puritan ideals were often in conflict with the fruits (material and ideal) of merchant endeavor. Some recent historical studies suggest that there was, if not a total acceptance, then at least a recognition of social mobility and, therefore, the power of this achieved status, while others indicate that there were more formidable social barriers.

Part of the merchants' problem was that there remained a taint associated with trade, as opposed to the traditional professions of the clergy, law, or the army, because it was too closely associated with physical labor rather than rent or other income. Added to this social conundrum was the fact that the wider benefits of mercantile activity were hotly debated. The merchants as an occupational group were championed by some contemporary observers, like Defoe or Steele and Addison, who were in favor of commerce and what it could provide for England and vilified by others, like John Brown or later, Adam Smith, who were concerned that the merchants caused a drain on national resources with the goods they imported. John Brown's statement that "commerce polishes manners but corrupts Manners" is revealing, suggesting that while their wealth refined the merchants, it thereby also debased the whole notion of mannerly behavior (1757: 152). The general view was that while merchants might accrue phenomenal wealth, akin to that of the landed elite, they could never be anything but polished middle-class pretenders to high status.

Despite their newly gained economic power, merchants tended to remain marginal figures in the highest society but were able to insinuate themselves as *gentlemen* (Hancock 1995: 279–280). About the same time as the emergence of the merchant class as a social entity, the definition of a "gentleman" was changing. The renewed interest in courtesy literature in the first half of the eighteenth century was linked to the social mobility that characterized these phenomena. After 1688 and the Glorious Revolution, with the development of a larger bureaucracy and increased fortunes from transatlantic commerce, a "deportmental rather than a hereditary or preferential definition of gentility gained currency. One was a gentleman if one looked and acted the part" (Hancock 1995: 280).

A hierarchical society remained, but rank was less clearly demarcated and the meaning of it varied with local context. Although wealth was essential in gaining social prominence and power, a new idea of personal improvement was an integral part of achieving this. One element of this improvement was the genteel education in, and refinement through, mannerly behavior. Another aspect of improvement had to do with the relationship of the new gentleman to his community. Urban centers were expanding and becoming increasingly important at this time, linking port cities with manufacturing towns and agricultural areas. Thus, it is not surprising that the rising merchant class had a profound effect on the physical shape of these cities. By improving the infrastructure (roads, wharves, warehouses, and public markets) of a town, the gentleman merchant was also improving his own lot. This underscored his interdependence with the community, something that strongly resembled the paternalistic interest of the landed gentry. Cities also concentrated change and provided a focal point for taste and fashion, and because they had more to gain in economic terms, cities received the new "gentlemen" with greater enthusiasm than more rural areas. By generating more goods and more cash, the merchants, in turn, accelerated urban growth, which, likewise, encouraged more trade.

In New England, the blurred nature of the English social structure was further complicated by the place of the Puritan clergy at the top of the social structure and the demographics of the Great Migration (1629–1642). Merchants eventually replaced the clergy in power through their growing influence in increasingly complex colonial economic matters. The merchant's rise was rooted in economic power, consolidated by political sway, and crowned by social eminence.

As a new elite acting in a role outside the prescribed hierarchy in England, this social eminence was structured by mannerly behavior and reinforced through social activities that consolidated and strengthened group allegiance through the use of luxurious and exotic artifacts. Use of these ideas, ideals, and artifacts established a way of life, if not an absolute right to power, and reproduced itself through the ritualized social behavior of the mercantile elite.

The data that support this study are derived from three principal sources. The first is my own archaeological work researching the Turner family (1650s–1784) in Salem, Massachusetts. The next is a group of letters from John Mascarene (in London) to his wife Margaret Holyoke Mascarene of Cambridge (and later Salem), Massachusetts, from 1761 to 1764. The final data set comes from a collection of letters that were exchanged between members of an expatriate English merchant house in Italy, the Earle-Denham correspondence (1763–1781).

Each of these brings a particular strength and they complement each other amazingly well. The historical archaeological research on the Turner family forms the basis of this work, with a set of documentary and artifactual data. The Turners first inspired my questions about the construction of merchant elite culture. The Mascarenes found themselves in Salem at the same time as the Honorable John Turner, Esquire. John Mascarene and Turner undoubtedly knew of each other: they both signed a letter welcoming General Gage to Salem in 1774 and were both Loyalists with connections to the customshouse in Salem (Phillips 1969: 324). The Mascarene letters also provide an American perspective of British society and merchant activities. The Earle papers and Joseph Denham's letters provide an English perspective of trade and merchant society, as well as the view of expatriates in Italy. Like the Turners, the Earles were also involved in the Atlantic trade and so were connected with the Americas as well.

Although the Turner family was the only group of these three to be examined archaeologically, there has been recently a growing body of work on merchants and merchant sites in the eastern United States, and particularly in Massachusetts. I describe some of this recent work, including that by Beaudry (1995; n.d.), De Cunzo (1995a), and Harrington (1989), and how it can be used to better understand the data provided by the Turners, Earles, and Mascarenes.

I conclude by explaining how the merchant class in Massachusetts used their privilege and status to consolidate and define their social identity. Through the use of imported models of behavior as well as artifacts, they defined and delimited their class and restricted access into it in significant ways. At the same time, I argue that they had a vested interest in demonstrating their allegiance to the larger community and by employing different strategems that revealed a canny use of polite distance and apparent disinterest, they signaled their responsibilities and ties to the community. They assumed patriarchal responsibilities as well as power, both of which were reinforced by the mannerly ideals that they claimed to share with the English landed elite.

MERCHANTS AND SOCIAL STATUS IN SEVENTEENTH- AND EIGHTEENTH-CENTURY ENGLAND AND NEW ENGLAND

At its broadest sense, a merchant is one who buys and sells commodities for a profit. The term *merchant* has been used to describe every sort of trader, ranging from street or market peddlers to sea captains to the very wealthiest international importers and exporters. According to Chambers's *Cyclopedia* (1738), a merchant is a "person who carries on merchandize, or sustains the mercantile profession." Under *merchandice* [*sic*] he continues, "[i]n republics, [the mercantile profession] is still more valued; but no where more than in England, where the younger sons and brothers of peers are frequently bred up to *merchandice* [*sic*]," (Chambers 1738, *s.v., merchant, merchandice*). In *A New Dictionary of Trade and Commerce*, Rolt rather less enthusiastically defined a *merchant* as:

> a person occupied in some commercial employment, for the purchase, trade, and exchange of commodities; by wholesale, or retail; by land, or by sea; or both conjointly. A merchant in England is one that buys and trades in any thing: and as merchandise includes all goods and wares exposed to sale in

fairs or markets; so the word merchant anciently extended to all sorts of traders, buyers, and sellers. (1761)

He later clarifies by stating that:

> every man who buys and sells goods, is not at this day under the denomination of a merchant; only those that traffic in the way of commerce, by importation and exportation, or carry on business by way of emption, vendition, barter, permutation or exchange, and who make it their living to buy and sell, by a continued assiduity, or frequent negotiation, in the mystery of merchandising, are esteemed merchants. (Rolt 1761, *s.v. merchant*)

Daniel Defoe (1660–1731) himself occasionally worked in trade and always was an enthusiastic supporter of merchants and the benefits of commerce to the Empire. He made the clear distinction between merchants, manufacturers or artists, tradesmen, peddlers, and shopkeepers in his *The Complete English Tradesman* (1725–27):

> In England the word *merchant* is understood of none but such as carry on foreign correspondences, importing the goods and growth of other countries, and exporting the growth and manufacture of England to other countries; or to use a vulgar expression, because I am speaking to and of those who use that expression, *such as trade beyond sea*. These, in England, and these only, are called *merchants*, by way of honourable distinction. (quoted in Curtis 1979: 382)

For the sake of the present study, the term merchant is restricted to those who traded on a wide scale, most often internationally, as opposed to a shopkeeper or retailer. While some of these merchants did keep shops, this was a by-product of their engagement in trade, and not the sum total of their profession. In specific, I refer to the members of the economically elite class in Massachusetts (and elsewhere in New England) who had achieved great wealth or social status as merchants.[1]

Part of the explanation for the economic rise of merchants in England at the beginning of the eighteenth century lies in the increasing profitability of owning ships. The most important cost of running a voyage was in the crew's wages and victualing, ships repairs and stores, port charges, and miscellaneous expenses (including ship ownership,

---

[1] I include the Mascarenes in this group even though they were not as wealthy as either the Turners or the Earles because they were engaged in international business and were of high status because of their antecedents: John Mascarene's father, Jean Paul Mascarene, was a respected commander in Nova Scotia, and Margaret Holyoke Mascarene was the daughter of Edward Holyoke, president of Harvard College for more than 30 years after his election in 1737 (Shipton 1945: 35–39). In fact, members of the Turner family and Joseph Denham, as well the Mascarenes, all suffered serious economic or social setbacks that were mitigated because of their (or their families') mannerly participation within the merchant community.

customs duties, etc.) (Davis 1962: 363–365). Although a merchant would expect to pay less at beginning of a ship's lifetime, the cost could eventually rise to almost £1 per tonne a year over the whole life of the ship (Davis 1962: 368). This does not include the cost of the merchandise to be bought or sold.

In light of these expenses, it is not surprising that merchants were at the top of the informal hierarchy of urban businessmen, and that those who succeeded usually had the help of a wealthy father to provide a good education, apprenticeship, and the capital to start out (Earle 1986: 50; Mitchell 1984: 277). Compared to other trades, sedentary merchants tended to live longer, either because of their greater wealth or the less arduous nature of their work, compared to say, haberdashers or artisans, and were accordingly able to accrue more wealth in their lifetimes (Earle 1986: 55).

The notion of "elite," on the other hand, is at once a little easier and a little trickier to define. It can refer simply to a particular ruling rank, or it can refer more vaguely to mere elevation; it is a modern term that I apply to contemporary definitions. In England there was a titled nobility, but there were also landed gentry who were wealthy but not part of the peerage. This landed elite, composed of both the titled and untitled landed gentry, was associated with heredity, longevity, wealth, exclusivity, and association with land. The definition used by the Stones in their discussion of England's reputedly "open elite" includes "all greater landowners, regardless of their titular rank" (Stone and Stone 1984: 3). It was usually from the ranks of this group that members of Parliament as well as local leaders were picked. The Stones suggest a further refinement of this distinction: one segment of the elite consists of the parish gentry, men whose interest was restricted to the village level, who were poorly educated and had no political power other than that of justice of the peace, while the other (the county gentry) had greater wealth, education, and local political leadership, including membership in Parliament (Stone and Stone 1984: 5).

But as wealthy as they were, the landed elite differed significantly from its continental counterparts in that its members did not receive special privileges in law, taxation, or ownership of land, nor were they barred from trade and industry (except by self-regulation) (Habakkuk 1953: 1). It was a social class with indistinct edges, sharing much in common culturally with the wealthier members of the middle class. There was no sharp break in wealth between higher ranges of one rank and lower ranges of the next, and there were plenty of impoverished peers and baronets who held their title with no estate, but they were more than simply the wealthier end of the middling class (Habakkuk

1953: 13). The grades of title within the landowning class, ranging from duke to plain gentry, were primarily social gradings, probably corresponding in a very rough way to gradations of landed wealth and the general notion of an estate sufficient to maintain a given rank.

Property formed the crux of the landed elite's identity, both in terms of their huge estates and the antiquity of the name associated with them. It was the rent from these estates, rather than living on the direct proceeds of the farm, as did the French nobility, that made the landed elite a leisured class. In England political power and social standing relied more on the ownership of real property than on lineage or royal favor, and while there was no legal restriction on the right to acquire land, lawyers or merchants or other new gentlemen could buy estates only if they were being sold (Habakkuk 1953: 15–16). The fact was, they did not usually put the capital aside from their businesses to do so.

Keith Wrightson's analysis of social order studies in England, including those relying on contemporary perceptions, social-distributional studies, and social relations research, tends to confirm these observations. He observed that these different approaches emphasized the recognition of local variation in social structures and the permeability of social "membranes" with the possibilities for social mobility, and that the "blurring" along boundaries between groups belies the rigid distinction implied by the use of the term "class." He also cautions that the term "class" is a nineteenth- and twentieth-century construct and that care should be used in how it is applied, as contemporary observers tended to use vague terms like "meaner," "better," and "sorts" (Wrightson 1985: 183).[2]

Rather than strictly enforced legal or social boundaries, rank was based on a number of factors, including birth, inherited or assumed title, wealth (and importantly, the nature of that wealth), occupation, and land tenure type (Wrightson 1986: 180). Because of this "blurring," Wrightson endorses the use of what Vivien Brodsky Elliott calls "social clusters" (Wrightson 1985: 190). Measuring the relative social distance between groups by charting marriage choices, apprenticeships, and other social contracts, Elliott demonstrated that there were not evenly graded hierarchies but "clusters" of status and occupational groups who were close enough to consider marriage or other social connections. These clusters, forming smaller milieux within a formal hierarchy, were contextually defined by association, relative wealth, locality, and kins-

---

[2]My use of the term "class" should be taken as synonymous with "group" or "sort" in this context; although hierarchies of some sort exist in virtually every society, they do not always contain the clearly defined notions of class that existed in nineteenth-century Britain.

hip and other relations (Wrightson 1985: 191). As the marriages that take place within a class are a better index of its social inclinations than the composition of its dinner parties, few children of the great families married into families far removed from them in rank and general standing (Habakkuk 1953: 19).

Similarly, Lawrence and Jeanne Stone examined the myth of the "open elite" to determine how permeable the landed elite really was. They discovered that while a few merchants had actually become part of that class, they had done so by taking part of their business capital and buying an old estate that was large enough and with grandeur suitable to maintain political connections through entertaining, the land of which also conferred the right to representation in the House of Commons (Stone and Stone 1984: 7). The Stones concluded that, contrary to popular belief, most of those who became "county elite" tended to be members of "honorable" professions—clergy, army, or law, with whom the landed elite had connections—rather than merchants or other businessmen (Stone and Stone 1984: 402). Although members of all three of these profession groups might share similarities in education, incomes, or lifestyles, the professions were respectable options open to the younger sons, who were constrained by primogeniture, while merchant life still carried the taint of business and labor. Contrary to Chambers's 1738 definition, it was rare even for the youngest son of a peer to go into trade; it was only among the gentry with large families that trade was at all a common occupation for a younger son (Habakkuk 1953: 19).

Only about 6 percent of the Stones' sample of merchants from a 340-year period bought their way into the landed elite. These were assimilated by the second generation. The rest "confined themselves to aping genteel culture and building themselves villas within commuting distance of their place of work in the city" (Stone and Stone 1984: 403–404). Those who did use their profit (or capital) to buy the country seat generally shared the characteristics of longevity and willingness to expend the funds. The success of the elite in surviving, then, was attributed to the increasingly flexible notions of gentility that united the landed gentry with the middle class and the lack of legal privilege for the peerage (Stone and Stone 1984: 406–407).

The cutoff point between these wealthy groups is vague, and anxiety about rank permeated society, particularly at the end of seventeenth century when an urban officeholder like Pepys could be thought of as a gentleman. "Even if the assumptions had become devalued, the concept of a ruling landed elite was preserved, as nearly all commentators were prepared to concede" (Stone and Stone 1984: 7). Although business still did not have the unimpeachable respectability of the professions, because of its association with physical labor, merchants at the beginning of the eighteenth century had the wherewithal on a scale heretofore unprecedented to purchase the cultural and material trappings of a gentleman (Borsay 1989: 228).

If the ranks of English social hierarchy (broadly drawn) had not changed significantly with the emergence of the wealthy merchant, then the notion of the "gentleman" had. Although it was hotly debated, it essentially came down to the fact that after the Restoration, if one dressed and acted like a gentleman, then one would probably be called such. In 1748 Guy Miège wrote: "The title of gentleman is commonly given in England to all that distinguish themselves from the common sort of people, by a genteel dress and carriage, good education, learning, or an independent station" (quoted in Borsay 1989: 227). Ever the promoter of trade and merchants, Defoe also noted rather early on that trade was so far "from being inconsistent with a gentleman, that, in short, trade in England makes gentlemen, and had peopled this nation with gentlemen" (quoted in Hancock 1995: 281).

Mercantile wealth might not have purchased titled status, but it could buy almost everything short of it. Even if the status of the landed elite remained largely inaccessible to the wealthiest merchants, they were able to claim the title "gentleman" as it became more broadly defined through the seventeenth and eighteenth centuries. The trappings of the gentleman resembled those of the titled landowner, and it was for this reason that the merchant was simultaneously applauded and abused by contemporary critics.

On one hand, the notion of the obligations (and even the character) of the landed elite still seemed to be the metric by which successful merchants were judged. Many writers attributed the weakening of morals and social order to what Samuel Johnson decried as "the great increase of money" brought in by merchants and trading (quoted in Porter 1990: 49). John Brown wrote that "[t]here are traders who are generous: nobles and gentry whose ultimate passion is for Gold: But such Exceptions affect not the general Principle ... and different Colours remain in their Nature distinct and invariable," suggesting that there would always be the distinction between nobility and the newly wealthy (1757: 160).

Courtesy literature contained sharp criticism of those merchants aspiring to a better rank. Although the criticism was often found in older texts, these were frequently reprinted and could not have been other than a slap in the face to the hopeful merchant who hoped to learn gentility. Brathwait warned, for example, that the "urbanity which becomes a Citizen, would rellish of too much curiosity in a Country-man.

That Complement which gives proper grace to a courtier, would beget derision or contempt, being personated by a Merchant or his Factor" (1631: 73–74).

But even as early as 1622, courtesy writer Henry Peacham was, somewhat reluctantly, willing to concede that merchants were necessary for the common good:

> No one Countrey affordeth all things, but must be beholden not onely to her neighbours, but euen the most remote Regions, and Common-wealths cannot stand without Trade and Commerce.... I cannot ... but account the honest Merchant among the number of Benefactors to his countrey, while he exposeth his life as well as his goods, to the hazzard of infinite dangers, sometime for Medicinall Drugges and preseruatiues of our liues in extremitie of sicknesse; another, four our food or cloathing in times of scarsitie and want, haply for usefull necessaries for our vocations, and callings. (Peacham 1968: 12)

On the other hand, poetry that sang the praises of the merchants began to emerge in the mid-seventeenth century and reached a peak by the 1750s indicating a wide acknowledgment of what the merchant had achieved. "The trader is a hero not only because he achieves the near impossible, going where even Nature almost dare not follow him, but because trade is intrinsically glorious and beneficial" (McVeagh 1981: 55). The writers of the time were able to project beyond the idea of the merchant filling only his own purse to seeing what the wealth they generated did for the entire country: in their minds, empire, commerce, and wealth were intermingled. Paeans to commerce and to the men who made it possible proliferated. One of the more rhapsodic was found in Edward Young's *Imperium Pelagi, a Naval Lyric* subtitled, "The Merchant" (1729). The author begins by stating that "merchants o'er proudest heroes reign" and that "priests pray for blessings; merchants pour them down," concluding with the question "Is 'merchant' an inglorious name? / What say the sons of letter'd fame, / Proud of their volumes, swelling in their cells? / In open life, in change of scene, / 'Mid various manners, throngs of men, / Experience, Arts, and solid Wisdom dwells" (quoted in McVeagh 1981: 73). Detractors of merchants became more vocal and combative in the later eighteenth century, but in the first half of the century, merchants received a very enthusiastic reception, at least in terms of what they did for the country, if not for their social aspirations (McKendrick 1986: 109).

There were also those who fell between the doubters and the promoters, seeing genetic distance from trade as the key to gentle status. In 1758 Josiah Tucker wrote that the son of a merchant could rise above his father "if he gives his Son a liberal and accomplished Education—

the Birth and Calling of the Father are sunk in the Son; and the Son is reputed, if his Carriage is suitable, a Gentleman in all Companies, though without serving in the Army, without Patent, Pedigree, or Creation" (quoted in Hancock 1995: 281). He believed that merchants could use their wealth to buy respectability and status, but only with generational distance from the source of that wealth. Defoe wrote that "trade makes gentlemen, after a generation or two the tradesman's children come to be as good statesmen, judges or bishops as those of the most ancient families" (quoted in McKendrick 1986: 118). His notion is that once the fortune was made, a merchant would leave his business and turn his hand to the service of the community. Defoe overstated the possibilities for elevation from merchant life into true gentility; his writings suggest that such upward mobility was not only possible but easy, and such was certainly not the case.

Defoe's notion of the merchant "rising" above trade was rooted in a commitment to the older principles of how a landed gentleman behaved, personally and in his relationship to the community: "The social criteria of ancient land, ancient lineage and ancient wealth gave way (in the face of threats from those who looked likely to acquire the least mimic forms of those requirements) to behavioural criteria based on taste, manners and acceptable conduct" (quoted in McKendrick 1986: 119). It was not just fine clothing and pretty manners, however, that made the gentleman; education and interaction with the community were also important. Successful appropriation of the duties of the landed elite (if not admission to their ranks), required public duty in the form of public works. By helping the poor of the community, particularly those involved in trade who had fallen on hard times through illness, natural disasters, or war, merchants not only protected their own investments but gained local currency as conscientious benefactors (Hancock 1995: 307–308). This was not always a disinterested investment in the community, as the improvement of roads, the construction of new wharves, or the raising of a new marketplace that fundamentally aided the merchants were generally as welcome as a new church or library. This development contributed to the "urban renaissance" of the eighteenth century and also helped raise polite culture to a new level and breadth: by taking on the responsibilities and the behavior of the landed elite, the new gentlemen merchants narrowed the gulf between their sorts (Borsay 1989: 225).

The relationship between the economic and social elevation of the merchants and the urban renaissance in England can neither be separated nor one said to be the cause of the other. The pace of economic development in commercial towns accelerated in the eighteenth century, causing even more inequalities between status and income (Ellis 1984: 192). The cities and growing towns were tolerant of the blur between status and wealth and the easing of the application of the term "gentleman" because, in purely economic terms, they had more to gain by the larger population of gentlefolk, with the necessities of genteel dress, living, and entertainment as well as the benefits of increased trade and improvements brought on by the resident merchants (Borsay 1989: 246).

In these urban situations, some trends can be seen in the way that both the merchants and town leaders carried on their affairs. In contrast to the rural landed societies, the urban centers of the eighteenth century were comparatively open and competitive, but "avenues of upward advancement" were still difficult to realize (Corfield 1982: 124). As with the landed elite, kin relations (by blood or marriage) were particularly important both in guild and town politics. Clark's research in Gloucester, England, revealed that the city fathers had up to four kinsmen sitting with them at any time, providing an effective political alliance as well as cooperation in business dealings (Clark 1984: 318–319). These links of kinship were crucial as the urban elite was increasingly restricted to a small pool of influential families throughout the seventeenth and eighteenth centuries (Ellis 1984: 206).

Members of these urban elites tended to live near one another, build similarly impressive houses, and band together to defend their common economic interests (Clark 1984: 319). Some also found it useful to live in proximity to workers, because this fostered notions of economic interdependence if not an actual convergence of interests (Ellis 1984: 199).

As indistinct as class lines were, merchants often did not penetrate the ranks of the landed elite in England. They became increasingly more powerful in urban contexts and in many ways appropriated some of the duties, and, therefore, the right to power of the landed elite, prescribed by tradition and found in courtesy books. The merchants' behavior and wealth allowed them to take on the title "gentleman," which also help cast them in a light similar to that of the landed elite, even as they struggled to have others see past the taint of trade. A similar strategy (with similar goals) was employed, although in a different cultural context, by the merchants in New England.

THE NEW ENGLAND MERCHANT ELITE

William Spengemann wrote that "the empire gave rise to a transatlantic cosmopolitanism, which found expression in London as well as in the provincial centers" (quoted in Shields 1990: 6). This was as much the case of the provincial urban centers on the American side of the Atlantic as it was of Liverpool or Exeter. As it was more convenient to construct the materials in New England and then ship them back to England, shipbuilding and the provision of ships' stores was a core of trade with England from the very earliest colonies, thus ensuring wealth from ship owning (Davis 1962: 66). By 1686 one-half of the vessels trading between England and New England were American-owned and American-built, and this inspired ancillary trades to support shipping as well (Davis 1962: 67).

By the end of the seventeenth century there was a powerful new social group emerging in Massachusetts maritime communities. What defined this merchant elite, besides their occupation and similar interests, was their social characteristics, a combination of selected European customs and sensibilities modified by the cultural and environmental necessities of life on the Atlantic frontier. Like their successful counterparts in England, the American merchants' status was more often achieved rather than ascribed solely through birth, and they employed similarly innovative material and ideal means to construct and maintain their social identity.

There were some differences, of course. Even in cities like Boston or Salem, the New England merchants were by nature provincials, and they were profoundly influenced by the Puritan idealogy, far more than those in England. The New England merchant elite was also different in that they were, aside from Puritan divines and a few Royal representatives, eventually at the very top of their local hierarchy. Without the physical presence of the peerage or even the untitled country landowners, the New England merchants would style themselves in the likeness of the landed elite, successfully appropriating some of the characteristics and responsibilities in the same way the English merchants did.

The nature and demography of the population of New England, and Massachusetts in particular, was distinct from old England as well as the other colonies in America. The Puritans imported a distinctly East Anglian culture with their Calvinism, including architecture and dialect, but other immigrants from elsewhere in England, Scotland, Ireland, and the continent also added to the mélange (Wertenbaker 1949: 6). The Puritan ideals that prompted the Great Migration shaped legislation and public deportment, but were gradually challenged by conflicts introduced by the increasing mercantilism. Social order that was considered divinely ordained was thrown off by the sudden appearance of new riches, sometimes in the hands of the those who were not of the saintly elect who could be reasonably expected to be rewarded with worldly signs of grace.

Not surprisingly, the highest populations of merchants were to be found in the port cities, such as Boston, Charlestown, and Salem, and initially these areas were where the merchants had the most political influence. The merchants were not dominant elsewhere because the rest of rural Massachusetts was largely ruled by those more inclined to Puritan sympathies in the 1650s (Bailyn 1964: 103). The merchants gradually accumulated political power to match their wealth, and this, as well as the goods and entertainments they were importing and popularizing, drew protests from the clergy. In 1663 the Reverend John Higginson decried the worldly excesses and distractions that the merchants brought: "My Fathers and Brethren, this is never to be forgotten, *that New-England is originally a plantation of Religion, not a plantation of Trade.* Let Merchants and such as are increasing *Cent per Cent* remember this ... that worldly gain was not the end and designe of the people of *New-England*, but *Religion*" (Bailyn 1964: 140). Increase Mather continued to condemn the merchants two decades later, vilifying not only the vain fashions they imported, including periwigs and "such like Whorish fashion," but the sorts of "mixed Dancings, light behaviour and expressions, sinful Company-keeping with light and vain persons," that occasioned the display of such ornaments (Bailyn 1964: 141).

By the 1670s, a clearly defined merchant class had emerged from what was essentially a medieval social order, causing tremendous change in New England society. Though the merchants never rejected Puritanism wholesale, they incorporated a secular aspect to their faith hoping to mitigate the potential corruption and luxury of their trade by emphasizing the values of honesty, industry, and enterprise, much like the classical virtues that were being embraced, or at least proclaimed, by their English fellows (Shields 1990: 18).

Although the traveler and journalist Madam Knight remarked that "they give the title of merchant to every trader" (quoted in Bailyn 1964: 194), in New England (as in England) those associated with trade sorted themselves out into a commercial hierarchy. In a roughly ascending scale, itinerant and market peddlers were found at the very bottom ranks, superseded by traders, shopkeepers, seamen, sea captains, and finally by merchants (Main 1965: 83). While these merchants were engaged primarily in international commerce, they generally also had secondary occupations connected with that business (such as shipbuilding, banking, or insurance) or resulting from their accumulation of capital (such as speculation in land). Intensive specialization was not a characteristic of the earliest, most successful merchants.

In New England, the best possibility for movement into this newly powerful merchant class existed at the end of the seventeenth century into the first two decades of the eighteenth century and was most often achieved through familiar connections. These links often extended back to trusted friends and family in England who could provide the information, goods, and finances to American relatives. The earliest generations who were able to situate themselves to the best advantage could, if the family survived, parlay the short tradition of their honorable name into social currency. An expanding "system of interlocking mercantile connections" developed between merchants of different towns, both in New England and elsewhere in America, and was also maintained through relatives (Bridenbaugh 1938: 187).

As with merchants in England, this community was consolidated by a tremendous rate of intermarriage among descendants of successful first generation merchants and tradesmen, forming what "amounted to a single interrelated family" (Bailyn 1964: 135, 137). Entrée into successful families became less of a possibility after the mid-eighteenth century, when they tightened their control of trade and politics. Members of the elite looked no further than their own close-knit circle for spouses and business partners. For example, traders who came to Gloucester as middling sea captains and became wealthy as merchants were kept out of the elite circles in that town—unless they could marry in. In Marblehead, local merchants stiffly refused to do business with their competition from other towns (like neighboring Salem), except with those men who married local women of the merchant class (Heyrman 1984: 167, 347). New wealth generally had to marry into older, more prestigious families (even if their arrival was only two generations earlier) who formed the "mercantile nobility of the metropolis" if they wanted to get in at all (Bridenbaugh 1938: 185).

Opportunities for social advancement were present in New England, even more so than in old England. The chain of events that could occur in New England (and did occur, as in the case of the Turner family) has taken on a nearly mythic quality in American history:

> An unknown, hard-headed colonial tradesman, sailor, or even farmer becomes a successful merchant, competes for the political and economic favors of the official group, attains power on the colonial Council, creates friendships with influential people in England, and passes on a fortune to his son. The heir grows up in a different society from that of his father, solidifies the family position in English officialdom, uses his family connections to advance in trade and to receive important political appointments, and becomes a colonial member of the British ruling class. Having reached through different channels the social and political position of the Englishmen who left the home country for careers in the colonial governments, he is tempted to

> end his career in the English countryside. But what is a return to his
> colleagues is an arrival for him, and most often he ends his career as a
> colonial merchant prince. (Bailyn 1964: 195)

This pattern also seems to reflect the goal described by Defoe, wherein
the "stain" of trade that secures the family fortune is wiped away when
future generations were empowered to take on the more worthy business of public service.

Without the presence of a landed or titled gentry in America, it was
not difficult for the merchant elite to style themselves not only as
genteel but as the landed elite themselves. This emulation incorporated
the same sorts of activities and pursuits as in England. The New England merchants bought large tracts of land and fine houses and attended
to the improvements of person, environment, and community with the
same sort of (dis)interested ideals of public service. In previous centuries, these social responsibilities would have been the sole province of
the peerage or even royalty.

In this respect (and many others), the merchants in Massachusetts
were similar to other provincial elites. In Edinburgh, for example, the
merchants also held sway in political and cultural affairs. The eighteenth-
century Glaswegian "tobacco lords" shared the same sorts of familial
connections with planters in the West Indies, and strove to accumulate a
fortune to buy their way into landed class, and the sons of the earliest
established families were the ones most likely to thrive and become even
more wealthy (Devine 1978: 47). This powerful oligarchy was made up of
kin and close friends, both from the planters in the Caribbean and the
merchants back in Scotland; correspondence across the ocean was filled
with inquiries about parents, siblings, and cousins. This made it extremely difficult for newcomers to break in to the circle (Devine 1978: 49).

As they looked to London as the cultural center of their world, these
provincial elites were anxious to not appear countrified or out of touch.
One contemporary observer wrote that he was "almost inclined to believe ... that a new fashion is adopted earlier by the polished and
affluent Americans, than by many opulent persons in the great metropolis" (quoted in Clive and Bailyn 1954: 209). Gossip and the news found in
the numbers of *The Spectator*, *The Tatler*, and *The Rambler* were consumed in attempts to keep au courant about London life. *The Spectator*
and *The Tatler* were particularly attractive to the merchant class because they promoted the Whiggish philosophy that was in favor of
commerce as well as universal gentility.

Grand as these provincial elites were, however, their lights would
have been dim compared with those in London. "There were a few of the

leading merchants, or, more frequently, their more leisured heirs like the versifier Peter Oliver or his politician-historian cousin, Thomas Hutchinson. These men, potentates on the local scene, were no more than colonial businessmen in the wider world of British society" (Clive and Bailyn 1954: 204).

The identity created by the merchants in the provinces, particularly in America, would not survive the trip back to England; as described by Bailyn, the journey would be an arrival and not a return. Locally, however, this creation served the merchants very well. In improving their own situations, taking on the public responsibilities of the landed gentry and wealthy merchants in England, they also changed the shape and face of their communities—physically, politically, and culturally. Charlestown, Salem, and Boston saw the construction of wharves and warehouses, highways, shops, and marketplaces (Figure 2). By hiring local laborers and artisans and providing a market for nearby farmers and husbandmen, the merchants profoundly affected the local population and those of surrounding communities. The merchants undertook the regulation of markets and the care and protection of the harbors and the easily accessible courts of laws (Bailyn 1964: 96). These improvements and the control that they implied were not always to universal benefit and it would not be too cynical to observe that there was, moreover, a healthy dose of personal interest in the undertaking of these works. The farmers who supplied the merchants were often constrained to sell at a dictated price.

Like their English counterparts, merchants on Boston's North Shore considered themselves gentlemen and aspired to the paternalistic responsibilities and rights of place that were held by the English landed gentry. This, to some extent, was achievable, falling short only of parliamentary membership. In both old and New England, newcomers were carefully scrutinized and seldom allowed into the merchants' ranks, but once accepted, they were quickly (and permanently) assimilated, to the mutual benefit of both sides. Marriage was the most likely avenue into this class of merchants, and most members of these classes were strongly connected by marriage or blood relation to their business associates. The notion of improvement, both in person and one's domestic and community surroundings, was vital to both groups. While in England even the wealthiest and most powerful merchants were not likely to join the ranks of the landed gentry, in New England and elsewhere in America, the merchants were able to style themselves as the ruling elite and did so with studied diligence. The significant degree of cultural solidarity between the middling sorts of people (to which the majority of

Figure 2. *Crowninshield's Wharf* (1806), by George Ropes, Jr. Although this early Republican painting postdates the Turner family's influence in Salem, it suggests how Salem's busy harbor might have looked when they lived in the nearby Turner house. Photograph by Mark Sexton. Courtesy, Peabody Essex Museum, Salem, Massachusetts.

merchants on both sides of the Atlantic belonged, no matter how elevated) and the landed gentry (titled and untitled) tended to perpetuate this situation.

> In each province they [the merchants] were the leading political interest, exerting a far-reaching influence on legislation; in each town they managed municipal affairs, whether through Corporation or Town Meeting; and in each community they constituted the cultured, aristocratic circle whose roots lay deep in the structure of the British Empire. (Bridenbaugh 1938: 340)

But while the New England merchant elite assiduously looked to London for its cues, it could never be mistaken for anything but a provincial interpretation of a high status culture. Both the demographics of the Great Migration and the Puritan influences in the population ensured this distinction from the start. The desire to appear as English as those still in England and the crossing of old status lines dictated by religion made the New England merchants more conservative in some instances of cultural expression. "As was appropriate for arrivistes, these expressions were archaic, modest, virtuous, and concerned with improvement and learning. They reflect the tightrope that successful men of affairs had to walk in the eighteenth century if they were to integrate themselves into society" (Hancock 1995: 381).

I suspect for this reason, the adherence to mannerly scripts, particularly those that could be used in social negotiation, would have been of special concern to the Massachusetts merchants. The innovative use of new ideas and imported goods to display wealth, proclaim status, and avert the most serious charges of provincialism was combined with a strain of the Puritan ethic and "a compensatory local pride" to shape the New England merchant elite (Clive and Bailyn 1954: 211). This is clearly apparent when examining the data sets that largely support this work.

THE DATA: THREE MERCHANT FAMILIES

Three families provide the core of supportive data for the present work. The Turners and Mascarenes were British-American and the Earles were English, living for long periods in Italy. Although the Mascarenes and Turners may have been associated at one point, the physical and chronological distance between them and the Earles does not diminish the way in which these sets of data reflect the generalizations about merchant life described above. These families all were acutely aware of what distinguished or failed to distinguish them from the rest of their communities and actively sought to cultivate and improve the qualities that, to their minds, set them apart as gentlefolk.

The Turner Family

Robert Turner, a shoemaker, departed from London on the ship *Blessing* and arrived in Boston in 1635. He was born in 1615, and it is possible he was from the eastern part of Suffolk, having left as part of the Great Migration (Moriarty 1931: 7). Most of the initial settlers of Boston were couples or families, and most of them were agricultural workers, moving from East Anglia to New England as a natural extension of the population movement within England (Bailyn 1986: 20). Robert joined the Boston church in 1643, but was not a freeman (Rutman 1965: 247). He held the office of "Sealer of Leather" in 1649, when his source of wealth was listed as his shop.

About 1642, Turner married Elizabeth Freestone (ba. 1619–before 1679), who was descended from Lincolnshire woolen drapers (Moriarty 1931: 8). She joined the First Church at Boston in 1646 after her marriage to Robert. Only three of the six children she bore survived to adulthood. The eldest son, John Turner, was born in 1644, probably also in Boston. His brother Habakkuk was born in 1647, and his sister Elizabeth came in 1648 (Moriarty 1912: 273).

Shortly after Robert Turner's death at age 36, probably about 1653, Elizabeth Freestone Turner remarried George Gardner (d. 1679), a wealthy freeman of Salem. Gardner owned a considerable amount of property and his family had amassed great wealth in the Atlantic trade (Gardner 1901: 213). This wealth would have an enormous effect on Elizabeth's young children in their later lives.

Before John Turner was 25, and presumably with the assistance of his Gardner relatives, he successfully established himself in the coastwise trade (Gardner 1901: 211–212). Favored by the economic and political climate, Captain Turner became one of the wealthiest men in the Commonwealth. Although historian Samuel Eliot Morison, in his *Maritime History of Massachusetts* (1921: 16), described the Salem community as suspicious that young Turner's rapid rise in wealth might be attributed to piracy, it is more likely that his success can be attributed to his family's connections in Salem and in Barbados, where a kinsman (possibly an uncle or cousin, also named John Turner) owned a plantation (Moriarty 1931: 7–14).[3]

[3]The Barbadian John Turner, like his Salem kinsman, was involved in local politics, representing Saint Philip's Parish in the Assembly in 1666, and was a member of the Council in 1667 (Moriarty 1931: 10). He bought one-quarter of the ketch "Speedwell" from his namesake and cousin in Salem on January 9, 1667/8, and was one of the most wealthy merchants in Barbados at that time, particularly invested in sugar. In the same way, Habakkuk Turner, when not at sea or tending to the Turner family business in Salem, took part in town management in various ways, at one point acting as a member of the jury of trials, chosen at the town meeting in June 1680. Habakkuk had married his stepfather's daughter Mary Gardner, on April 30, 1670 (Patch 1861: 235).

Described as one of the most important shipping men in Salem by the end of the seventeenth century, Captain Turner was business partners with his brother Habakkuk (Phillips 1933: 286). Habakkuk often commanded the vessels that went to Europe, Barbados, and other destinations in the Caribbean, where he exchanged the Turners' fish, lumber, shingles, and ships' stores for sugar and rum (Cheever 1859: 172). In one transaction, Habakkuk Turner is recorded as having exchanged fish for "450 pounds of good Muscovado sugar, per tun" (muscovado was raw sugar, from the juice of the sugarcane with the molasses drained off) (Records and Files of the Quarterly Courts of Essex County, Massachusetts V 1916: 48) (hereafter RFQCEC). As a result of this trade, the Turners were also involved in distilling and John was licensed to sell "strong waters" from 1673 to 1680.

With this solid foundation of wealth, in 1668 the 24-year-old Captain John Turner bought about three-quarters of an acre of property from Ann More, a widow to whom the Salem town council granted the land for her support in 1637 (Belknap 1928: 49–50) (Figure 3). On the deed of sale, Turner was described as a "marrenear" (Goodwin 1993: 30). On this property the Captain built a splendid "hall and parlor" style house overlooking his wharf and warehouses on Salem Harbor. Captain Turner married Elizabeth Roberts of Boston. They had five children who survived their infancy: John (born in 1671), Elizabeth (born in 1673), Eunice (born in 1676), Freestone (born in 1677), and Abial (born in 1680).

With their rapidly growing family and business, Captain Turner soon found it necessary to expand his home, so he added a large lean-to and a kitchen to the north side of the house, and around 1678, a two and one-half-story addition to the south. Turner also bought land across the road (then called Turner Lane, now Turner Street), where he built two warehouses. In addition to the Turner Lane house, the captain owned three more houses and various parcels of land (including a farm at Castle Hill in Salem), the lease of Baker's Island (in Salem harbor), a warehouse on Winter Island, and 200 acres in Haverhill. He also owned ships and shares in ships, including the ketches *Blossom*, *Fraternity* (one-eighth share), *Friendship* (one-quarter share), *John and Thomas*, *Prosperous*, and *Society* (three-eighths share); the pink *Speedwell* (one-quarter share); the *William and John* (three-quarters share); and *Willing Mind* (Perley 1924: 360–373).

Captain Turner was a devoted member of the Salem civil and spiritual community as well. He attended the First Church in Salem, where, on January 27, 1672, he was allowed to build a pew for his family (*Essex Institute Historical Collections* 1907: 35) (hereafter *EIHC*). In June of 1680, he and his brother Habakkuk signed the petition, later granted, to build a new meetinghouse to meet the needs of the growing town (RFQCEC VII 1919: 402).

Figure 3. Detail of James Duncan Phillips's *Map of Salem in 1700* (Phillips 1933). The location of the Turner house and its wharf is near the center; note property belonging to Abial Turner at the top of the illustration. Photograph by Jeffrey R. Dykes. Courtesy, Peabody Essex Museum, Salem, Massachusetts.

John was elected to be on the "jury of tryalls" in 1669, 1671, 1673, and 1676 (*EIHC* 1906: 60). Perhaps his obligations as a businessman interfered with his civic duties: in 1671 and 1676, Captain Turner, his brother-in-law Eleazer Gedney, and friend John Grafton were fined for failing to appear for jury duty (RFQCEC VI 1914: 430; VI 1917: 145). And in 1673, Captain Turner was elected to be constable but arranged for another man, John Clifford, to take the position instead. As well as being elected to the committee of selectmen in 1679, John was also involved in other civic duties, such as overseeing the construction of fences and draining swampy land (*EIHC* 1912: 18; Perley 1924: 401; *EIHC* 1913: 77).

In 1680 at the age of 36, Captain John Turner died, having accumulated one of the largest fortunes in Essex County (around £2000) and considerable prestige as a town leader as well as a merchant. His widow, Elizabeth Roberts Turner, subsequently managed the family and the business, probably with the help of trustees and guardians (Jedry n.d.). Elizabeth paid the £3 rent on Baker's Island in 1680 and she was also granted a license to sell liquor after her husband's death (*EIHC* 1926: 182; RFQCEC VIII 1921: 48). When Mrs. Turner married her second husband, Major Charles Redford in 1684, he replaced her as the manager of the estate (Moriarty 1931: 11). Both Elizabeth and Major Redford died in 1691, and it was revealed that Redford (who had died at Bridgetown, Barbados), had been borrowing against the Turner fortune, leaving very little to his charges.

The eldest of the children the second John Turner, was only about 20 when his mother and stepfather died. He took over the family's affairs, and in 1693, as executor of his father's will, he inventoried his father's unsettled estate. The bulk of the value of this inventory was the more than £1,100 that was vested in land, houses and warehouses, and rents. Of the rest of the estate, £335 was in bonds owed to Captain Turner and £100 was invested in silver plate. A poorly repaired ketch worth £80 was another significant entry, and the rest of the inventory consisted of household items and some shop stock.

Family connections with the Gardners and the Gedneys, another important Salem merchant family into which his aunt had married, probably helped smooth the way to economic recovery. It seems that John remained heavily committed to the West Indian trade. Later evidence of this appears on October 4, 1723, when Nicholas Burrough in Nevis received £23 14 shillings on the account of "Col. John Turner of Salem to be shipped by the first opportunity for Boston or Salem in good sugar or mallaces" (*EIHC* 1909: 92). Like his father and mother before him, John was "among those appointed retailers of strong drink in ye Town" in 1712 (Waters 1876: 263). He continued in this trade at least until 1714 (Perley 1924: 86). The Gedneys, as well as the Brownes and Gerrishes, to whom John was related by his sisters' marriages, also had family members licensed to sell liquor, again demonstrating the strong links between family and business in many instances.

In 1701 John married Mary Kitchen, who was the daughter of Lieutenant Robert Kitchen (a merchant and town clerk) and Mary

Boardman of Cambridge. She was baptized in 1683, making her at least 18 years old at the time of her marriage (John was 30) (Perley 1924: 135). In addition to marrying into another influential Salem family, Mary was traditionally described as one of the most beautiful women in Salem (Emmerton 1985: 20). John and Mary had eight children, six of whom survived to adulthood: Elizabeth (b. 1704), Mary (b. 1706), John III (b. 1709), Eunice (b. 1713), Robert (ba. 1715), and Habakkuk (Moriarty 1931: 14) (Figure 4, Figure 5).

Most of John's sisters also married into the most powerful families of Salem. Elizabeth Turner married Benjamin Gerrish, a successful merchant and deacon in the First Church at Salem in 1696. Eunice married the Honorable Colonel Samuel Browne in March 19, 1695, at the age of 19. She is briefly mentioned in Samuel Sewall's diary entry of January 17, 1701/2: "We hear that Mrs. Sam. Brown of Salem is dead, and the first child she had. She earnestly desired a child, having been a pretty [one] while married" (Sewall 1878: 51). Freestone married Major Walter Price in 1699.

Abial remained unmarried until her death sometime after February 1723/4, when she sold some of her common rights to her brother (Dow 1903: 61). She probably lived in the Turner family house with her brother and his family (Moriarty, 1931: 12–13).

While heavily involved in commerce, the second John Turner also took an active role in local affairs, particularly as a constable and a member of the Salem watch and troops. His military career was distinguished and colorful. During June 1704 the diarist Samuel Sewall described how his brother Major Stephen Sewall and John Turner led a party of 43 men against the pirates in the crew of Captain Quelch. The mission went smoothly, "without striking a stroke or, firing a Gun.... Twas all order'd and Tim'd and effected by the Singular all-powerfull gracious Providence of God" (Sewall, 1878: 106). Once the crew and their cargo had been seized, all of the pirates were taken to Boston and most were eventually executed (*Boston News Letter*, June 25, 1704). Turner and Sewall were rewarded with shares of the pirates' cargo.

There was no lack of opportunities for advancement in the military in Massachusetts at the turn of the eighteenth century. In 1708 Reverend Joseph Green of Salem recorded in his diary that between September 26 and 27, "We had news of 300 Indians having beset Haverhill ... we found there was by 20–30 seen—none hurt.... I walked with Major Turner & 20 men to several garrisons in Haverhill" (Fowler 1866: 94). Major Turner had much to fear from a raid in Haverhill, as he had inherited 200 acres of land there.

John's continued success with the Essex troop of horses brought appreciable results. He and his brother-in-law Colonel Samuel Browne

Figure 4. *John Turner* (1737) by John Smibert (1688–1751). The third John Turner (later, the Honorable John Turner, Esquire) was painted as a wealthy and expectant young man of about 26. He is gesturing to two vessels that represent his family's commercial endeavors. Although both were capable of transatlantic travel, the sloop (on the left) was probably restricted to the coastwise trade. The full-rigged ship (to the right) could have been employed in both areas of the Turners' trade. Gift of Mrs. Horatio A. Lamb, in memory of Mr. and Mrs. Winthrop Sargent. Courtesy, Museum of Fine Arts, Boston.

Figure 5. Eunice Turner Browne Balston, by John Smibert (1688–1751). Eunice, daughter of Colonel Turner, married into two important merchant families in Salem and Boston. Collection of the Colby College Museum of Art, Gift of Mr. and Mrs. Ellerton M. Jetté.

rode to Lynn, Massachusetts, on October 15, 1716, and escorted Samuel Shute, the Royal Governor, to Salem. The governor was said to have been greeted with the boom of cannons and to have enjoyed "splendid entertainment that night and the next morning" at Colonel Browne's (Felt 1849: 2: 64). It was some time after this that John was made colonel of the Essex County regiment, the highest military rank that he would attain.

In a parallel to his active military career, Colonel Turner was equally busy in Salem's civil affairs, rising steadily as the years progressed. In 1705 he became a selectman in Salem; by 1712 he was appointed justice. Turner was the deputy from Salem to the Massachusetts General Court in 1713, and shortly thereafter, in 1714, was made a judge of the Massachusetts Court of Common Pleas for the County of Essex (Moriarty 1931: 13). This admirable list of duties was at last crowned by a 20-year stint as a member of His Majesty's Council, beginning in 1721.

Like his English contemporaries, Colonel Turner also contributed to the changing face of his community. In 1712, he and his friends Major Stephen Sewall and Colonel Samuel Browne were charged with the construction of a watch house for the town. This was built "nigh the meeting house," and had a "handsome wooden soldier" carved on top with "Anna Regina, 1712" in gold (Perley 1903: 247). Building such a structure had the effect of conferring further prestige on men who were already well known to their community, and by investing themselves in the "collective image of town," this elite group enhanced their own image as leaders of it (Borsay 1989: 254).

Colonel Turner eventually acquired all the land between Turner, Hardy, and Derby Streets. It seems that he employed his family's various properties as settings for a variety of lavish entertainments. In about 1720, the same time as his appointment to His Majesty's Council in Boston, John renovated and redecorated his house on the harbor, providing a suitably large and elegant setting in which to conduct business and socialize with the rest of Salem's elite community. Reverend William Bentley, the Salem diarist, recalled that Baker's Island was a "delightful" and cultivated garden while Colonel Turner owned it, and it is possible that at least part of it was designed to be a pleasure garden (*EIHC* 1902: 241). Benjamin Lynde, Jr., recorded in his diary that the colonel also used his "farm" land at Castle Hill for barbecues.

Colonel Turner died on March 4, 1742, at the age of 71, a wealthy and respected man. The documentation describing the division of his land and property is considerable; the probate inventory taken after his death is 11 pages long; the value was more than £10,600.

There is a portrait of Colonel Turner's son, the third John Turner, painted by Smibert in 1735 (Figure 4). It depicts a deeply self-satisfied and elegantly clad gentleman gesturing to the ships in the background that are an allusion to his family's mercantile wealth. The portrait was painted when he was about 26, suggesting that the third John Turner fully expected to enjoy the riches and position that his father and grandfather had amassed before his birth. Although he would later be styled the Honorable John Turner, Esquire, honorifics that suggest rank and wealth, his expectations were not to be realized and his hopes for a life as a gentleman were at odds with his political and economic situation.

John married Mary Osborne on April 22, 1738. They had four children who survived to maturity: John IV (ba. 1744/5), Elizabeth (ba. 1748), Edward Kitchen (ba. 1751), and Osborne (ba. 1752) (Essex Institute, *Vital Records of Salem* 1918: 366) (hereafter, *VRS*). Mary Osborne Turner died around 1752, probably as a result of her last pregnancy. John remarried to Katherine Berry on September 29, 1752 (*VRS* 1924: 406). They had four children together: Woodbury Osborne (ba. 1753), Mary (ba. 1754), Elizabeth (ba. 1756), and Charles (ba. 1757).

The third John Turner inherited part of the Turner house (in 1744) at the age of 33 but apparently decided that it was too old fashioned for use as anything but a summer home. By this time the house was nearly 80 years old and, while the neighborhood was still respectable, the growing trade and bustle at the wharves rendered the atmosphere increasingly noisome. The more genteel and newly fashionable center of town a few blocks away from the harbor was more attractive to a young gentleman interested in putting physical and social distance between himself and the family wharves and business. In 1743, a year after the Colonel's death, John built himself an expensive new home (described as "the mansion house") with a gambrel roof on Prison Lane, fitted out with stables and yards (Dennis 1903: 21). It is not difficult to imagine that John wanted to establish himself as a gentleman and as an individual in his own right, outside his father's considerable shadow of reputation, and that he had been waiting only for his patrimony to construct this new house.

Because his father Colonel Turner died intestate, it is possible that John did not receive as much property and land as he expected to. He did receive a double share as the eldest son, which amounted to only £1,225. If the old house on Turner Lane was valued at £565 when Colonel Turner died in 1742, then a new, more extravagantly appointed home in a quieter, more elegant part of town would have eaten up the Honorable John's share of the inheritance at an alarming rate.

It appears that the costs of the new mansion house, the goods to furnish it in an equally high style, and the entertaining that in all likelihood took place there expedited a tremendous drain on the family resources. With a huge young family and John's apparent neglect of the family trade, new expenses and taxes began to weigh uncomfortably on his purse. By 1759 John found it necessary to use family contacts to secure a paying position in the colonial government.[4] In a diary entry dated May 3 of that year, Samuel Gardner recorded the following:

> Pickman was at Boston, and by Mr Epes who was there, learned that Mr. Vans has been turned out as the Naval Officer, and Mr Turner placed in his Room, and what is even more remarkable that Mr Nutting had a commission sent him to be Naval Officer and accordingly went to take the Oath, but Mr Turner obtained another commission which surplanted Mr. Nutting. (Moriarty 1913: 7)

Depriving Mr. Nutting of his commission and Mr. Vans of his position would have violated the very code of polite behavior that John sought to emulate and revealed deeper personality traits in this Turner that were at odds with the notion of a gentleman. By eschewing his connections with business matters and by moving away from the house and wharves that were the source of his family's wealth for two generations before him, John had undercut the wealth that made his status as a gentleman possible. Ironically, it was probably his father's reputation in business and the community that helped him get this position, as there are indications that the Honorable John himself was held in light regard.

The tax valuations for 1760 (the earliest extant for Salem) indicate that John was paying taxes on only one house, so that it is likely that he was forced to move back to Turner coincident with his assuming the post of naval officer. There is no mention of the grand house on Prison Lane, and it was probably either sold or seized.

The Honorable John's mother, Madam Mary Turner, had also received a share in the old Turner house, but it was probably at the time that John and his family returned that Madam Turner moved to Ipswich, where she lived until her death in 1768. Perhaps the move was provoked by antipathy toward her improvident son, but her departure may have taken the form of a strategic retreat, as her son's family had

[4]John's titles probably came from his family's importance in Salem and his post as a naval officer. According to J. T. Main, nonmilitary titles like "esquire" usually were given only to men of property and respected name before the Revolutionary War (Main 1965: 215–216). His use of the prefix "honorable" was associated with his place in the naval office, "for it was attached to miscellaneous persons of repute, especially high civil officials, many of whom were self-made men" (Main 1965: 218–219). Similarly, the wives of high officials were addressed as "Madam" (Carson 1966: 45). Although Colonel Turner's rank was genuine, Dr. Alexander Hamilton noted the propensity for assuming military titles in Salem: "Mr. Malcolm and I ... went to the Ship Taveren where we drank punch and smoked tobacco with severall collonels; for collonels, captains, and majors are so plenty here that they are to be met with in all companys, and yet me thinks they look no more like souldiers than they look like divines, but they are gentlemen of the place, and that is sufficient" (Bridenbaugh 1948: 121–122).

mushroomed during the intervening 13 years. At the time of the last child's baptism date (presumably soon after his birth) in 1757, there were eight children under the age of 12 in the house. Four of them were under the age of five. It is conceivable that a woman who had already raised her own large family would have had little interest in sharing the peacefulness of affluent late life with a houseful of toddlers.

When John's position was threatened by a political rival, Turner fought to keep it. He wrote to Governor Thomas Hutchinson, begging that he be allowed to keep his post, reminding the governor that he "never took a bribe ... that is a fack & have had them offered by severall [to] which they can attest [I never took]" (Jedry n.d.: 16; Felt 1849: 265). He remained in this post from 1759 to 1772 until the age of 63, in spite of the danger to an avowed Tory levying the Crown's taxes on ships returning from abroad in rebellious Salem (Felt 1849: 265).

It was an unfortunate time to be a professed Anglican (his father, grandfather, and great grandfather had been Congregationalists) and a staunch Tory in an American port city economically hurt by prohibitive taxes, but still the Honorable John Turner, Esquire, persevered in his beliefs. He was one of several hosts of a ball and parade held in honor of General Gage when he visited Salem and the British troops quartered there on June 11, 1774 (Moriarty 1931: 14). Many other Loyalists were forced to leave for England or other less volatile British possessions. Those who remained suffered abuse (in the form of snowball attacks, house arrest, or floggings) at the hands of citizens dedicated to the rebellion.

Curiously, John Turner does not seem to have been subject to these persecutions. Local legend has it that the only reason that the old Turner house was not burnt to the ground by anti-Loyalists was that two of John's sons were particularly active and popular proponents of the American cause. John Turner IV took part at the Battle of Chelsea in 1775 and later commanded the privateer ship *Franklin* in the early 1780s (Allen 1927: 137). On May 19, 1782, this fourth generation Captain John Turner took a "ship after a fight of forty minutes, had one killed and one wounded. The prize had two killed, eight wounded" (Felt 1848: 272). Edward Kitchen Turner was a surgeon, possibly on the *Massachusetts*, an American naval brig (Morgan 1986: 61).

The Honorable John's luck did not hold, however. On September 30, 1782, he was forced to sell the Turner Lane house. Events went from bad to worse thereafter. On September 23, 1785, William Pyncheon records that John Turner sold his remaining furniture at auction (Oliver 1890: 223). In 1787 the authorities seized the mortgage to Baker's Island, which had been meant to remain in the Turner family's possession for "one thousand years and a day," and during that same year, John's right to a particular piece of property he claimed was his own was investigated and seized (Oliver 1890: 279, 281).

Ultimately, the Honorable John Turner, Esquire, was willing to openly break with his community, flaunt his political and religious differences, wheedle, cheat, and finally sell off the house and land that had been in his family three generations. In his quest to be perceived as a wealthy gentleman, free from the irksome title "merchant," he shattered every unspoken rule of personal and public deportment. This dishonor may be further mirrored in the fact that the Reverend William Bentley of Salem, who wrote from 1784 to 1819, almost always refers to the Turner house in terms of *Colonel* Turner, even though the Colonel had died 40 years before the diary was started. Bentley seems to have written off the third John, although the Honorable John was alive the first two years during which the diaries were written and constantly refers to Colonel Turner in terms of awe and respect. Such is the staying power of a good reputation.

Impoverished and living in lodgings, John died of asthma in 1786, caught between his aspirations and harsh reality (*VRS* 1925: 287). The tattered remnants of his family's wealth (his probate inventory was worth just £58) found in this setting of dishonorable insolvency is a striking contrast to the previous state of the family. After all of his furniture had been auctioned the only traces of his former wealth lay in his fine clothing, which included a green velvet coat, silk stockings, seven caps, silk breeches, and a "surtout coat," a silver watch and buckles, gold buttons, and two silver spoons. His inventory also listed a pair of knitting needles, a cheese toaster, a coffee mill, and a "mackarel line," mundane items for which there was little room in his father's probate inventory. This may also be suggestive of the notion that he was forced to manage his own housekeeping on a stingy level unimaginable by his immediate forebears. One item that does seem to have been passed down to the Honorable John is "a money scale," possibly the same one from which a weight was recovered at the site of the Turner house, a sad reminder of what trade had meant to his family.

When Captain Samuel Ingersoll bought the house from the Honorable John Turner in 1782, it retained some of the cachet with which Colonel Turner imbued it. Although the house was in a neighborhood that now could be considered, at best, respectably middle-classed, the home had made the transition in the community's imagination from "old fashioned" to "venerable." Having been associated with Salem's trade and one of its most important families for over a century, the house conferred an element of status on its newest occupants, just 40 years after it had been considered too antiquated for the last member of the Turner family to live there.

Captain Ingersoll made considerable alterations to the property, including the construction of a seawall, the removal of the "back part" of the house, presumably the seventeenth-century kitchen ell, and the extension of the first floor of the new parlor to meet the second floor overhang (Bentley 1907: 463). Susannah Ingersoll, Samuel's daughter, eventually inherited the house in 1811 (Bentley 1907: 216). It was she who invited her kinsman Nathaniel Hawthorne to the house and, as local legend has it, regaled him with stories of the house's history, inspiring among other works, *The House of the Seven Gables* (1858).

The house went through the hands of several other owners until it was bought by Salem philanthropist Caroline Emmerton in 1908. She hired Joseph Chandler to restore it to its seventeenth-century appearance in 1909 and the property is to this day an historic site that continues to raise money for her settlement work (Figure 6).

Figure 6. The Turner house after restoration, ca. 1910. Courtesy of the House of Seven Gables Settlement Association.

The Mascarene Family

Much of the nonarchaeological data that was collected for the present study came from two collections of letters. One of these sets of correspondence, between John Mascarene and Margaret Holyoke Mascarene was written while John was in London pursuing business matters. He was starved for news of his home in Cambridge, Massachusetts, and in return for tidings of his family, he wrote to his wife, Margaret, about every detail of his existence in London so "that You may know how we live." These letters included mention of fellow New England merchants who frequently met in the New England Coffee House in London, his opinions of the London merchants he encountered, and how his meals and evenings out compared with what he was used to in Massachusetts. His homesickness was extraordinary and touching. When John left Boston at the end of August 1761, he anticipated being in London for just a few months. He did not return until October 1764, more than three years later. But his longing for home and family generated a series of inquiries that inform us about what he missed and why.

John Mascarene was born in Annapolis Royal in April 11, 1722, the son of General Jean Paul Mascarene, a refugee Huguenot who went to Nova Scotia to be the commander in chief of the province (Shipton 1945: 35). While Jean Paul was regarded as a great letter-writer and conversationalist, apparently John did not share his gift. He was shy and his letters to his father during his apprenticeship to a successful merchant were long, pious, and uninteresting, though it should be pointed out that these mundane details provide the researcher with more quotidian information than a "clever" letter might (Shipton 1945: 36). By 1743 John was handling the family mercantile business, and in 1750 he married Margaret Holyoke, daughter of Edward, once president of Harvard College, and Margaret Appleton Holyoke. The new couple bought a house and shop, but in 1752, John left for England for the first time to make his claim for £5000 that his father was owed for his military service in Nova Scotia. John had hopes that the income from that sum would allow him to retire from business altogether.

The results were nightmarish: not only was Mascarene unsuccessful in his suit, but the trip contributed to his bankruptcy and he suffered a breakdown as a result (Shipton 1945: 36). To make matters worse, he was accused of having property that he had been given by his father made over to Margaret's name in order to protect it from his creditors. Both John and Margaret denied this accusation strongly. After a protracted struggle, he cleared his reputation, regained his health, and recouped a modest fortune through manufacturing and retailing of potash, upon which he wrote a sound treatise recommending it as a staple to balance trade with England (Shipton 1945: 37).

In 1761 Margaret and John moved to the Wadsworth house in Cambridge with their two children Paul and Elizabeth. It was at this time that John again undertook his suit for the £5000 and set off for London.

While he was away, John copied nearly 150 of his letters to Margaret into a series of carefully stitched copybooks. He recorded each of the letters in order, numbered them individually, with a description of by which ship the post was sent, and included occasional checklists of what letters he received from Margaret and what she had received from him. When he heard of the loss of a ship that was carrying some of his post, John would dutifully summarize what he had sent in that letter in the next so that Margaret might not miss any of the details of his daily life.

Considering that John was abroad under stressful circumstances, with his friends and family at least four weeks away by ship, it is not surprising that he was lonely. He constantly encouraged Margaret to write more often, praised her letters when they were exceptionally good, corrected them, and, occasionally, complained of her poor handwriting. His only other steady companions were fellow merchants from Cambridge, Salem, or Boston, or elsewhere in New England. John dined with these friends frequently, sometimes once a day, and when they returned to America, he took the opportunity to send small presents and letters to his family with them.

Aside from meeting with a few fellow New Englanders, John also occasionally dined with his landladies and their families. He made a few new friends in London in the course of the prosecution of his "memorial" (as he referred to his suit), and dined with them as much for companionship as to press his case.

Because there were often long delays between stages of his petition, John was very conscientious about making the most of his sojourn in what he viewed as one of the greatest cities of the world. He read, attended lectures on philosophy, listened to music, and visited the theater, all in the name of self-improvement. "I have I think now seen almost all the public diversions & Entertainm'ts worth notice in this town & if you have receiv'd all my past Letters believe you will find some account of what I judg'd remarkable at the Museum which contains Sr. Harry Sloane's Collection of Curiosities" (Mascarene May 18, 1762). These public diversions included several evenings at Ranelagh, where he noted, "the whole thing Strikes with Grandeur & Magnificence[,] drinking Tea or Coffee walking round & attending to the Musick," and Vauxhall: "It was suppos'd not less than five thous'd people were there this

Evening. [T]he charge of the Boat, Gardens, Entertainment & coach home stood us in 4/4 a piece" (Mascarene April 18, 1762; May 22, 1762).

John Mascarene also made a few brief tours outside London. One was to Oxford where, he noted to Margaret, he "had breakfast in room in which [Joseph] Addison lived when he was at Magdalen" and where he spoke "very freely" with master and fellows of Trinity, two of whom, he was careful to point out, were titled, about "our college [Harvard] and theirs" (Mascarene July 25, 1762; July 7, 1762). On another occasion, he traveled with several friends to Hampton Court, Kew, and Windsor. On that trip, he marked his letter "from Mr. Pope's grotto, principally for the sake of dating it from hence as it may give you perhaps some pleasure to receive a line from so celebrated a habitation.... I flatter myself I could by staying here a little while catch some small spark of that noble fire which perhaps may be still hovering here, tho' the Genius who grac'd it is now numbered among the Dead" (Mascarene April 5, 1762). This underscores his, and coincidentally, Margaret's, literary tastes and the importance of education and improvement to the Mascarene family.

Finally in 1764, John Mascarene had the results of his suit. While he was not granted the £5000 he sought, he was given the Comptrollership of the Port of Salem, with its small income, and 10,000 acres of land in Nova Scotia. This arrangement was disappointing on several levels: John had asked for 20,000 acres and also was ambivalent about having to move his family to Salem (Shipton 1945: 38).

John did not become a member of the uppermost circles in Salem society, possibly because of his shyness, his reduced financial circumstances, or his job in the customs office, or possibly the fact that like the third John Turner, he signed the letter welcoming General Gage, but there are still indications that he was held in some regard by the local community. When the port of Salem closed during the Revolution, the Mascarenes became even more impoverished. He sought work in Boston at the customshouse there, and even moved his family to that city, but died soon after in September 1779 (Shipton 1945: 39).

Ironically, the Revolutionary War had rendered it impossible for him to recover his lands in Nova Scotia, as most of it now fell in the new province of New Brunswick. Although the Massachusetts governor made attempts to secure a pension for Margaret after John's death by stating the Mascarenes' loyalty to England, the Crown coldly replied that since the Mascarenes had remained in the colonies, they were now subjects of the United States and not any responsibility of Britain's (Shipton 1945: 39). In an attempt to raise money for her support, Margaret advertised John's "valuable and elegant" library of "History, Classics, Mathematics, Astronomy, and Miscellaneous Pieces in English

Latin and French, Chamber's Dictionary, Mathematical Instruments, &tc" (Shipton 1945, 39). She eventually donated what she could not sell to Harvard. Margaret died on December 21, 1792, a resident of Boston (Shipton 1945: 39).

A good deal can be discovered about the characters of the Mascarenes, from context and direct contemporary observation. In a letter of introduction, John was described as "a very worthy Gentleman, of a liberal education, & of Singular Modesty; which is so great that it may perhaps prove a disadvantage to him, where he is not known, tho' it highly recommends him where he is" (Mascarene October 23, 1761). This recommendation of John carefully mentions his famous late father and his connection to President Holyoke of Harvard and his shyness was transformed into restraint rather than awkwardness. John's observations of the "sluttish" and "gaudy" behavior of the nobility at court are tinged with prudishness, yet these are comments on *public* behavior and may not be entirely at odds with his frank appraisal of a friend's lack of sexual capacity, his erotic memories of his courtship of "Peggy" and their honeymoon, and his sending "Burlesque" prints home to her. His letters are honest, anxious, observant, hopeful, dutiful, and affectionate.

Margaret too seems to blend this combination of sense and sensibility, perhaps with more grit than her husband. In one of her few letters in the collection, she describes a devastating fire at Harvard College, an event that is of great personal consequence to all of her family. "We are all Real mourners on this occasion and I doubt not your attachment to alma mater, will make you feel Sorrowful upon this Conflagration[.] As the Father, he had very near lost his life on the occasion, the Snow was in drifts in many places four and five feet high, papa went thro' it all with nothing more upon him than he sets in the house" (M. Mascarene January 30, 1764). Yet, after her moving description, all the more harrowing for her father's near death, she takes a hardheaded approach to rebuilding. Even as she is demurely circumspect in her direction of her husband, Margaret explicitly outlines how John can help to raise resources to restore the loss:

> I hope the King will give Something to repair the Loss as he has never done any thing for this College, yet, and my Dear (tho I would not dictate to you) I believe if you was to try among your acquaintance for some donations by way of Books, or mathematical Instruments, it will be very acceptable[.] Mr. Winthrops thinks that 3 H[undre]d p[oun]d Sterl'g would buy a compleat apparatus, and there are books which are of no great use in a private Gentleman's Library, which are ornamental and useful to an ancient and Public one[.] Cahill is generous, and Loves Show, Suppose you was to ask him, if he gives any thing worth while, he will have the Public thanks of the

college, and his name will be enroll'd among the worthy Benefactors to this Luminary, and will live when the Building themselves are Crumbled into Dust, but I need say no more, I know you will want no Stimulus in this affair[.] our Country men at the Coffeehouse I doubt not if properly applied to, would subscribe something Handsome, and [the] wealthy Lady that is minded to make her Fame Immortal, cant have a more favourable opportunity. (M. Mascarene January 30, 1764)

Margaret was extremely literate, resourceful, and economical, taking what measures she could to maintain the family's circumstances while John was away. On several occasions Margaret also assisted John in his potash business.

In the Mascarenes' case, it was not great wealth but education and important family connections that determined their social status. John Mascarene's letters reveal his concern for social improvement, his awareness of his public image, and, above all, his desire to win his suit so that he and his family could retire genteelly. He clearly considered himself a gentleman and was proud of his achievements in researching and selling potash.

The Earle Family and Joseph Denham

While the Mascarenes provide a rather domestic view of merchant social life on both sides of the Atlantic, the Earle family gives us insights into the English merchant world, set off by the foil of expatriate life in Italy. The Earle family was rooted firmly in Liverpool, and though various members of the family lived abroad for long periods, they always returned to England. Although the letters to Mary Earle from her husband's junior partner Joseph Denham are not as intimate as those between the Mascarenes, their formal distance informs us about the role of social connections in merchant life. In fact, the very courtesy that permeates Denham's half of the correspondence provides vital clues as to how these connections were maintained. His letters, written with a dutiful gallantry about friends' lives and activities, political events and gossip, and offhand comments about business opportunities, reveal the formulae.

This collection of data is particularly significant as the Earle family's rise almost coincides with the development of Liverpool as a major port in the eighteenth century. Liverpool became the preeminent slave port in England in the 1730s, because of her more diverse trading base and better communications with midland cities over competitors in London and Bristol (Corfield 1982: 41, 42). Liverpool was called "the

Darling Child of Fate" (in 1706) and "the emporium of the Western World" (in 1773) because of her staggering business success (Corfield 1982: 125).

The Earle family originated in Warrington (just to the south of Liverpool), but in 1688 John Earle (1674–1749) moved to Liverpool, working for a wealthy merchant and ship owner there. His own mercantile endeavors began around 1700, and John dealt particularly in wine, but also in iron, tobacco, sugar, and slaves (National Museums & Galleries on Merseyside, Maritime Archives & Library 1995: 1) (hereafter NMGM). Eventually he became mayor of Liverpool.

John married Ellen Tyrer and they had seven children, four of whom survived them: Ralph (1715–1790), Thomas (1719–1781), William (1721–1788), and Sarah (n.d.) (NMGM 1995: 2). The brothers were partners in a trade that included timber and slaves. Thomas is of particular importance for it was his sojourn in Italy that provides the characters and the setting for a remarkable set of letters between his junior partner Joseph Denham and his wife Mary Earle. Thomas dealt in coffee, wine, hides, and marble from his first merchant house in Livorno (sometimes called Leghorn by the English), eventually establishing another house in Genoa with the brothers Thomas and Robert Hodgson, and John Denham, who eventually expanded the business to Civita Vecchia (NMGM 1995: 2)

The long-distance connections between different members of the Earle family and their partners were maintained through social engagements as well as business transactions. The bonds were seen in terms of courtesy, mutual obligation, and mutual advancement. These bonds tied Liverpool and Italy together, not falling away when different members of the extended family moved from one place to another. The connections were reinforced by constant letter writing, visiting, favors—including procuring hard-to-get items from England for those who remained in Italy, or sending back curiosities and novelties for show in England—and the exchange of presents—food, personal items, or gossip.

Little is known about Joseph Denham. From his letters, it is clear he was well educated, well read, fluent in Italian, French, Latin, and possibly Portuguese, and numerate. He was skillful in business matters. He was familiar with notions of courtesy of the day and offered scathing remarks on the behavior of the Earles' friends as well as the English nobility in Italy. He claimed in another set of letters to be in the English army at one point, but as it turned out, he quite intentionally misrepresented several important aspects of his life to the Earles and their associates.

In his letters to Mary Earle, Denham corrects her Italian, her spelling, and her penmanship, keeps her up to date with court politics in Genoa and Livorno, suggests whom she might cultivate, and offers her the most salacious of gossip. His descriptions are pointed and witty. In his letters, Joseph occasionally tiptoed on the edge of propriety by considering whether to tell Mary some dirty joke or rude anecdote, and then convinces himself that he will amuse rather than distress her by doing so. His tone is frankly flirtatious and often charming, and occasionally throughout the correspondence, Denham asked Mary to intercede on his behalf to her husband about matters of business.

Denham wrote several times a year to Mrs. Earle and the letters that exist are dated between August 1763 and August 1781. There does not appear to be a significant gap in information between the letters that are in the collection, suggesting that the group is relatively intact (apart from the missing half of the correspondence written by Mary Earle). When Mary returned with her husband, Thomas, and their two daughters to Liverpool in 1766, she remained there at least until the correspondence ended in 1781.

On more than one occasion Denham had reason to chide Mrs. Earle about her failure to write back to him. This suggests possibilities that she was a poor correspondent, that her letters were lost, or that she was uninterested in communicating with him that are presently unprovable. But there is a particularly long gap between 1768 and 1772 that seems to correlate with the Earles' discovery that Denham had a wife who was still living in England. By 1771 he had married an Italian woman and had two children with her. Joseph Denham was an engaging liar, a debtor, and a bigamist as well.

Throughout the course of his correspondence with Mr. and Mrs. Earle, Denham made no reference to the fact that he was married. Indeed, he occasionally made veiled, though highly recognizable, references to Mrs. Earle about his love (possibly unconsummated or unrequited) for another Englishwoman in Italy, implying his unmarried state. After the revelation of the existence of his first wife, Denham's final few letters (separated by a few years) to Mrs. Earle have a melancholy character, reflective, perhaps penitent, but resigned, and in each of them he requests her to speak to Mr. Earle on his behalf on some business matter. The brash assurance and dashing flirtation of his earlier letters is unmistakably missing.

A group of twelve letters to his English wife, Sukey Denham, sporadically written by Joseph between 1762 and 1771, also survives in this collection. In them, Denham describes his serpentine attempts to avoid creditors. He first fled from England to Ireland, then to Portugal and Italy; he changed his Christian name and explained to Sukey that it was a bureaucratic mistake, and he even instructed Sukey how to fold and seal her letters so that they could not fall open to curious eyes. He recounts his attempts to look for work and, in the same sentence that he denies her charges of infidelity, avers his continuing love for Sukey.

Denham keeps Sukey at more than arm's length. He mentions the Earles to Sukey and his hopes for bringing her to live with him in Italy, but consistently refers to the dreadful plagues, fevers, wars, famines, or work troubles that prevent him from doing so. These calamities do not appear in his letters to Mrs. Earle. At one point in 1767, Joseph was apparently in some fear that she might have followed him to Italy, for he wrote an anxious and obsequious letter to the English ambassador at Venice inquiring if his wife had been in service there (NMGM D/Earle/ 3/3/6). The next month he wrote to Sukey in London, complaining that she had not written to him for a year.

During the next few years, Joseph Denham seldom wrote to his wife and then only when he had a favor to ask of her. Finally, after a gap of more than two and a half years, between September of 1768 and April of 1771, he wrote a letter to Sukey explaining that because he had not heard from her in some time and after attempting to reach her and her sister with no success, he assumed that she was dead. Furthermore, because he believed she was dead, he had kept company with ladies of "unblemished character," and eventually one of them became pregnant. Joseph claimed that he was forced to marry his Italian wife after her family beat him, and he complied only because he feared how the Earles might react after they had welcomed him to their home and business (NMGM D/Earle/3/3/15). Denham was now living in Civita Vecchia with his Italian wife, whom he had married with a papal dispensation, and their two children, but continued to protest his love for Sukey.

The last letter from Denham to Thomas Earle, who apparently had helped the newly resurrected Sukey Denham with her living expenses, is remorseful, as he wrote of the death of his "dearest friend," probably Sukey. He reiterated a desire, previously communicated to Mrs. Earle, that the Earles burn all of his letters, something that they obviously did not do. The fact that his letters to his wife Sukey are *also* preserved in the Earle Collection suggest that Sukey gave them to Mr. Earle after he began to help her financially.

As titillating as the story told by these letters is, these data also support several of the premises of the present work. The first is the consistent references to the health, whereabouts, and activities of English and Italian friends, which suggests just how important maintaining relationships, founded as much on amity as business, were, particularly during physical separation. Denham's continuous and passing descriptions to Mrs. Earle of the Hodgson brothers and their families and the Lawrences (all partners of the Earles) indicate the role that familiar intimacy, often maintained by the women in these merchant communities, played in business connections. These were maintained through correspondence and the exchange of small gifts or food from England to Italy, and vice versa, which tended to reinforce the identity of the Anglo-Italian merchants as well as their personal relations.

The references that Denham makes in his descriptions of various court or public occasions, and particularly his comments on the behavior of the English nobility in Italy, also underscore the attention that was being paid to public decorum and deportment by "gentle" folk at the time. The correction of Mrs. Earle's spelling and punctuation, and Denham's recommendations that she could best learn to write well by reading well (he recommends Swift and Addison to her, and had been translating poetry by Tasso for her perusal), in addition to his remarks about his own studies, also imply how thoroughly the merchant class, as well as other upper middle-class folk, had embraced the notion of gentility through self-improvement. This was equally visible in the letters from John Mascarene to his wife.

The final point, although a small one, is vital. Joseph Denham had represented himself to the Earles in a particular way for many years before they discovered the truth. Yet, they did not insist on his entire withdrawal from their company (business or social) when they might have done so with perfect justification. I believe that this supports the notion that once one had been accepted into a particular status group and had demonstrated one's ability to function successfully in it, the acceptance was permanent. This was the case with the third John Turner, spared by the community for his sons' and his father's sake, and the Mascarenes, who were Loyalists, but still commanded respect for their behavior and their families' sakes as well. This enclosure, although potentially dangerous, served both parties well. Any missteps that might emerge after joining the community would be easier to correct from the vantage point of elevated status.

HISTORICAL ARCHAEOLOGY AND MERCHANT SITES

There has been a gratifying amount of historical archaeological work conducted on sites in the eastern United States that were associated with merchants, including Beaudry (1995; n.d.), De Cunzo (1995a),

Garman (1994), Goodwin (1992a; 1992b; 1993, 1994a, 1994b, 1996, 1997, 1998), and Harrington (1989). In some cases, the merchants have been examined specifically as social beings playing particular roles in their respective communities, rather than simply the fortuitous inhabitants of a site.

I conducted the archaeological work at the Turner house with a volunteer crew of professional and amateur archaeologists in the summer of 1991. About 15m² was excavated, uncovering features from the eighteenth and nineteenth centuries. We recovered nearly 17,000 artifacts from all periods of occupation, from the late Woodland period to evidence of the use of the site as an historic attraction in the early twentieth century. The range of types of artifacts and their generally small size suggest that the site was a busy place throughout its history, not only a fine residence but an active seat of commercial activity as well.

While a full description of the artifacts has been given elsewhere (Goodwin 1992a, 1993, 1994a), (and some classes of artifacts are discussed in detail in Chapter 4), a brief mention of certain other artifacts is warranted here. With the long and consistent history of occupation of the site by the Turner family (and the documentary references to their entertainments), it is no surprise that most of the artifacts that we unearthed were related to food preparation, service, and storage.

The location of the house on the harbor is itself the best reflection of the Turner families' involvement in trade, but there were several small indications of the mercantile life that appeared in the excavations. A fishhook and a lead fishing weight were discovered in early nineteenth century contexts (fishhooks were being sold in the Turner shop as early as the seventeenth century) (Goodwin 1993: 196, 198). The probate inventories of both Captain John Turner and Colonel John Turner listed equipment both for fishing on a small scale and for preserving fish at commercial levels.

Another artifact that was related to mercantile endeavors, which was also a direct link between the archaeological and the documentary record, was a brass scale weight. This weight, about 1.3cm², is marked with fine lines running diagonally across the surface. The word "scruple" and the numeral "2" appear on it, indicating its weight, which is roughly two-thirds of a dram or about 2.5g. Although "scruple" is a term frequently used to describe the weight of drugs, it was also employed by goldsmiths. In the probate inventory of Colonel John Turner, there is an entry in the "accounting room" with a listing for "a pr Pistols 60/ a pr Silver Scales & weights 40/." The niceness of the weight's manufacture, its location in the accounting house with pieces of armor, firearms and

Figure 7. The scale weight (marked "Scruple" and "2") and molded silver wire were excavated from the Turner house in 1991. The weight is 1.3cm square. Photograph by Jeffrey R. Dykes. Courtesy, Peabody Essex Museum, Salem, Massachusetts.

bullets, and a silver-hilted sword, and the value of the scale set (40 shillings) suggest that the weight was an important piece of equipment. Also in that probate inventory are several entries of silver, measured out to the ounce, pennyweight, and grain, and in a context near to where the weight was excavated, a molded piece of silver wire was also uncovered (Goodwin 1993: 200) (Figure 7).

The great quantity of architectural debris and most of the features on the Turner site indicate the amount of labor invested in the renovation of the Turner house and its grounds through the centuries. Colonel Turner's 1743 probate inventory mentions that the house possessed a garden, and other documents show that there was also a garden of some sort on the property in the nineteenth century as well; a stone pathway was uncovered, and a post from a fence that marked it were uncovered.

Evidence from Captain Ingersoll's enclosing of the gable ends of the house was recovered, as was a large French drain also constructed by him, that cut through layers of eighteenth- and nineteenth-century artifacts (Goodwin 1993: 246–247).

A particularly interesting artifact is associated with the earliest construction of the Turner house by Captain Turner in 1668 and its remodeling by his son Colonel Turner about 50 years later. A fragment of a window lead was found to have been milled with the date "1664" on the interior face (Figure 8). Although this dates to four years prior to the construction of the Turner house, research by Egan, Hanna, and Knight (1986) suggests that leads were often stored before they were used or shipped and that there was a four-year lag between the changes of dates or locations in the vise wheel. Found in an eighteenth-century context, the window lead may be part of the assemblage generated from a remodeling episode that Colonel Turner undertook about the time of his appointment to His Majesty's Council in 1720.

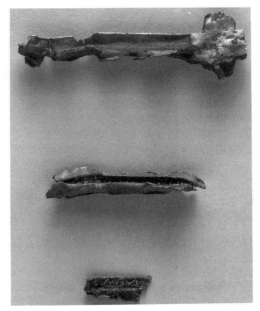

Figure 8. Window leads from the Turner house excavations. The lead at the bottom is marked "1664." Photograph by Jeffrey R. Dykes. Courtesy, Peabody Essex Museum, Salem, Massachusetts.

In addition to the work conducted at the Turner house, several other sites nearby have been excavated, all of the inhabitants being closely involved in the mercantile activities in Salem, Massachusetts, during the seventeenth and eighteenth centuries. Several of these projects, including a citywide survey of potential archaeological resources (cf. Mrozowski, Shaw, Holland, and Zisk 1988), have taken place within a mile of the Turner house. While some work has focused on the wealthy Derby family, especially at the advent of Salem's involvement in the China Trade (cf. research by Friedlander 1991; Garman 1994), other research has explored the part that farming and husbandry played in Salem's trade (cf. Hood's 1991 research on the Skerry house and the role of artisans and other professionals (cf. work on the Narbonne house by Moran, Zimmer, and Yentsch 1982).

A few miles up the coast in Newbury, Massachusetts, Mary C. Beaudry has explored the changing image of the property and the Spencer-Peirce-Little house since 1986. The property has been a working farm since it was acquired by John Spencer in 1635, and over many years it gained a reputation of gentility as the "country estate" of the Peirce family (who lived on the site from 1651 to 1772) and especially of the Tracy family who were among the most wealthy of Newbury's merchant elite (Beaudry 1995: 24). The house was constructed by Daniel Peirce, Jr., after he inherited the property from his father in 1677. Its impressive structure was built in about 1690 in a style that was outmoded in England and unique in North America: it is cruciform in plan, built with local stone and a brick porch entry, and has decorative details in molded brick (Beaudry n.d.: 14–15).

The house and property were inherited by successive generations of Peirces (entailed by Daniel Sr.'s eldest son in 1722) and remained in the Peirce family until 1772 when Nathaniel Tracy purchased it. The Tracy family treated the property as "a country estate" until the late 1780s when the family was forced, through a series of financial setbacks, to "retire" to the country house.

What is particularly relevant to the present study is Beaudry's discussion of the construction of identity of the Newbury "prestige elite" and her employment of McCracken's notion of "patina" (Beaudry n.d.: 49). The Tracys' ability to express their social and economic power was boosted by their ownership of a house and property that had acquired an association with gentility and wealth over the course of more than a century. This long-term association with the "gentry" of Newbury conferred on the house's owners (even to the present day) a status reminiscent of English nobility that survived the economic insolvency of the

Tracys. This identity, maintained and enhanced by the "antiquity" of the house, supported claims to status through longevity (Beaudry n.d.: 43). This notion of antiquity, continuity, or longevity repeatedly has been shown to be important to the merchant-class identity in Massachusetts, including that of the Turners.

The life of Portsmouth resident Joseph Sherburne (1680s–1745) in many ways mirrored that of Colonel John Turner's career (Harrington 1989). A merchant with an elaborate home close to his wharves, Sherburne was also a colonel in the militia, a member of the king's council, and an active representative in the colonial legal process as a supreme court justice. Like members of the Turner family, Sherburne was involved in the trade with Virginia and the Caribbean. He remodeled his house around the 1730s to use it, as well as other material signs of his wealth, including his dress, diet, and slaves, to indicate his high status in the community and the colony (Harrington 1989: 5). Faith Harrington makes the point that the Portsmouth merchant elite manipulated their landscapes and portable artifacts in the same ways as the Connecticut Valley "River Gods," while relying heavily on their wharves, warehouses, and important goods to establish their precedence in that community (Harrington 1989: 11).

Another important example of merchant research comes from Lu Ann De Cunzo's 1995 "The Culture Broker Revisited," which studied the White family, who were merchants who lived in Duck Creek, Delaware, from 1760 to 1815. The Duck Creek merchants dealt with local (rural) goods primarily, and secondarily with consumer goods (imported through Philadelphia). Unlike the other merchants described here, they did not deal to any large degree with direct international trade, and the center of their business was their shops. Both the Duck Creek merchants and the North Shore merchants extended their influence well beyond the limits of their commercial structures. Both had access to information from the world beyond their localities and to a certain extent, filtered it to suit those communities. Both had architectural and landscape investments in their communities, with keen, localized meanings. Material culture (in the Whites' case, fences as well as portable artifacts) was also used to segregate the community, but also to inform and instruct about the class and provide a model of what could be attained.

In her analysis of the relationship between world-systems theory and ethnographic studies, De Cunzo employs the term "culture brokers" to describe the role of the merchants as negotiators or middlemen "between producers, consumers, and other middlemen in the local-global exchange systems" (De Cunzo 1995a: 181–182). Citing Paine (1971), she states that there is more than a simple, inequal relationship between client and patron (or merchant and consumer), as "each complements the other for mutual gain" (1995a: 182). By trading literally and figuratively on the four "funds" described in Villamarin and Villamarin (1982), including wealth, social position, political affiliation, and religious alignments, the Duck Creek merchants were able to communicate their power and facilitate their brokering activities in a highly effective manner.

Land had a particular significance, in terms of wealth and capital, for inhabitants of rural Delaware, as did high-style architecture. Merchants William White and his son-in-law Darrach purchased many parcels of land between them and manifested their wealth through the construction of permanent, brick buildings to maintain continuity as social and economic leaders (De Cunzo 1995a: 195–196). Inside the home, material culture, such as clothing, furniture, carriages, and silver tea sets, was on display to intimate acquaintances and business partners, and their elite brokering status was reinforced though the bonds of marriage, political connections, and church appointments. The more connections each merchant shared, the more likely both would benefit through access to goods, information, or services (De Cunzo 1995a: 199–200).

While scale and context may vary, there is a great similarity in the way that merchants in different parts of Atlantic America interacted with their communities. Merchant culture remained flexible enough to accommodate local tastes and mores, while still retaining the overarching structure of the elite. Merchants used material culture in similar ways. The permeation of power beyond commerce into realms of religious, civil, and social participation was apparent in the above studies, as did the oft-observed necessity of elite bonding through marriage, apprenticeships, partnerships, and other social connections.

CONCLUSION

Although the place of the merchant in seventeenth- and eighteenth-century English society was debated, the reality was that the wealth possessed by that class allowed them to comport themselves with all the (expensive) characteristics of gentlemen, an identity that was becoming more flexible and accessible at the time. By accepting the self-regulation that was part of this widening culture of politeness, as well as by emulating the elite's association with land, material display, and public service, merchants were able to establish a recognizable, if not entirely comfortable, place in society. This place was further reinforced by the familiar habits of the urban elite who, like the landed elite, tended to rely on marriage and kin relations and longevity in order to maintain their social status and power.

In New England, where the presence of merchant elite was thrown into high relief by the lack of a resident landed elite, the merchants who gained power also manipulated family and marriage ties and other cultural elements, but in an American fashion. Part of this new design was derived in concession to the prevailing influences of Puritanism and Whig philosophy, part was related to the conservatism of the provincial nouveau riche, which appeared as a mixture of anxiety and pride in local identity, and part was caused by the conscious trampling of old social lines. All of these elements disposed the merchants toward a strict adherence to accepted codes of behavior. By remarking on and criticizing the actions and manners of others, as seemed to occur regularly in the data, presented here and elsewhere, these new gentlefolk demonstrated their understanding of mannerly behavior, proclaimed their acceptance of it, and, at the same time, announced the peculiar character of their own brand of manners. This comparison of virtuous and industrious American merchants with decadent English nobility served to offset, I believe, any anxiety that might have come from seeing one's own occupation or social group held as a negative example in courtesy literature.

For the reasons described above, mannerly behavior, if taken as a means of negotiating social interaction along social boundaries, would seem to be particularly important, then, to merchants in New England. There were also other reasons to believe this. One would be social distance, or more correctly, the lack thereof in several instances. For example, so many of the merchant families who became the ruling elite in Massachusetts were merely a generation or two from much humbler circumstances. The Turners, although assisted by their stepfather George Gardner, were the children of a shoemaker. The same could be said for virtually every family in the first generation of successful Salem merchants. While "the English memory for social origins was ... shorter than was general on the Continent; since few families were very old, newcomers were less conspicuously new," this was doubly so in New England, where even a generation or two made the difference (Habakkuk 1953: 18).

What also might have added to this necessity for mannerly behavior was the potential for rapid change in fortunes, either up or down. While wealth was a key factor in determining status, a merchant could maintain some semblance of his rank when the fluctuating market place worked against him, through mannerly behavior. Thus, loss or gain of wealth did not always mean a corresponding change in status. If acceptance to a class was permanent, it was because of the associations one maintained. This is evident in the misfortunes of the Mascarenes' lives. Similarly, the Honorable John Turner, Esquire's, failing of fortune or the revelation of the truth about Joseph Denham's background also could have been much more disastrous—they received assistance because they had been already assimilated into the community.

Merchants in New England were successful in importing and adapting many of the luxuries and habits of deportment and gentility that were enjoyed in England. Some of these diversions, like the theater, were not permitted by Puritan regulation; others, like the cultivated delights of Ranelagh or Vauxhall, would not have been sustained by the relatively small population who could afford such things. But if the polite distractions that amused English merchants and their friends were not available in Massachusetts, there were other, homegrown and peculiarly New English recreations that maintained the bonds of the community.

The virtues that the merchant elite embraced were the codified notions of deportment and noblesse oblige found in courtesy literature, which had its origins in the instruction of the landed elite. Even when North Shore merchants actually did not own the courtesy works, they were recognizing and employing the same ideals. By harkening to the emblems, activities, and behavior patterns of the ruling classes in England, the Massachusetts merchants took on the power and trappings of the landed elite. This can be seen in the artifacts, architecture, and observations of the Earles, Mascarenes, Turners, Tracys, and Whites. Bourdieu observed that:

> Legitimate manners owe either value to the fact that they manifest the rarest of acquisition, that is, a social power over time which is tacitly recognized as the supreme excellence: to possess things from the past, i.e. ..., accumulated, crystallized history, aristocratic names and titles, chateaux or "stately homes," paintings and collections, vintage wines and antique furniture, is to master time, through all those things whose common feature is that they can only be acquired in the course of time, by means of time, against time, that is by inheritance or through dispositions which, like the taste for old things, are likewise only acquired with time and applied by those who can take their time. (Bourdieu 1996: 71–72)

Archaeology, by its nature, tends to focus on the material. Having established the historical context of the ideals that the merchant elite imported and adapted, the material manifestations of those ideals demand attention. Merchants were consumers as well as importers of artifacts and manners. They also interpreted the use of those goods to establish and maintain their elite identity in America. This was expressed partly in the public sphere through public displays, dress, and elections and partly in more private areas for members of the same merchant class. Similar expressions were seen in England at the same time, and the ritualizing of events, heightening the appeal to the senses through gorgeous costume, free (or exotic) food and intoxicating drink, bonfires, musket-fire and cannons, elaborate speeches, and processes, cemented these ideas for the group itself and for the community. By participating in these events, the merchants acknowledged their allegiance to their social class as well as to the wider community, welcomed new members, excluded other outsiders, and provided displays for emulation by potential consumers, simultaneously reinforcing their social place and providing a continuous market for some of their imported wares and manners.

Material Expressions of Mannerly Behavior | 4

> *Tradelove: One merchant is of more service to a nation than fifty coxcombs. The Dutch know the trading interest to be of more benefit to the state than the landed.*
> *Sir Philip: But what is either interest to a lady?*
> *Tradelove: 'Tis the merchant makes the belle. How would the ladies sparkle in the box without the merchant? The Indian diamonds! The French Brocade! The Italian fan! The Flanders lace! The fine Dutch Holland! How would they vent their scandal over their tea tables? And where would you beaus have champagne to toast your mistresses, were it not for the merchant?*
> *Prim: Verily, neighbor Tradelove, thou dost waste thy breath about nothing. All that thou hast said tendeth only to debauch youth and fill their heads with the pride and luxury of this world. The merchant is a very great friend to Satan and sendeth as many to his dominions as the pope.*
> *—Susannah Centlivre, A Bold Stroke for a Wife*

INTRODUCTION

Susannah Centlivre brought a number of social contentions to the stage with *A Bold Stroke for a Wife* (1718). As well as castigating the impolite extremes of Anne Lovely's four guardians and revealing their inherent flaws through the stratagems Colonel Fainwell employed to gain their consent to marry Mrs. Lovely, she also discovers contemporary arguments about the role of merchants in contributing to luxury and decadence, the social nuances of (and gender associations with) polite drinking, the way men and women consumed newly available imported and manufactured goods, and how, in a very short time, such things as tea, fans, and notions became "necessities" rather than luxuries. In a few brief lines she delineated the desires for commercial goods and the dangers therein.

That the merchant Tradelove should provide one of her caricatures is not surprising. Merchants were not only controversial as the source of the goods described, but they were, in some ways, some of their own best customers. Eager to acquire the trappings of wealth and polite gentility, their access to a wide range of goods, novel or luxurious, provided them with a social camouflage that helped obscure the difference between mere wealth and traditional definitions of high status. Especially in America, where they could become the "landed gentry," merchants armed with these goods and the knowledge of the behavior that properly accompanied them could be effectively described as the "makers of manners."

This chapter is about the merchant class and the ways that they used some types of objects as meaningful ways to create and indicate identity. After beginning with some general statements about material culture, I will then discuss contemporary and current issues of the construction of identity and consumption. Then, by examining the qualities of *luxury*, *novelty*, and *patina* in an early modern context (in American and England), I provide an idea of the range of debate that went on at that time as well as its context in order to better identify the meaning in the past. I have chosen an artifact category as an example to discuss each of these qualities, to demonstrate how they were perceived by contemporary people, and to show how merchants might have used these artifacts in mannerly ways. The selections of artifacts associated with clothing, foodways, and architecture and landscape are not original choices, but they are useful because these groups are the most visible both in courtesy literature and in the archaeological record. I believe that combined with the general comments that go before, they may especially underscore some of the social components of the merchant class. I concentrate on the most public aspects of the polite rituals associated with these goods because *personal* intent cannot be elicited from their presence in the archaeological record or probate inventories. Unless there is an individual statement of that intent, then all else is speculation at best.

I am by no means suggesting that these objects can be interpreted in only this one way. I believe that the data I have gathered suggest that these artifacts and their polite usage were important, but only one part of the picture. Certainly objects convey public messages, which may or may not be intended on the part of the owner, but they also may have multiple private associations. Personal choice, no matter how rationalized, reflects sentimental, aesthetic, or philosophical associations as well as functional capabilities. I think that as researchers we are phenomenally lucky to recover any of these subtler, personal expressions, which generally are revealed only through documentary sources, but in this discussion, I focus on the broadest, most public aspects of these uses.

Emulation is a topic that is inevitably linked with consumption, particularly in this period. Based on the data I have found and other secondary sources, I believe that, for the most part, the agency of the consumer allowed him or her to selectively adopt different elements of what had previously been part of elite culture, investing them with new, locally contextual meanings. This is particularly true with the Massachusetts merchants, who chose certain components of the culture of the landed elite and adapted them to fit the New English social context. Even the burgeoning interest in polite behavior and civility in the early modern period was adapted from elite courtesy literature, broadened, and applied to new definitions of gentle behavior for the middling classes. There was no wholesale acquisition of goods in a rush to become "elite," but certain types of items were purchased and used to demonstrate comparable qualities that were thought to characterize the elite.

The material culture used in polite social rituals was used to identify knowledgeable members of a social group, exclude pretenders to that group, and celebrate group solidarity:

> [Objects] do so first by demonstrating the owner's power, vital erotic energy, and place in the social hierarchy. Second, objects reveal the continuity of the self through time, by providing foci of involvement in the present, mementos and souvenirs of the past, and signposts to future goals. Third, objects give concrete evidence of one's place in a social network as symbols (literally, the joining together) of valued relationships. In these three ways things stabilize our sense of who we are; they give a permanent shape to our views of ourselves that otherwise would quickly dissolve in the flux of consciousness. (Csikszentmihalyi 1993: 23)

I believe that as much importance was attached to understanding the polite use of an artifact as to the fact of its ownership.

MATERIAL CULTURE, CONSUMPTION, AND IDENTITY

There has been so much written lately about consumption and consumers in history, the ways and reasons for which they purchased goods, the effects, and ultimately, the results of all this acquisition that I

will not attempt to summarize the discussions here.[1] Because it is such
a provocative topic, one that often is met with strong feeling, tied up with
issues of identity, agency, and politics in the early modern period as well
as today, I believe it is important to try to establish a contemporary
context for the present study, both in terms of its subject matter in the
seventeenth and eighteenth centuries and in my approach to it at the
end of the twentieth century. Although merchants were the focal point of
much of these debates as the importers and owners of goods, in this
chapter I treat them particularly as consumers who employed material
culture in the creation of their identity. I believe the changes that were
being made throughout the social structure contributed in part to the
fascination with newly available goods in a quest to define individual
and class identity within an expanding range of potential choices.

What Is Consumption?

The definition of consumption that I employ is "the desiring, acquiring and enjoying of goods and services which one has purchased," further clarified the as "active seeking of personal gratification through
material goods" (Appleby 1994: 162, 164). Conscious choices may not be
conspicuous and even that which is inconspicuous may be making a
profound statement (Burke 1994: 148). I would also suggest that with
this conscious or subconscious personal gratification, comes self-definition,
as Marshall Sahlins put it, "by satisfying our own individual needs we
create society" (quoted in Mintz 1994: 267).

Whether there was a genuine "revolution" in consumption in the
eighteenth century remains a subject of debate (see the arguments
made in Styles 1994: 529). Certainly there was an unprecedented level of

---

[1]Historical archaeologists will be familiar with the tremendous energy exerted in examining the topic, including Spencer-Wood (1987), Henry (1991), Klein (1991), LeeDecker
(1991), Wurst and McGuire (1998), and Gibb (1996). Martin (1996) not only thoughtfully
discusses issues of consumption and emulation, but also considers the relationships
between scripted behavior and material culture props. Miller (1987) delineated the
relationship between consumption and industrialized society. Work by Douglas and
Isherwood (1982) focused on the marking of identity through the use of goods. There is
also a huge and important body of literature by historians on material culture as objects
of consumption. McKendrick, Brewer, and Plumb broke ground with their *Birth of a
Consumer Society* (1982). Weatherill (1996) and Shammas (1990) both examined the
probate inventories from Britain and America to identify trends in consumer behavior in
the early modern period. Brewer and Porter (1994) in their edited volume provide a
splendid overview to the theory, history, and discussion of consumer behavior worldwide,
and Carson, Hoffman, and Albert (1994) have approached the topic from the American
side of the Atlantic.

access for a larger percentage of the population with the drop in price of some goods (Porter 1994: 65). Shammas suggests that while there was no more money being expended on consumer goods than previously, the falling prices may have allowed more purchases with the same available funds, but she remains cautious, remarking on the shortcomings of probate inventories as sources of data (1990: 294–296; 1994: 192). Weatherill points out that a larger percentage of consumers was to be found in the middling sorts, not universally through the entire social spectrum from laboring poor to landed elite, and that it was those people (tradesmen and merchants) who were most likely to be handling the new goods who were also more likely to own them (1996: 193, 195).

What was driving the upswing in consumption remains unclear, but this was not a phenomenon restricted to Europe. About this same time, newly emerging wealthy groups in Asia also began to consume on a large scale, often acquiring more goods than those who had rank as well as wealth (Burke 1994: 158). There were significant differences between these phenomena, because the consumption was on a smaller scale in the Chinese, Japanese, or Indian situations and was often constrained by strict legal regulation (Wills 1994: 134). The ways that Asian consumers made their choices were also very different from those in Europe, as discussed further below. What is apparent is that in both situations, the increase in social mobility and wealth was matched by a parallel use of goods to define personal and group identity. In Europe, this may have been increased by the growing emphasis placed on the individual as described by Johnson (1996).

It was not only purchased goods or new goods that were consumed and given meaning, the transfer of material culture of a personal nature was also very important. Elizabeth Shackleton of Lancashire, for example, thought of her household goods as either mundane or celebrative, and used new clothes and older objects with sentimental value to mark family celebrations (Vickery 1994: 284). She also described how small handmade gifts given by members of the same social circle served to cement relations, the investment of time and personal effort in this case being more meaningful than a purchased gift (1994: 287). Similarly, the venison pasties and beer sent by Mary Earle to Joseph Denham and the potatoes and other produce he sent to her were more effective (and affective) ties than other objects might have been, reflecting personal connections, as well as identity, within a larger group.

In terms of recovering the meaning of the artifacts being consumed, researchers are faced with the uncomfortable knowledge that the simple presence of an object on an archaeological site or in a probate inventory cannot be used to infer meaning of any sort. It might be possible only to learn about one of the more public meanings of a particular object from contemporary primary documents, because the meaning of material culture is fluid and often personally as well as culturally meaningful in many ways. Difficult enough in the present, our ability to perceive the meanings of goods in the past is obscured in part by not knowing the principal use of those goods. Weatherill, for example, suggests that window curtains could be used for warmth, privacy, or decoration, while mirrors could be used for lighting, decoration, or to feed vanity (1994: 211). Most consumer goods do not have intrinsic meanings but are assigned them by their users (and observers), who continuously negotiate interpretations for the objects (Breen 1994b: 250). This mutability confers power on the consumer to actively manipulate the meaning of artifacts in the service of personal or class identity, which is successful only to the extent that others recognize and accept the statement being made or to the extent that the individual making the statement is content that it has been effective.

Although certainly some consumer choices were made with the desire for novelty, fashion, or social emulation in mind, I believe strongly that most decisions about the acquisition of goods were carefully considered in light of personal issues such as expense; suitability of class, gender, age, among many others; durability; and individual taste (see, for example, Vickery, 1994). John Mascarene, shopping for his wife in London, made it very clear that fashion and richness were considerations, but personal suitability was paramount in choice:

> I am glad you mention what sort of Gown you would chuse as it will influence me in my choice which I would endeavour to regulate by what I thought might be agreeable to you, but hope I shall not be oblig'd to go to Monmouth street as I should think it better to purchase one thing new & fashionable tho less rich than that you should appear in what might be called borro'd Feathers[.] [T]he extent of my purse must however be the principal direction in this and many other affairs which I doubt not you will readily submit to. (Mascarene February 22, 1762)

I believe this was particularly the case of American consumers, by whom English manufactured goods and styles were valued, but not blindly taken up. Kevin Sweeney makes a convincing argument that certain styles were embraced but given peculiarly local meanings, while others were retained when newer styles were introduced, suggesting that American consumers were filters of English style, rather than sponges (1994: 13).

While I believe that in many respects, colonial merchants in Massachusetts (like their English counterparts) were taking cues from the social and material behavior of the landed elite in England, I believe they were, for the most part, selecting what they perceived as evocative and meaningful and using it to suit their situation. Their audience was American, not English, and their own culture, generally speaking, was British-American. An uncritical appropriation of goods and manners would not have succeeded in this cultural milieu, which was formed by different philosophies and religions, demographics, and distance from the taste-makers of the metropolis of London. Sweeney's (1994) use of the term "high-style vernacular" is an effective descriptor for the sort of material goods, and the attendant mannerly use of them, used to convey a variety of messages (including historical right to rule) in this context. The use of courtesy literature, in fact, might make the best case for emulation of elite society, but based on John Mascarene's observations, it is clear that the differences between American and English manners suggest this same sort of selective, adaptive behavior seen in earlier instances of adoption.

While emulation of the upper classes has been traditionally cited as the main spur to the increased consumption of goods in the late seventeenth and eighteenth centuries, this notion, derived from Veblen (1994) and employed by McKendrick, Plumb, and Brewer (1982), and so passed on into many studies, has been demonstrated to be incomplete. Martin found that simple emulation could not account for the differences between the probate inventories of eighteenth-century backcountry Virginians and their eastern counterparts (1996: 73, 87–93). Weatherill (1994) has shown that new goods more often appear in the homes of tradespeople and merchants than they did in the gentry household. These well-off folk were not part of the landed elite and although Elizabeth Shackleton paid attention to elite fashions, she found much that was worthy of her criticism (Vickery 1994: 290–291). Similarly, the Mascarene and Denham correspondences are filled with criticisms of the "better sort."

The Veblenesque view of emulation tends to remove agency and individuality from the consumer at the very time when these characteristics were being so vigorously explored in the social world. This view has also reduced the role of consumption to a thoughtless, frivolous, empty activity as opposed to production (Veblen 1994: 57–59; Shammas 1994: 177). The role of women as consumers similarly has been severely mitigated. Breen suggests that women were perceived as avid consumers because they could, for relatively little expense, acquire manufactured goods that would relieve them of hours of tedious labor; these choices demonstrated an agency that was unappealing to the male observer (1994b: 256–257). It is possible, too, that women were more frequently associated with portable goods because of the general rules of inheritance: women tended to inherit portable objects rather than real estate (Vickery 1994: 294). If ready-made goods had the taint of luxury, then women were more likely to be seen as consumers, profligate or otherwise, because of the long historical association of women and luxury since Eve's reputed commission of the first sin of "luxuriousness" (Sekora 1977: 24).

If Vickery's observations are correct, however, there are certainly differences in the way that women and men made purchases. Women, as part of a family household, tended to shop for quotidian items, goods that were smaller, more mundane, and likely to be needed repeatedly. Men tended to purchase luxuries, shopped more impulsively, and usually bought the family's "dynastic" goods (1994: 281). The fact that are there are differences seems to be supported by Weatherill's research (1986: 143–144; 1994) and strongly suggests that there is certainly more going on than women simply attempting to "keep up with the Joneses," particularly if men were purchasing the luxuries. Consumption—luxurious, emulative, or otherwise—was not the exclusive purview of either gender.

It would be an interesting exercise to substitute the word "luxury" whenever the word "consumption" is used, either in present-day research or in contemporary essays on the topic. While I agree with Campbell's (1994: 50) assessment that consumption in the seventeenth and eighteenth centuries was not necessarily the same as modern consumption because of its links to hospitality and gentle status in the past, much of the criticism focuses on a moral discussion of spending and excess, which is not at the heart of all consumption.

There was a wide range of opinion on consumption that often blurred with luxury or antitrade rhetoric in the early modern period. Defoe gave it much consideration as early as 1728 with his *A Plan of the English Commerce*:

> In England, the Country is large, populous, rich, fruitful; the Way of Living, large, luxurious, vain and expensive, even to a profusion, the Temper of the People gay, ostentatious, vicious, and full of Excesses; even criminally so in some Things, and too much encreasing in them all. Hence comes as a Consequence, a vast Importation of foreign Growth of every kind, either for Eating or Drinking, for Fancy or Fashions, and this so great, as not to be equall'd in any Part of the World. (1967: 193)

He in fact used the word "consumption" to describe the quantities of goods and foods that were purchased and expended by the English people.

Some period writers believed that commerce, and the communication that resulted from it, promoted the ideals of the Enlightenment, which should lead to a "fulfillment of natural rights" (Lieberman 1995:

145). James Sterling wrote in 1752: "Necessaries grow in sterile Lands, / To answer Nature's prime Demands. / Ev'n there some Superfluities are made; / That Arts and Elegance may spring from Trade" (quoted in Shields 1990: 16–17). Addison, using Sir Andrew Freeport, his alter-ego in discussing matters of trade, wrote in 1711: "My friend Sir ANDREW calls the Vineyards of *France* our Gardens; the Spice-Islands our Hot-Beds; the *Persians* our Silk-Weavers, and the *Chinese* our Potters. Nature indeed furnishes us with the bare Necessaries of Life, but Traffick supplies us with every thing that is Convenient and Ornamental" (Steele and Addison 1988: 439). Others, looking at more detrimental effects closer to home, were not so convinced. Henry Fielding, in his *Enquiry into the Cause of the Late Increase of Robbers* (1751) referred to the "vast torrent of Luxury which of late Years hath poured itself into the nation ... [and] almost totally changed the Manners, Customs, and Habits of the People, more especially of the lower Sort" (quoted in Sekora 1977: 5).

The upper classes perceived several threats to the social order. Not only were existing hierarchies threatened when the poor desired what they could not have and the middling sort appeared to ape the dress and manners of the elite, but there was a more concrete danger in theft, burglary, and other violence of the sort described by Fielding. Bernard Mandeville in *The Fable of the Bees: or, Private Vices, Publick Virtues* (1732) replied to those who railed against consumption and new luxuries that vices could be found in the poorest of situations and, if trade ceased, England would be bankrupt. He claimed that:

> Frugality is ... a mean starving Virtue, that is only fit for small Societies of good peaceable Men, who are contented to be poor so they may be easy; but in a large stirring Nation you may have soon enough of it. 'Tis an idle dreaming Virtue that employs no Hands, and therefore very useless in a trading Country.... Prodigality has a thousand Inventions to keep People from sitting still, that Frugality would never think of. (Mandeville 1966: 104–105)

He further insisted, rather self-righteously, that "where good Sense is fashionable, and a genteel Behaviour is in Esteem, Gluttony and Drunkenness can be no reigning Vices" (1966: 121–122). He pointed out that merchants encouraged navigation and domestic manufacture but admitted that "his [the merchant's] greatest Dependence is Lavishness and Drunkenness." He dismissed that point, however, insisting that merchants could not be held responsible for vices resulting from their trade any more than "a Druggist may be to Poisoning, or a Sword-Cutler to Blood-shed" (Mandeville 1966: 85).

Not entirely separate from the historical debate over the virtues or dangers of consumption, the new power of the consumer was a significant force to contemplate. This power was immediately noticeable in visible identity creation and agency, but later in the century, consumers found they had the ability to formulate protests that demanded response (see Breen 1994a). As more people were able to afford imported and manufactured goods, however, the need to maintain separate class identities caused some distinctions to be made in the way that material culture was perceived and used.

Some Important Qualities of Goods: Luxury, Novelty, and Patina

The availability of cheap goods introduced a new vocabulary of materials, qualities, and forms to the consumer. At the same time, new questions that paralleled those being asked about the changing social structure of the early modern period arose around those goods. Just as the social order was being renegotiated, the goods that, in part, helped create blurred distinctions in that structure fell under that same critical scrutiny. It is impossible to separate issues of class from those of access and morality: what was deemed "appropriate" for one group was redolent of "greed" and "waste" in another. Increasing individuality made a new mode of communication necessary, one that could sustain a new hierarchy while preserving the integrity of the individual. Increasing interest in the "proper" use of these artifacts led to an interest in behavior that was deemed "polite" or "civil," especially in the popular press. Mannerly behavior was thus used to express as much of the status of the objects as the goods themselves and provided subtle or not so subtle clues as to the rank of the user, as well as his or her aspirations and background.

I propose that there was a scale of statement that could be made about individual identity based on artifacts and the way they were used by their owners. This involved self-identification and the association of an individual with a social group through inclusive and exclusive polite rituals. The least convincing statement one could make was that of *luxury*: anyone could buy, borrow, be given, inherit, or steal a luxurious item. It became a matter of concern to make a distinction between those who could afford to buy a luxurious object and those who appreciated the social ramifications of the articles and their proper use. This was visible in the elevation of the "subtle" and in the quest for *novelty*. The most remarkable distinction was that of *patina*, an enduring indication of the historic legitimate right to high status.

I have chosen clothing as a means of discussing luxury, artifacts related to celebrative foodways as an example of novelty, and architecture and landscape as being emblematic of patina. These are not entirely arbitrary choices. These categories are prominently discussed in the courtesy literature and abundantly visible in the archaeological record. There is also a scale of intent in these objects: clothing speaks most about the individual's state and aspirations, the use of tea wares or punch bowls is seen in group statements of identity, while architecture and landscape, particularly in the colonies, were important dynastic statements about heredity and long tradition.

Luxury and Dress

In the seventeenth and eighteenth centuries (as well as before and since), the notion of luxury evoked a morass of conflicting responses. Associated with decadence, the exotic, and the inherently immoral, luxury was also supremely desirable. This makes a precise definition difficult. It can be said that a luxury is anything above and beyond what is strictly necessary for survival, but as Weatherill thoughtfully points out, there is more to life than meeting physical needs (1994: 207). McCracken describes luxury as "consumption that exceeds physical and most ordinary cultural needs" (1990: 115). Trying to describe objects in a probate inventory or other document as necessities, decencies, or luxuries (sensu McKendrick, Brewer, and Plumb 1982: 1) does not seem to help, as many commodities, in the sense of artifacts or services, may slip imperceptibly between these categories as fortunes change (for better or worse), prices are altered, or fashions shift.

The idea of luxury is further complicated by class issues. Luxury was so long a social marker of the elite that most of the furor surrounding it in the early modern period was generated because of the rapidly changing material world in Europe and America. Elite groups have always consumed to receive self-gratification, to establish identity, and to create privacy. It was widely believed (or at least, put forth) that luxuries did not harm the upper classes, who ostensibly were accustomed to them. It is important to realize that luxuries were usually deemed indecent, corrupting, and tasteless when they were used by a person with whom one had some dispute, and the luxurious artifacts were perceived as ennobling an already virtuous character and behavior (Vickery 1994: 286).

The public outcry against luxuries was most vocal when it was the lower classes (or women) who sought them. These desires were generally portrayed solely as either greedy emulation or crass intraclass competition, and it was the fear of social disorder that arose from this consumption that spurred a shrill response: "Its [luxury's] baleful influence extends even to inferior ranks of people, who vie with each other in furniture, eating, drinking, and apparel" (quoted in Raven 1995: 304). Luxury for the "lower sorts" was dangerous because members of the elite were forced to surrender the visual cues of their status and to reckon members of the lower classes as individuals with agency and because it "destroyed harmony" (Appleby 1994: 167, 172). Fielding and Defoe both lamented about how more of the middling sort of people were able to afford luxuries and imitate their betters, which increased popular anxiety about the "upward spiral" of consumption, when the enjoyment of luxuries only increased the appetite (Borsay 1989: 231). Sekora suggests that luxury historically has been seen as anything unneeded or something to which one has no right, and therefore inherently contains the seeds of overthrow of hierarchy and order (1977: 23–29).

Explicit discussion of luxury appears in the first half of the eighteenth century. George Cheyne wrote: "Since our Wealth has increas'd, and our Navigation has been extended, we have ransack'd all the Parts of the Globe to bring together its whole Stock of Materials for Riot, Luxury, and to provoke Excess" (quoted in Porter 1994: 64). "Luxury is the spreading Contagion which is the greatest Corrupter of Publick Manners and the greatest Extinguisher of Publick Spirit" (John Dennis 1711, in Porter 1994: 58–59). This extravagance was perceived to lead to a breakdown of national as well as personal character, and consumption was blamed for literally weakening the physical constitution of the population. Porter observed that according to eighteenth-century literature, the consumption of luxuries promoted physical consumption by weakening the constitution with rich, unhealthy food, thin clothing, and artificial heating and lighting (1994: 67).

But, even with all its potential pitfalls, luxury, in the sense of a surplus, or a freeing from heavy or dreary work, could also improve the world, depending on the character of the goods and, most important, the quality and character of the possessor. I have mentioned some of Mandeville's arguments for the benefits of luxuries (keeping vice at bay with self-restraint), and there were others who believed that good could be found in luxury. David Hume wrote: "Luxury, when excessive is the source of many ills, but is in general preferable to sloth and idleness, which wou'd commonly succeed in its place, and are more pernicious both to private persons and to the public" (quoted in Raven 1995: 303). Observing the relationship between polite behavior, commerce, and the "Whig humanism" in the works of such writers as Steele and Addison in the 1710s, Lawrence Klein remarked that while "material progress ... widened the traps of dissipation and luxury encountered by the wealthy, it freed many from the morally deadening effects of poverty" (1995: 226).

Luxury was also connected to the debates about commerce and trade. In 1691 Nicholas Barbon commented that "the main spur to Trade, or rather to Industry and Ingenuity, is the exorbitant Appetites of Men which they will take pains to gratifie, and so be disposed to work, when nothing else will incline them to it, for did Men content themselves with bare Necessaries, we should have a poor World" (quoted in Appleby 1994: 165). Many people, especially merchants, claimed luxury promoted industry, navigation, and international goodwill, but for others it was associated with foreign vices and believed to have an effeminizing effect on men as well as weakening the general populace. Later, at the end of the eighteenth century, the import of luxuries was seen as creating unwanted international bonds. A notion of being enslaved to goods was given political currency in the amplified neoclassicism of revolution-period America, where tea, British textiles, and other "baubles" had become politicized and were converted to "public vices" (Breen 1994a: 475).

Luxurious clothing was the most obvious target for attack; it represented the most visible expression of personal identity and aspiration and upset visual clues of the social order. According to a 1733 *Boston Gazette* writer, "We run into ... Extremes as to Dress so that there is scarce any Distinction between Persons of great Fortune and People of ordinary rank" (quoted in Breen 1994b: 255). Clothing was also the example most frequently cited in the courtesy literature that discussed the pitfalls of luxury. According to those works, not only was sartorial superfluity uneconomical for *all* classes, it promoted a vanity that smacked of idolatry. At the same time, however, it was imperative to dress according to one's social station, neither better nor worse. The negotiation of this balance required some effort. Brathwait wrote that even if it kept the cold out, clothing made of thin tissues and gaudy colors would only bankrupt the wearer and one who wore apparel "above degree" was "lifting self proudly against God" (1631: 12–13). But, he continued to say:

> For albeit, some have affirmed that all gorgeous attire is the attire of sinne, the *quality of the person may seeme to extenuate the quality of that sinne. For Noble and eminent personages were in all times admitted to weare them; and to be distinguished by them.* Neither indeed, is the sumptuousness of the habit, so reprehensive, as the phantastickness of the habit respect of the form or fashion. It is this which derogates highly from the repute of a Christian. (Brathwait 1631: 91–92, emphasis added)

Increase Mather also spoke passionately against the false god of fashion in 1679:

> A proud Fashion no sooner comes into the Country, but the *haughty Daughters of Zion* in this place are taking it up, and thereby the whole land is at last

infected. What shall we say when men are seen in the Streets with monstrous and horrid *Perriwigs*, and Women with their *Borders and False Locks* and such like whorish Fashion, whereby the anger of the Lord is kindled against this sinful Land! (quoted in Bailyn 1964: 141)

In testimony of the power of fashion over parental advice, Samuel Sewall remarked with disappointment that Increase Mather's son, Cotton Mather, wore a wig (Carson 1966: 15). In spite of the influence that the elder Mather had, the sumptuary laws that were enacted in Massachusetts from 1651 to 1653 were never successfully enforced (Calvert 1994: 259).

In addition to being expensive, fashion was also regarded as foolish by some writers. "The Mode destroys itself; it aims always at what is perfect, and never finds it, at least it will not stop there, should it even find it," wrote Fenelon. "It would be Reasonable if it chang'd, only that it might change no more after having found Perfection, both for Convenience and Comeliness; But to change for the sake of Changing, is it not to seek rather inconstancy and Irregularity, than true Neatness and Decorum?" (1707: 205). This argument could be subtly employed to denigrate those who purchased goods to appear better off than they were, as fickle fashions were only for those who did not know any better.

True neatness and decorum were at odds with the gaudiness of new, cheap finery. With the wide range of goods available, the wearer had to beware of excess. "The True Graces depend not on a vain and affected Dress," wrote Fenelon. "It is true none are to be blam'd for seeking Neatness, proportion, and Decency, in the Habits necessary for covering their Bodies. But after all, these Stuffs which cover us, and which may be made both convenient, and handsome, can never be the Ornaments that give a true Beauty" (1707: 202). The character of the wearer was what gave the dignity to the clothing, and no amount of finery could make up for personal coarseness.

For the elite reader of courtesy literature, it was a matter of finding the middle ground in clothing between what was appropriate to one's station and what was "apish," "affected," or "antick." Being able to afford items of luxurious clothing did not mean one should wear them indiscriminately. Not surprisingly, restraint was the watchword, along with dressing to suit the company one was in. In 1749 Lord Chesterfield, a firm believer that dress was "a thing of consequence in the world," cautioned his son that "a man of sense carefully avoids any particular character in his dress; he is accurately clean for his own sake; but all the rest is for other people's. He dresses as well, and in the same manner, as the people of sense and fashion of the place where he is. If he dresses better … that is more than they, he is a fop; if he dresses worse, he is unpardonably negligent" (Chesterfield 1992: 128).

Lady Pennington also advised following local taste:

> By decency, I mean, such an habit as is suitable to your rank and fortune; an
> ill-placed finery, inconsistent with either, is not ornamental, but ridiculous: a
> compliance with fashion, so far as to avoid the affectation of singularity, is
> necessary; but to run into the extreme of fashions, more especially those
> which are inconvenient, is the certain proof of a weak mind. (1794: 127–128)

Knowledge, awareness of fashion and of one's own limitations, was imperative.

Although the upper classes were allowed their luxuries by most social commentators and writers of courtesy literature, this did not mean that they were not exempt from criticism by right of their station. The middling sorts might have watched fashions worn by the elite and may have emulated them on occasion, but they were critical observers to be sure. John Mascarene wrote to his wife Margaret about the nobles he saw at Court in London:

> As to the Lords & Ladies they were vastly rich & gayly dress'd but many of
> them very gaudy & finical[.] [A]s to the Ladies way of dressing themselves,
> and tho there was scarce one among them tolerably handsome yet it seem'd
> as if they were afraid they should be too tempting and endeavor'd to make
> themselves by their dress as disagreeable as possible[.] [T]hey put on so
> much on the Forepart of their heads that they look as if they were in a Bush,
> they wear their stays very low & some look as if they had none on[.] Over
> their bosoms is thrown a thin handkerchief & then a Tippet drawn away as
> far towards their Shoulders as possible which makes them appear to me like
> so many Nurses who had just suckled their Children and had not had time to
> compose themselves. (Mascarene November 15, 1761)

His reference to the physical restraint of clothing is key, and the importance of self-restraint in one's physical person and emotions is discussed further below.

Elizabeth Shackleton also kept abreast of what the elite were wearing and also found that high rank was no proof against bad taste. She thought some of the more absurd fashions a good joke, and had no qualms in commenting that clothes were "very ugly for all they are the Queen's" (Vickery 1994: 291).

In Fielding's *Joseph Andrews* (1742), Mr. Wilson reveals that he once believed that clothing was of the first importance to the gentleman: "The character I was ambitious of attaining, was that of a fine gentleman; the first requisites to which, I apprehended were to be supplied by a taylor, a periwig-maker, and some few more tradesmen, who deal in furnishing out the human body" (Fielding 1985: 196–197). Although luxuriousness in dress was easily acquired, the ability to wear certain elements of clothing took skill and practice: posture and ease (that is, control over the body) were what gave the fine clothes true elite cachet (Calvert 1994: 269–271). Brathwait recommended that "for your Carriage, it should neither be too precise nor too loose" (1631: 42), and Lord Chesterfield, not surprisingly, was vehement on the subject, scornful of those who were overwhelmed by their own clothing and fashionable accessories.

> The very accoutrements of a man of fashion are grievous incumbances to a vulgar man. He is at a loss what to do with his hat, when it is not upon his head; his cane (if unfortunately he wears one) is at perpetual war with every cup of tea or coffee he drinks, destroys them first, and then accompanies them in their fall. His sword is formidable only to his own legs, which would possibly carry him fast enough out of the way of any sword but his own. His clothes fit him so ill, and constrain him so much, that he seems rather their prisoner than their proprietor. He presents himself in company like a criminal in a court of justice; his very air condemns him; and people of fashion will no more connect themselves with the one, that people of character will with the other. This repulse drives and sinks him into low company; a gulf from whence no man, after a certain age, ever emerged. (1992: 163)

Items of material culture were used as props to display character and access to certain types of information, but they also provided a distraction and gave something to which one might pay attention when otherwise at a loss in company, as illustrated by Wildeblood and Brinson: "Men and women of the seventeenth century used the snuff-box and the fan for ... reasons unconnected with mere physical pleasure; their modern equivalent might light a cigarette or pipe, knowing as they did, that such little actions give a sense of release from tension" (1965: 217). The narrator of *The Tatler* observed this snuff habit in 1709 when he remarked that "when a Person feels his Thoughts are run out, and has no more to say, it is as natural to supply his weak Brain with Powder at the nearest Place of Access, viz. the Nostrils" (Steele and Addison 1988: 98). This could be well done, with the charismatic nonchalance of the *je ne sais quoi*, or it could be badly done, further compiling the negative image of a socially inept individual.

Books like Nivelon's *The Rudiments of Genteel Behavior* (1737) (the subtitle of which is *An Introduction to the Method of attaining a graceful Attitude, an agreeable Motion, an easy air, and a genteel Behavior*) and Pierre Rameau's *The Dancing Master* (1744) (very similar to Nivelon) were designed to teach graceful movement. This was to be found in careful posture and self-control, and if the head were properly held, the rest of the body would follow. Nivelon wrote that "A Person, whose Head is rightly placed, is capable of Standing, Walking, Dancing, or performing any genteel Exercise in a graceful, easy and becoming Manner; the Person, whose Head is wrong place, is wholly incapable of Standing, Walking, Dancing, or performing any Exercise but with Difficulty, and in a Manner very aukward and unbecoming" (1737: 2). Sometimes, however, mechanical methods of bodily restraint were substituted, to no good effect.

> If the Head be improperly situated, by projecting forward, it spoils the true Proportion of the Neck, which can never be remedied by fastning Collars or Bandages to draw it back (a Custom too prevalent in the Infancy of the Female Sex) but on the contrary, by confining the Neck in such a Manner, it is not only painful to it, but of bad Consequence, for it is thereby deprived of due Nourishment, and the free Communication between Head and Body is greatly obstructed. (Nivelon 1737: 2)

Control of the body and control of the emotions were absolutely related, just as clothing reflected the true character of the attired. The way one carried oneself (literally and figuratively) spoke of one's relationship to the world and was of consequence in polite communication. Rameau wrote "a Woman, how graceful soever she may be in her Deportment, may be differently judged of: For example; if she holds it upright, and the Body well disposed, without Affectation, or too much Boldness, they say there goes a stately Lady; if she carries it negligently, they accuse her of Carelessness; if she pokes her Head forward, of Indolence" (1744: 23). Chesterfield adjured against "loose" (sloppy) behavior and its social ramifications:

> In mixed companies with your equals (for in mixed companies all people are to a certain degree equal), greater ease and liberty are allowed; but they too have their bounds within *biensèance*.... You may have your hands in your pockets, take snuff, sit, stand, or occasionally walk, as you like: but I believe you would not think it very *biensèant* to whistle, put on your hat, loosen your garters or your buckles, lie down upon a couch, or go to bed and welter in an easy chair. These are negligences and freedoms which one can only take when quite alone; they are injurious to superiors, shocking and offensive to equals, brutal and insulting to inferiors. That easiness of carriage and behaviour, which is exceedingly engaging, widely differs from negligence and inattention, and by no means implies that one may do whatever one pleases; it only means that one is not to be stiff, formal, embarrassed, disconcerted, and ashamed, like country bumpkins, and people who have never been in good company. (1992: 232–233)

Part of this self control, whether managing a powdered wig, wearing a sword, or walking in heels, translated itself into the material world. Undergarments like stays reinforced posture, but so did the cut of fine clothing: "men's coats pulled the shoulders down and back into the prescribed postures, and under their suit coats, men wore snug waistcoats" (Bushman 1993: 65). Buckles, pins, buttons, and laces were common to clothing of both sexes.

Tightness in clothing was proof that there was nothing loose about the character of the wearer, either in terms of thoughtlessness or sexuality. One example of this control over the self (and in this case, one's sexuality) can be seen in Defoe's *Roxana*. Clothing, and one's interest in or attention to it, reflected internal character and was visible through all exterior signs of poverty. When Roxana prepares for a dinner with a landlord who may proposition her, she worries that her appearance betrays too much of her miserable circumstances and desperation, but consoles herself with the "restraint" of her garb: "By this time I had dress'd me, as well as I could, for tho' I had good Linnen left still, yet I had but a poor Head-Dress, and no Knots, but old Fragments; no Necklace, no Ear-Rings; all those things were gone long ago for meer Bread. However, I was tight and clean, and in better Plight than he had seen me in a great while" (Defoe 1991: 29). Roxana had not at this point decided to sleep with the man, and her clothing pronounced the fact of her as yet unimpeachable virtue.

At the same time that tightness and uprightness were desirable qualities, stiffness of the body or the spirit were equally as repellent as slovenliness and looseness. Stiffness or unease announced only a pedantic understanding of polite behavior rather than the thoughtless ease and grace, the *je ne sais quoi* that proclaimed a true mastery of the social graces: "*Les manieres nobles et aisées, la tournure d'un homme de condition, le ton de la bonne compagnie, les Graces, le je ne sçais quoi qui plait*, are as necessary to adorn and introduce your intrinsic merit and knowledge, as the polish is to the diamond; which, without that polish, would never be worn, whatever it might weigh" (Chesterfield 1992: 164).

This quality was also described by the Chevalier de Méré (1607–1685):

> This civility is perceived in the features, the manner, in the slightest actions of the body and mind; and the more one considers it, the more one is charmed by it, without realizing where it comes from…. For everything that is done out of constraint or servitude, or has any trace of coarseness, destroys it. And to render a person amiable in his ways, you should please him as much as you can and take care not to burden him with tedious instructions. (quoted in Bourdieu 1996: 71)

Particularity of knowledge—a pedantic knowledge—was quite different from the shared, polite in-group knowledge. Bookish specialization was too extreme and too exclusive, denying the free exchange of ideas. It revealed too much of the self where the subjection of the self was paramount.

Simone de Beauvoir similarly wrote of the ideal that could be achieved through clothing, both for the wearer and the observer. This was found in body discipline and in clothing that revealed the attitude of the wearer to the public, either of conformity or rebellion.

Even if each woman dresses in conformity with her status, a game is still being played: artifice, like art, belongs to the realm of the imaginary. It is not only that girdle, brassiere, hair-dye, make-up, disguise body and face; but that the least sophisticated of women, one she is "dressed," does not present herself to observation; she is, like the picture or statue, or the actor on the stage, an agent through whom is suggested someone is not there—that is, the character she represents, but is not. It is this identification with something unreal, fixed, perfect as the hero of a novel, as a portrait or a bust, that gratifies her; she strives to identify herself with this figure and thus to seem to herself to be stabilized, justified in her splendor. (De Beauvoir 1989: 533)

Fragments of some clothing artifacts were recovered at the Turner house. A buckle fragment, several silver-gilt, wrapped-headed pins, and buttons were found on the site (Figure 9), and even when there was no clothing listed in the probate inventories, the Turners always had textiles and notions for sale in their shops. Captain John Turner's 1693 probate inventory included: "2 pr Silk bodyss & stomacher 9/" and "2 ps 8 oz ribbon" worth 12 shillings (Essex County Probate Records, vol. 303) (hereafter ECPR). Colonel Turner's 1743 inventory included "8 felt hatts," "230 Doz'n Buttons best Coat @ 2.6," "258 ½ pr Doz'n Do. Brest @ 15," "165 Doz'n old fashion Buttons @ 4d," bolts of "Check holland," "Mohair," "Kersy," silk, "crape," leather, "satten," silk, and serge, hooks, and caps (ECPR, Docket 28,367). The range in choices (and quantities) in this short selection, just in terms of buttons, is highly suggestive of how great the demand was.

Madam Mary Turner's 1768 inventory had the most detailed descriptions of clothing, much of it very costly. Among her many gowns she had owned "a flower'd Sattin Gown" worth £ 5.8s.6d. and a "Claret" worth £ 4.8s.0d. A number of caps, a fan with its case, aprons, waistcoats, leather gloves, cotton hose, and shoes rounded out her wardrobe. Attention to the finishing details to her dress can be seen in the listing of "Sewing Silk & 3 Ribbands & Quality binding" (ECPR, vol. 345). The Honorable John Turner, Esquire, owned two wigs, surtout and summer coats, waistcoats, breeches, silk gloves, buckles, black stockings, garters, five pairs of shoes, and a pair of slippers in his 1790 probate inventory. He also had fragments of "old" gold lace, gold buttons, a pair of silver knee buckles, and a snuffbox (ECPR, vol. 361).

The scale of demand for consumer goods in the early modern period thrust merchants into the ranks of the wealthy. They purchased luxuries to distinguish themselves from those who were less successful, but soon learned that there was, literally, a balance to be maintained between marking rank and showing oneself to be a pretender with no sense of the restraint required of the genteel. Clothing became more subtly made, with rich but subdued fabrics, to show this restraint

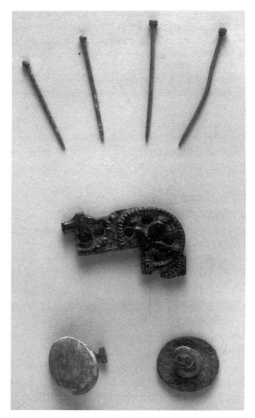

Figure 9. Clothing-related artifacts from the Turner house excavations. Several of the pins (*top*) have wrapped heads. The buckle fragment (*middle*) is probably from a shoe. The cuff link and the button (*bottom*) are made of white metal. Photograph by Jeffrey R. Dykes. Courtesy Peabody Essex Museum, Salem, Massachusetts.

(Calvert 1994). As bearing and clothing and one's use of other luxuries revealed personal character, the demonstrated knowledge of novelty also became important to discover the individual within the context of social rituals.

Novelty and Celebrative Foodways

In an age where many more people could acquire goods that were formerly only available to the elite, one distinguishing and, therefore, coveted characteristic in material culture was novelty. Closely associated with notions of luxury, novelty, at least according to one study, seems to have been a peculiarly European preoccupation. Whereas consumers in Asian urban centers wanted the same Indian fabrics every year, the European market demanded variety in patterns and colors, even at the expense of the quality of the cloth. The English Company's directors instructed their servants in India in 1681:

> Now [Know?] this for a constant and generall Rule, that in all flowered Silks you change ye fashion and flower as much as you can every year, for English Ladies and they say ye French and other Europeans will give twice as much for a new thing not seen in Europe before, though worse, then they will give for a better silk for [of] the same fashion worn ye former years. (Wills 1994: 134, 137)

Foreign fashions were not the only source of novelty. Daniel Defoe described the ways in which members of the Royal household could ignite interest in a new fashion:

> The queen brought in the custom or humour, as I may call it, of furnishing houses with china-ware, which increased to a strange degree afterwards, piling their china upon the tops of cabinets, scrutores, and every chimney-piece, to the tops of the ceilings, and even setting up shelves for their china-ware, where they wanted such places, till it became a grievance in the expense of it, and even injurious to their families and estates. The good queen far from designing any injury to the country where she was so entirely beloved, little thought she was in either of these laying a foundation for such fatal excesses, and would no doubt have been the first to have reformed them had she lived to see it. (1986 [1724–26]: 175)

I suggest that part of the craze for novelty might have arisen from a desire to stand out (in a favorable sense) from a crowd of dedicated consumers. Subtlety of clothing was one effective method, as was a knowledge of the arts, sciences, and social graces. "Not just 'outward Appearance, Clothing and Equipage' but 'rational Abilities [and] real knowledge' of the arts also distinguished 'the well-bred Gentleman'" (Hancock 1995: 347). These required understanding that could not be imitated, and the ownership of either the objects themselves or the appreciation of them implied a greater social cachet than mere access or ownership. Refinement set off the use of luxuries and considerably elevated the practitioner in social estimation. Knowledge of novel things—material culture, technology, or manners—also hinted at fashionability, being au courant. Those in the know could speak to others similarly informed, building a group identity through exclusion of others who were not so educated.

Novelty was also a partial solution to the problem of patina for the newly rich. Novelty had more status than mere luxury but still lacked the enduring and thoroughly convincing social legitimacy of *patina*.

McCracken suggests that the dictates of fashion, like novelty, overcame patina in terms of status weight for all but the very wealthiest in the eighteenth century (1990: 31). I argue below that the merchants in New England created a sort of retroactive patina to lend further legitimacy to their social position. "Such presentation served as social camouflage by which the merchant instructed others and reminded himself of the legitimacy of new wealth in polite society" (Hancock 1995: 360).

Procuring novel or exotic goods would have posed no problem for the merchant class: they were eager to do so. Joseph Denham stressed the novelty and the artistic nature of a gift of prints of Florentine statues he sent to Mrs. Earle in England. The gift consisted of a set of "30 Prints, 10 of which come out once a Year. As soon as the Fourth comes out it shall be sent you. I intend them for Furniture of the Best room in your House & they must be put into very handsome Frames such as they deserve for no Body in Liverpool except Mr. Hodgson will have the like. They were chosen for me by a famous Artist at Florence" (NMGM, D/Earle 3/2/24). Not only were the prints exotic (being from Italy) and novel, they also had the imprimatur of "a famous Artist."

John Mascarene's time in London helped to dress Margaret Mascarene in the latest fashions:

> I have sent you a Copper Plate sack which may at first sound a little odd but the reason of its being so called is that the pattern is stamp'd as I am told by a copperplate[.] I was very much pleas'd with it and hope it will please you, this way of stamping it is of no longer Date than last Summer so that imagine there will not be many of the kind with You as the Sack is made with a Trail. (Mascarene March 21, 1762)

Sometimes the novelties were quite rare and indeed odd. In 1762 John Mascarene had some shoes sent to his wife that had been made from "pieces which were left of the lying-in-bed of the Queen & the tops lin'd with the young prince's Cradle lining which for the novelty of it cannot I believe be matched in our Country except by Mrs. Barrell who will have a pair nearly the same" (Mascarene October 13, 1762). Apparently he had been given some of the remnants made from the birthing-suite of Queen Charlotte.

Entertaining became more popular with the increase in wealth and polite society through the eighteenth century. Opportunities to practice mannerly behavior escalated in formality, providing occasions to demonstrate knowledge and wealth through the material culture that proliferated in the home and in special settings outside the home. In this section, I describe some of the material dimensions of celebrative foodways that were part of that social life in the late seventeenth and early eighteenth centuries. Although these phenomena were not restricted to the merchant class, they were used, among other things, to help define this class, which would have had the first access to any of the latest goods and modes of using them. I will not go into detail about the origins of the materials, as they are generally better described elsewhere, but rather will focus on some aspects of colonial material life, as well as the somatic constraints that the artifacts and landscapes sometimes enforced. I will focus on the gender roles associated with these rituals and their importance in reproducing the merchant community in Chapter 5.

Anthropologist Mary Douglas wrote:

> A code affords a general set of possibilities for sending particular messages. If food is treated as a code, the messages it encodes will be found in the pattern of social relations being expressed. The message is about different degrees of hierarchy, inclusion and exclusion, boundaries and transactions across the boundaries.... Food categories therefore encode social events. (1971: 61)

Here I briefly discuss different aspects of three components of early modern foodways using archaeologically recovered material, courtesy literature, and documentary evidence. Not only did these situations involve material culture that is often archaeologically visible, but each offered a "script" for heightened occasions that could be improvised (within certain limits) depending on the situation. Although the courtesy literature at this time does not delineate these rituals (that would come into play later in the nineteenth century), there were distinct social penalties for failing to follow the "script," either through ignorance or clumsiness. These ritualized situations, sometimes public, sometimes more intimate, all included elements that were intended to sensually heighten the experience to mark it as a significant occasion.

Joseph Denham wrote to Mary Earle in July 1765 about the lengths to which he and his fellow hosts went in order to make an occasion of dinner for Mrs. Strine, someone for whom he did not care but still felt obliged to impress:

> We give them a very elegant Dinner ... Fowls, Ducks, boiled Beef, Plumb Tarts & Pudding, Roasted Venison (good for nothing), a Dish of Sweet Breads, &tc. Memorandum—give no more dinners—the Cook's bill terrible. Live upon the Bricks all this week to bring up the Credit side of the Acc't. Bellamy sent us a bottle of fine old Burgundy. Her Ladyship [Mrs. Strine] drank about half a Bottle, three of our Bumpers of Beer, & a Quantium Sufficit of Punch. In high Spirits after Dinner, nothing but ogling & Fun going forward. Within an Ace of playing Cards, but put it off being a red Letter Day. The Harpsichord out of Tune, but the Keys touched a little to shew the fine Diamond Rings & white hands all over piano. (NMGM, D/Earle/3/2/17)

The expense, the quantity and variety of food (and no doubt its presentation), and the discussion about the entertainments all suggest what the meal meant: an opportunity for folks on both sides of the table to impress and be impressed in the creation and maintenance of social group identity.

On the other hand, there were limits to which these displays could go and still maintain legitimacy. Mrs. Strine's excessive behavior made her a target for criticism and ridicule: self control and polite behavior were still of paramount importance to maintain the air of ceremony at the table. In 1749 Lord Chesterfield, acutely alive to personal impressions, warned his son:

> If you are absent in mind, I will soon be absent in body; for it will be impossible for me to stay in the room; and if at table you throw down your knife, plate, bread, etc., and hack the wing of a chicken for half an hour, without being able to cut it off, and your sleeve all the time in another dish, I must rise from table to escape the fever you would certainly give me. (Chesterfield 1992: 156–157)

Not only the wares and the food itself, but behavior at the table was crucial to the ambiance.

There was a thin line between maintaining a meal lavish enough to suggest ceremony and upsetting the subtlety that marked polite restraint: "Many dishes breed diseases, dulleth the mind and understanding, and not only shorten, but take away life.... Contrary to our feast-makers, who suppose the glory of entertainment, and giving the best welcome to consist in needlesse superfluities and profuse waste of the good creatures ... Be liberal and merry in taking meat, [it] is healthy and comely, and guests will be cheered by your cheer and not your meat" (Peacham 1968 [1622]: 192–195). John Brown in his *An Estimate of the Manners and Principles of the Times* was more scathing in his criticism of overconcern with dining:

> Splendid Furniture, a sumptuous Side-board, a long Train of Attendants, an elegant and costly Entertainment, for which Earth, Air, and Seas are ransacked, the most expensive wines of the Continent, the childish Vagaries of a whimsical Desert, these are the supreme Pride of the Master, the Admiration or Envy of his Guests.... Luxury is not idle in her Province, but shares with her Sister Vanity, in the Labours of the Day. High Soupes and Sauces, every Mode of foreign Cookery that can quicken Taste, and spur the Lagging Appetite, is assiduously employed. The End of Eating is not the allaying of natural Hunger, but the Gratification of sordid and debasing Appetite. Hence the most inflaming Foods, not those which nourish, but those which irritate, are adopted, while the cool and temperate Diets that Purify the Blood, are banished to inferior Tables. To this every Man of Taste now aspires, as to the true *sçavior vivre*. (1757: 37–38)

Certainly there were profligate meals in the seventeenth and eighteenth centuries. There were, however, situations where the restraint and decorum of the meal was in some ways more important than the food itself.

Tea. Although it might have been enjoyed alone, in a family context, or for purposes other than ritual or celebrative consumption, here I focus on tea when used in company.[2] Initially a luxury and novelty, the tea ceremony required specific artifacts to store, make, and serve the beverage as well as the knowledge of its preparation and service if it were to realize the full force of social impact. The beverage could have been made and served with rudimentary equipment: an iron pot for boiling water and coarse earthenware mugs for drinking in the kitchen. But by using a particular sort of ware or service (silver and porcelain), tea suddenly became emblematic of gentility, luxury, grace, elegance, and true *savoir vivre*. The physical nature or setting of the service, in addition to the attendant ceremonies, speaks about the server and whoever he or she has for company; it is not only about display and cost but is shared identity. I wish to emphasize, as other scholars have done, that the meaning of tea drinking changes in time, context, and company. Before 1750 tea was still considered a luxury, after that, it was a commonplace necessity, and so for the purposes of this study, tea drinking is treated as an elite activity with, particularly in mixed company, social reproduction at its heart, based on knowledge, physical grace, and intimacy.

Tea was introduced to England sometime before 1650, was popularized by Catherine of Braganza after 1662, and became recognized as a beverage by 1685, before which it was used for medicinal purposes (Brown 1995: 53–55). It was being served in public and increasingly popular for home socializing in England in the early 1700s and was more widely available in America only after 1740 (Roth 1988: 440–441). Polite tea drinking required knowledge of the ritual, wealth to afford the imported porcelain and silver wares, and the leisure to indulge in it. It was a status symbol with important social uses and implications.

Archaeologists have often dealt with the presence of porcelain tea wares on a site, but surprisingly few have attempted to discuss the social meaning of them. "The taking of tea in such a formal way is certainly a social event rather than a contribution to the survival in a direct, technomic way, of the people drinking it, so that ... Porcelain tea sets were probably socio-technic" (Deetz 1977: 60). Yentsch (1991) and Wall (1994) are two sterling examples that move beyond this simple statement, examining the meaning of tea taking (and its material remains) in terms of gender and social reproduction. Spurred by Deetz's discus-

---

[2]I particularly direct the reader to Roth (1988) for a complete discussion of the ritual of tea-taking in all its aspects, and to Brown (1995), Kowaleski-Wallace (1994), Shivelbusch (1993), Mintz (1986), and Smith (1992) (for an interesting but unconvincing argument) for further information and the contemporary meaning of tea, coffee, and chocolate consumption.

sion of porcelain tea wares, too many archaeologists, however habitually, employ the glossing formula "teacup sherd = British tea ceremony," but as Bushman reminds us, "the material indicators of refinement ... must not be given too much weight. The presence of a teacup in a household did not mean that the owner practiced all the genteel arts or even aspired to do so" and that "gentility vaguely represented improvements and dignity" without indicating a desire to "transform a life" (1993: 184–185).

A little more evidence is required to believe that the tea ceremony had any particular meaning for the inhabitants of a site, or in this case, a particular class of people, best found in the documentary evidence, particularly letters and diaries. Such an example of this meaning is found in the famous incident described by Dr. Alexander Hamilton. He encountered a rough fellow in Pennsylvania who was desirous of being treated as he perceived himself, as a gentleman. Unfortunately, neither his manners nor his clothing proclaimed this to his audience, and he was forced to explain things explicitly to them, completely abrogating the value of the symbols.

> He told us that tho he seemed to be but a plain, homely fellow, yet he would have us know that he was able to afford better than many that went finer: he had good linnen in his bags, a pair of silver buckles, silver clasps, and gold sleeve buttons, two Holland shirts, and some neat night caps; and that his little woman att home drank tea twice a day; and he himself lived very well and expected to live better. (Bridenbaugh 1948: 14)

No tea wares were listed in Captain John Turner's 1693 probate inventory, although this might have been a result of the long period between his death in 1680 and the time the inventory was taken. But this was not the case in Colonel Turner's inventory. Signs of his affluence and social status lie in the amount of porcelain, especially as tea wares, listed in his 1743 inventory. Their presence in the "best room," listed in the first two pages of the probate inventory, along with other descriptions by their friends of social eating and drinking, suggests how large a role polite entertaining, and, therefore, by inference, tea, played in their lives. The colonel had a matched set of "blue & white china" cups and saucers and a service set with a tea pot, milk pot, "canoo and saucer," and sugar pot. This set may have been of porcelain or another ceramic, as there was no modifier indicating that it was silver or some other metal (as suggested by Beaudry 1988: 44), and in the early eighteenth century, tea pots were not commonly made of silver (Roth 1988: 449). The wares and other collections of china cups were found in the "best room," "great chamber," and "kitchen" and were worth more than £15. The "Tea table and Handmaid" were worth an additional £4 (ECPR, Docket 28,367).

Several fragments of these wares might have been discovered during the excavations at the Turner house (Figure 10). Very early fragments of Chinese Imari (ca. 1725), blue and white Kang Xi (1720s), and brown glazed with iron red enameling (1720–1730) suggest that the Turners would have been at the vanguard of tea use in Massachusetts (pers. comm. William R. Sargent 1998).

Madam Mary Turner had six tea pots in her Ipswich home at the time of her death in 1768: two were porcelain, one was "delph," one of pewter, and two of stoneware. These tea pots were probably the remnants of a long history of entertaining, possibly even reflecting Madam Turner's continuing use of them. She also died possessing a set of silver teaspoons (as well as several single ones) and one "old fashioned" tea table listed in her probate inventory of 1768. This "old fashioned" table may have been the one referred to in her husband Colonel Turner's probate inventory (Goodwin 1993: 85). Her son, John Turner, Esquire, had no tea pots listed in his 1790 probate inventory, but he did have two tea kettles, a tea chest, and a single silver teaspoon. I suspect these were all that were left over from his family's extensive array of goods.[3]

Although the social aspects of tea taking are more particularly discussed in Chapter 5, one solid example of the intimacy that tea taking engenders comes from the Denham-Earle correspondence. The Duke of York, while in Genoa in 1764, was remarked by Joseph Denham to be taking liberties with some of the ladies in town: "Yesterday he ran into Mrs. L's room at breakfast, kissed her and sat down to tea, then ran into all the rooms, and down stairs again by himself" (NMGM, D/Earle3/2/8). The duke had kissed a married woman ("Mrs. L" may be Mrs. Lawrence, the wife of an associate of the Earles) and moved through the house unescorted, suggesting a good deal of intimacy, as did the taking of tea. Although kissing as a mark of honor and familiarity between social superiors and inferiors was falling out of mode by the eighteenth century, it was still fashionable for a lady to receive a guest in bed or while at her dressing table (Bushman 1993: 43; Wildeblood and Brinson 1965: 228).

John Mascarene's letters also mention tea on several occasions, generally of drinking it at breakfast. His other reference to it is in the

---

[3]Although I have elsewhere (Goodwin 1993, 1994a) suggested that these wares were purchased by the third John Turner, a reexamination of the fragments suggests an earlier date that is better attributed to Colonel Turner. I believe that my hypothesis about the Honorable John using smaller, less permanent wares to express his high status (when he could no longer afford to keep a finer house downtown), based on Bernard Herman's work at the Thomas Mendenhall site (1984), is still viable, however, based on other wares found on the site.

Figure 10. Archaeologically recovered tea cup fragments from the Turner house excavations and intact analogues from collections of the Peabody Essex Museum. The sherds are probably associated with Colonel Turner, and the careful descriptions of teawares, services, and furniture in his probate inventory, and later that of Madam Mary Turner, suggest how important the ritualized and social drinking of tea would have been to that family. *On the left*: A coffee cup and saucer, blue and white Kang Xi (*not en suite*). The saucer (1720–1730; Museum Purchase) is later than the coffee cup (ca. 1725; Gift of Mrs. Gordon Abbott). *In the middle*: A brown-glazed (traditionally called "Batavia ware") tea cup and saucer (dates to between 1740–1750 and is famille rose; Gift of Mr. and Mrs. William P. Wadsworth). The excavated sherd is decorated with iron red, which dates to between 1720 to 1730. *On the right*: Chinese Imari coffee cup and saucer date to ca. 1725 (Gift of Mr. and Mrs. William J. Flather). Photograph by Jeffrey Dykes. Courtesy, Peabody Essex Museum, Salem, Massachusetts.

pleasure garden of Ranelagh, where, with coffee, it is described as being served as part of a scene of heightened elegance. In both cases, it has associations either of intimacy or of celebration, shared with close members of the same social group.

Imported Chinese porcelain is light and thin and its decoration, whether polychrome or monochrome, produces a marked contrast against its white background, which makes the ware, like silver, visible and admirable in low light. Because of its fragility, one mishandled vessel leaves immediate, irreparable evidence of clumsiness. Handleless tea bowls filled with hot liquid add to the necessity for care. In addition to its expense—the tea itself, porcelain wares, and silver implements—tea taking provides the opportunity to display physical grace as well as knowledge of the intricacies of the sugar tongs and strainer. Posture and self-control, as part of the special knowledge of tea drinking, was imperative.

This also can be seen on a larger scale, in terms of the furniture involved. Care was needed in moving near a tea table in a wide skirt or with a sword or walking stick. Although furniture (or indeed, houses and landscapes) were not necessarily in themselves polite, they shaped and directed the movement and behavior of the participants in polite rituals.[4]

Other activities associated with tea taking, such as the performance of vocal or instrumental music, provided opportunities for the display of other accomplishments as well as dainty hands or throats. In the letters written by both Joseph Denham and John Mascarene, there are descriptions of these occasions, and the portrait of an unidentified family in Figure 11 supports this as well. Each of the family members is doing something to demonstrate correct posture and physical grace. The gentleman looks remarkably like the example provided by Nivelon (Figure 12) to demonstrate the correct attitude and posture (see Calvert 1994: 274) for giving or receiving something. He offers something to a seated woman (perhaps his wife), who similarly resembles Nivelon's model (Figure 13) with her hand curved at her waist and her other gracefully extended. The woman seated at the tea table displays the silver tongs while the third sits at the piano ready to play. Even the dogs are slender and lithe. The man-servant lugging the heavy kettle of water is immediately recognizable as being on the outside of this group, physi-

---

[4]Leone (1988: 244–247) and Shackel (1993: 151) also discuss how material objects associated with the table shaped the behavior of their users, but come to different conclusions than I about the significance of this.

Figure 11. *A Family Being Served with Tea*; British School, ca. 1740–5. Dinners or teas, such as those described by John Mascarene and Joseph Denham, provided the opportunity to display many accomplishments at once. The sitters, including their pets, seem to demonstrate the rigorous posture and grace required by courtesy literature. Yale Center for British Art

Figure 12. *Standing* [men]. From F. Nivelon's *The Rudiments of Genteel Behavior* (1737). Courtesy, The Winterthur Library: Printed Book and Periodical Collection.

Figure 13. *To Give or Receive* [women]. From F. Nivelon's *The Rudiments of Genteel Behavior* (1737). Note the attention paid to the details of dress and accessories. Courtesy, The Winterthur Library: Printed Book and Periodical Collection.

cally, artistically, and socially, but still quite necessary to maintain the infrastructure of this polite situation.

Tea taking was expensive, socially meaningful, and an embodiment of all the qualities that were desirable in polite society: refinement, ritual, restraint, and rarity. The investment in tea taking was an important social investment, being, as Roth describes it, imbued with the notion of "welcome" (Roth 1988: 446). It was a way to express one's abilities as well as to screen others who claimed to have the same knowledge, and therefore, some of the same claims to status. It was elite allegiance building at its most intimate, while the celebrative use of alcohol and special feasts were for a larger audience, in-group and out.

Punch Drinking and Toasting. Alcohol-based punch was another new development that appeared in England as a result of the increase and stabilization of trade with Asia around 1680. The name possibly is derived from the Persian *panj* or the Hindu *pànch*, meaning "five," probably referring to the number of ingredients: arrack or some other liquor, fruit, sugar, spice, and water (Brown 1996: 45). In some ways public or semipublic alcohol consumption shared many of the characteristics of tea in terms of celebration of shared identity. The complexity and expense of punch making (both in the costly liquor and tropical ingredients as well as the porcelain and tin-glazed earthenware serving bowls), as well as toasting (with its implied connotations of restraint, fortitude, courtesy, and obligation), is at distinct odds with the everyday beverages of beer, peery, and cider (and later, gin) that were consumed by virtually everyone. While punch was consumed in mixed company at dinners or parties, in all male gatherings, particularly those involving politics or the military, it took on other dimensions, involving a quite different sort of mannerly behavior.

Colonel Turner and Benjamin Lynde, Sr., were frequent hosts at Moor's, Lutwich's, and other public houses after political business was concluded with the Essex representatives (Figure 14, Figure 15). On May 30, 1733, Lynde recorded: "Eleccon ended, with Mr. Cook and … [elected] reps, whom Colo. Thaxter, Dudley, Turner, Cushing and myself treated at 5s per man; I paid Lutwiche" (Lynde and Lynde 1880: 42). Drink was also used to consolidate other sorts of relations in Salem and elsewhere. The Reverend Joseph Green gives us evidence that the officers also enjoyed refreshment after a dusty day of military exercises; in 1713 he and Colonel Turner dined at Phillip's ordinary after "trooping and training" (Fowler 1870: 102). Unlike the parties that were hosted after political meetings, however, training parties almost always were

Figure 14. *Judge Benjamin Lynde* (1666–1745), by John Greenwood (1727–1792) (after Smibert). The senior Benjamin Lynde was a close friend of Colonel John Turner and, along with his son, recorded some of the Turners' activities during the first half of the eighteenth century in their diaries. Photograph by Mark Sexton. Courtesy, Peabody Essex Museum, Salem, Massachusetts.

characterized by boisterous revelry, if not downright violence. Militia training days were often recognized as notorious excuses for drinking and carousing and had caused problems with rowdiness since the first settlements in America. "One must begin by recognizing that the militia did provide both an important means of formalizing authority in society and assemblies at which the male fraternity of warriors might get drunk together" (Isaac 1982: 107).

Figure 15. *Mary Browne Lynde* (1679–1753), by an unidentified artist. Mrs. Lynde was a member of the Turners' circle of friends and business associates. She and Madam Mary Turner shared the same obligations of polite entertaining. Photograph by Jeffrey R. Dykes. Courtesy, Peabody Essex Museum, Salem, Massachusetts.

The English admiral Edward Russell, after crushing a French invasion fleet, celebrated with:

> a mighty bowl of punch made at his house on October 25, 1694. It was made in a fountain in the garden ... in the fountain were four hogsheads of brandy, eight hogsheads of water, twenty-five thousand lemons, twenty gallons of lime juice, thirteen hundred weight of fine Lisbon sugar, five pounds of grate nutmegs, three hundred toasted biscuits and a pipe of Mountain malaga. And there was built on purpose a little boat, in which was a boy who rowed

round the fountain and filled the cups of the company, who exceeded six
thousand in number. (P. Brown 1996: 46)

Rhys Isaac described similar situations in colonial Virginia: "at
the Muster of his Company, after the Exercise was over, he [Captain
Wager] usually treated them with Punch, and they would after that
come before his Door and fire Guns in Token of their Gratitude, and then
he would give them Punch 'til they dispersed, and that has been a
frequent Practice for several Years" (1982: 107).

Although there are significant cultural differences between Virginia plantation society and New England merchant society, Isaac
makes another point that is pertinent and applicable here: mustering
and interaction with "the gentlemen officers" consolidated bonds within
the community. The provincial militia was a place where both the elite
and the rest of a community relied on each other for mutual support and
success. The largess of the officers and their communal drunkenness at
such times as training days mitigated the usual formal distinctions
between different classes.

This can also be said of drinking in merchant society. Figure 16
illustrates such riot that one is tempted to say that these merchants and
sea captains were a long way from home, literally as well as spiritually.
It is not the sort of decorum being practiced here that I have described
previously, but that would have been as out of place in this situation as
these antics would have been at a tea. Here the mannerliness lies in setting polite distance and detachment aside.

To judge from the documentary and archaeological evidence, Captain Turner and Colonel Turner both understood the value of alcoholic
entertainment, whether at home or abroad. This should be no surprise,
considering how large a role rum played in their trading system. Figure
17 shows some of the remains of alcoholic beverage service and storage
vessels found at the Turner site, including fragments of wine glasses,
tall mugs of white salt-glazed stoneware and brown luster stoneware,
and tin-glazed earthenware punch bowls, all reflecting the considerable
amount of entertaining in which the Turners engaged. The wine bottle
fragment with its seal ("1715") dates to the period of Colonel Turner and
his family; in his probate inventory was also listed "a flowd [flowered]
Decanter 12, 6 Wine Glasses @ 4"; elsewhere are listed innumerable
bottles and jugs (of stoneware and glass), a "decanter," "A Sullabub
[milk with wine or cider] pott," beakers, and "Earthen muggs with
pewter Covers" (ECPR, Docket 28,367). He also had stored in his cellar,
"three pipes Cyder," "½ Pipe Pricked [soured] Wine," and "a pipe with 15
gallons Wine." In Captain Turner's inventory was an entry for "1 case of
bttles 12/. 4 doz small Juggs & glass bottles 10/5, Lg. Juggs 3/e" (ECPR,
vol. 303). Madam Mary Turner had listed "2 Earthen half Pint Bowls,"

Figure 16. *Sea Captains Carousing in Surinam* (1758), by John Greenwood (1727–1792). Although public drunkenness was frowned upon, the ability to hold one's liquor was admired, especially with the rapid inebriation caused by toasting with punch. Some of these revelers were sea captains from Rhode Island, and the artist, holding the candle in the upper right-hand corner, was from Massachusetts. Occasions like this would have added significantly to the archaeological record. Courtesy, The Saint Louis Art Museum.

Figure 17. Drink-related artifacts excavated at the Turner house. *Top row (left to right)*: A rim and base from white salt-glazed stoneware mugs and a rim from a brown luster stoneware mug. *Middle row*: Tin-glazed earthenware base and two fragments from small punch bowls. The fourth sherd is manganese-colored stoneware from a jug. *Bottom row*: Two wine glass base fragments and a green bottle fragment with part of the seal: "1715." Note the bottom loops from letters from the missing half of the seal. Photograph by Jeffrey R. Dykes. Courtesy, Peabody Essex Museum, Salem, Massachusetts.

"two Madeira Baskets," beaker glasses, jugs, mugs, and basins (ECPR, vol. 345).

Evidence from the Boardman privy at the Spencer-Peirce-Little house and documentary evidence associated with that site again demonstrate the importance of social drinking to the merchant class. Along with remains from 30 punch bowls, bottles from wine, beer, gin, and aquavit suggest the range (and depth) of liquid hospitality that was available (Beaudry, n.d.: 40).

In spite of his strenuous objections against intoxication, Samuel Johnson believed that "the true felicity of human life is a tavern" (quoted in Porter 1990: 226). Many taverns have been excavated, particularly in port cities and political seats, and they reveal the variety of services as well as food and drink that could be offered to facilitate community and communication (Ekholm and Deetz 1971; Rockman and Rothschild 1984; and Vogt 1994).

Contemporary courtesy literature stressed moderation in drinking as well as eating, but not to deny oneself the pleasure of good food and drink. Henry Peacham wrote in 1622 that one should "avoid excessive drinking then, which there is no one vice more common and reigning, and ill beseeming a Gentleman ... remembring thereby you become not fit for any thing, having your reason degraded, your body distempered, your soule hazarded, your esteeme and reputation abased, while you sit taking your unwholesome healthes" (1968: 193). After going on for some time about the ills of intemperance, he then advised that one "not be so abstemious that won't remember a friend with a hearty draught. Moderately taken it preserveth health" (1968: 193, 195).

The Reverend Cotton Mather disagreed, believing that, in addition to the sin attending the drinking of healths (with its similarity to heathenism), to drink someone's health was to wish them illness. "Men pretend Charity to another in Drinking his Health, whereas many times thereby they Destroy their own and their Neighbour's too.... And it is against Reason for a man to drink for anothers Health. Suppose he should be required to Eat a Pound of Flesh, or of Cheese, when he is not Hungry, and that for the health of his Friend, How Irrational would the Proposal be?" (Mather 1953 [1687]: 24).

Similarly, a contributor to Matthew Carey's magazine wanted to abolish drinking healths: "I sincerely wish that we may abolish many disgustful, embarrassing, destructive English customs ... [among them] calling out across the table to know the name of mr. and mrs. such-a-one, that you may have the pleasure of drinking their healths." Men would become "disguised with liquor" and also risked illness from drinking from a communal vessel (Carson 1966: 29).

But in spite of these considerations, health-drinking and toasting remained important parts of social drinking. John Mascarene was careful to inform Margaret when he and his roommate had remembered their wives with a bowl: "We live together in good Company keep but one fire and are as sociable as Chumms at Colleges our Circumstances being somewhat parallel[.] [N]o day passes without some mention of our Dearys and the first toast we give of an Evening over a pot of Porter is that of our Beloved" (Mascarene October 8, 1762). He also told her of a new popular toast: "Instead of drinking their Majesties' health, the fashionable Toast now is The King & his Wife, and a late one is a speedy release to the Royal Prisoner, the meaning of which you will I trust easily discover" (Queen Charlotte was pregnant) (Mascarene after August 2, 1762). Margaret also returned the favor: "I gave them a little Supper which was genteely Serv'd and they seem'd perfectly pleas'd, we wish'd for and drank your Health" (M. Mascarene January 30, 1764). Similarly, Joseph Denham and his English friends drank to the absent Mary and Thomas Earle in 1763: "Yesterday we dined aboard an English Vessel and the Consul was w. us and we drank your health and Mr. Earle's under a Discharge of five guns which made the Doge and all the Senate start out of their selves" (NMGM, D/Earle3/2/1).

Most eighteenth-century writers seemed to believe that drinking was acceptable as long as one did not lose control. Samuel Johnson despised what drink did to men, causing them to commit the greatest sin of polite society: to forget themselves. "Before dinner men meet with great inequality of understanding; and those who are conscious of their inferiority have the modesty not to talk. When they have drunk wine, every man feels himself happy, and loses that modesty, and grows impudent and vociferous: but he is not improved; he is only not sensible of his defects (Boswell 1986: 212). He also wrote that "a man, who has been drinking wine at all freely, should never go into a new company. With those who have partaken of wine with him, he may be pretty well in unison; but he will probably be offensive, or appear ridiculous, to other people" (Boswell 1986: 197).

There were occasions where it was imperative to drink socially and sometimes even to excess. For the most part, however, self-restraint, even in drunkenness—as seen later in the eighteenth century in those who would subject themselves to excess to earn the title "dandy"—was again the hallmark of polite society (Campbell 1994: 50–51).

Feasts.   Samuel Johnson summed up the difference between eating and dining in company gruffly and concisely. In 1763 Boswell remembered that "when invited to dine, even with an intimate friend, he [Johnson] was not pleased if something better than a plain dinner was not prepared for him. I have heard him say on such an occasion, 'This was a good dinner enough, to be sure; but it was not a dinner to *ask* a man to" (Boswell 1986: 121). A noticeable degree of effort marked a true occasion. While some social occasions were made for inclusion (or exclusion) on a personal level, others, like feasts, were specifically to promote group solidarity. Entertaining had also become entertainment.

One such institution peculiar to the New England merchant class was the "turtle frolic," a celebrative expression of wealth, privilege, access, and solidarity. The sea captains who had voyaged to the West Indies brought back to New England large sea turtles, which tasted "between fish and flesh of veale," as an early visitor to Barbados described it (quoted in Dunn 1972: 5). Even if they were only touching at a West Indian port, it was expected that they would send the necessary ingredients, including turtles, as well as rum and limes for punch, back home for their families and associates to enjoy. Alice Morse Earle described a "turtle" that took place in Rhode Island in the mid-eighteenth century.

> In no seaport town did the turtle frolic come into a higher state of perfection than in Newport. Scores of turtles were borne to that welcoming shore. In 1752 George Bressett, a Newport Gentleman, sailed to the West Indies, and promptly did a neighborly and civic duty by sending home to his friend Samuel Freebody, a gallant turtle and a generous keg of limes. Lime juice was the fashionable and favorite "souring" of the day, to combine with arrack and Barbados rum into a glorious punch.... The frolic was held at Fort George, on December 23 ... fifty guests sailed over in a sloop and welcomed with a hoisted flag and salute of cannon. Dinner at two tea at five, then dancing begun ... and the keg of limes and its fellow ingredients kept pace with the turtle.... Upon the whole the entertainment had the preference over all turtle frolics before it, and Mr. George Bresett's health with "Honest George" was freely drank in a cheerful glass by every person. (Earle 1924: 221–223)

John Mascarene wrote to Margaret Mascarene about enjoying such a feast on his way to London: "I had the pleasure yesterday of dining with the Cap't of the Man of War Capt of the Mast shipps & a number of Gentlemen & Ladys of this Town upon a Barbiqu'd Turtle & Shote which were dress'd upon an Island where we had a Tent erected for the purpose" (Mascarene September 1–2, 1761). The Salem diarists William Bentley and Mary Vial Holyoke also recorded turtles that took place in Salem in the second half of the eighteenth century. On July 24, 1761, Holyoke recorded briefly, "Went to Johnson's to a turtle, 80 people present. A dance at Jefferies. Not there" (1911: 51). The Reverend Bentley was a little more detailed in his description of a turtle feast in 1801:

> A turtle feast of the Marine Society at Osgood's in S[outh] Fields. The Turtle was given by a Gentleman in Havana. The Clergy [Bentley included] were invited. Our chief Cook was Prince Hall, an African, & a person of great influence upon his Colour in Boston, being Master of the African Lodge, & a person to whom they refer with confidence their personal affairs.... The

Clergy were introduced to him, & the principal gentlemen took notice of him. (1962: 2:379)

In this case, not only was the feast a vehicle for class allegiance building, but it also provided a (temporary) bridge between races that might not otherwise have existed.

The distinction of having access to tropical ingredients, the singularly maritime quality that characterized the feast, and the extraordinary degree of effort in hosting such an event (note that the Newport turtle took place in December) made the turtle frolic a novelty. It was clearly an event meant to bring the merchant elite together: the turtles that were brought back weighed in excess of several hundred pounds. One shell was recorded as measuring three feet by three feet, seven inches (Holyoke 1911: 129). There was so much food that it simply would not be possible for one family to eat it all. The feast was designed to be shared by a like-minded group who would have understood the references to mercantile trade and wealth from the Caribbean. I suspect this access to exotic goods is also associated with the pineapple motif in New England material culture as a symbol of welcoming and hospitality.

Documentary evidence associated with merchant Nathaniel Tracy, who was one owner of the Spencer-Peirce-Little farm, confirms the amount of trouble to which a host would go to provide an opulent, courteous, and symbolic repast for honored guests in 1778:

> Mr. Nathaniel Tracy, who lived in a beautiful villa at Cambridge [now the Craigie-Longfellow House], made a great feast for the admiral, Count D'Estaing, and his officers. Everything was furnished that could be had in the country to ornament and give variety to the entertainment ... two large tureens of soup were placed at the ends of the table.... Tracy filled a plate with soup which went to the admiral, and the next was handed to the consul. As soon as L'Etombe put his spoon into his plate he fished up a large frog, just as green and perfect as if he had hopped from the pond into the tureen. Not knowing at first what it was, he seized it by one of its hind legs, and, holding it up in view of the whole company, discovered that it was a full-grown frog.... The company, convulsed with laughter, examined the soup plates as the servants brought them, and in each was to be found a frog. The uproar was universal. Meantime, Tracy kept his ladle going, wondering what his outlandish guests meant by such extravagant merriment. "What is the matter?" asked he, and raising his head, surveyed the frogs dangling by a leg in all directions. "Why don't they eat them?" he exclaimed. "If they knew the confounded trouble I had to catch them, in order to treat them to a dish of their own country, they would find that, with me at least, it was no joking matter. (quoted in Beaudry n.d.: 21–22)

This "frog frolic" was important because of the degree of effort that went into providing what Tracy believed would be a polite gesture to his guests and also a way of demonstrating his (supposed) knowledge of

French cuisine. His disastrous mistake, exposing his lack of in-group knowledge, was further compounded by the augustness and worldliness of his company.

When the Turners gave a hog barbecue at their country seat at Castle Hill on August 26, 1730, Benjamin Lynde, Jr., described the carriages that came from miles to the event (1880). Having also been hosts at many other social events, it is no surprise that the Turners' probate inventories list goods sufficient to entertain many of their friends and associates at once. The means to entertain a number of guests might be surmised from Captain John Turner's 1693 probate inventory. He owned £100 worth of silver plate and had 12 leather chairs, 17 "Turky work" chairs, and three tables in his hall and parlor, with twelve tablecloths in his parlor chamber (ECPR, vol. 303). There was no mention of knives or forks in this inventory, but it was taken thirteen years after his death and many factors might account for the absence of such things.

Colonel Turner, in addition to his extensive wares for tea and wine taking, also had 3 tables (in addition to the tea table), 12 black cane chairs, 6 in white, and 1 large 1 in white in the "best room" (probably the large southern addition). The hall had a long table and 3 more tables, 12 leather chairs (probably those having belonged to his father, now only worth half their original value of 60s), and 2 more chairs, as well as 30 knives and forks. In the Turner's house on the harbor, at any rate, they could probably accommodate about 30 guests, and possibly more at an outdoor party on Castle Hill, supported by the wide variety and amount of cooking equipment found in the "new kitchin" at the same time (ECPR, Docket 28,367).

Without even considering the available information on faunal evidence, it can be observed that the elaboration of meals that strengthened intraclass allegiance involved special elements that were theatrical "appeals to the senses." Peter Borsay, in describing city celebrations in English provincial towns from 1600 to 1800, discussed the ritual use of rich or unusual props and stimulants to appeal to the sense of sound (with cannons, trumpets, gunshots, music, or church bells), sight (with lights, special clothes, architecture, banners, or other artifacts), taste (food, drink, and tobacco), and movement (in posture, processions, or dance) that "elevated the occasion with corporate human movement" (1984: 237). All of these dramatic devices can be found in the turtle (or frog) frolics and barbecues as large-scale appeals to elite solidarity, and in smaller, more intimate occasions at the tea table.

Borsay points out that while these public celebrations were frequently used to consolidate group feeling in the upper echelons, they could also be used to forge bonds of wider community between social classes (Borsay 1984: 242–243). The raucousness of military training days allowed vents to ease stress that might occur within a divided society. By providing the liquor for training days and by obviously, consciously exercising their prerogative to set aside elite markers of polite distance and mannerly behavior, officers and town leaders could nominally ignore the usual stratification of society, so necessary in the provincial military, in order to create a sense of unity and community of purpose with the common soldiers.

One last thought about celebrative food, mannerly behavior, and material culture should be considered. Part of the reason that gentlefolk could act with ease and nonchalance at meals was their ability, in many instances, to delegate work to servants or slaves. This provided time for the leisure to study, practice, and master mannerly behavior, and it also relegated heavy and unseemly work to those not participating in rituals. Having servants or owning slaves also carried a solid measure of prestige.

Servants were also necessary for the maintenance of the profusion of artifacts that were dedicated to entertaining and eating with individual settings (as opposed to earlier communal eating). The profusion of goods made housekeeping considerably more complicated and the rituals of social dining or drinking, as well as the maintenance of valuable objects, were greatly aided by a servant who was well versed in their structure. Books like *The Complete Servant Man* (1758) not only instructed servants in the care of the house and its furnishings ("when you clean your Plate, take care to leave no Whiting in the Chinks," (anon., 1758: 58)), but also explained the niceties of service in company and the deportment expected of them to servants, and probably to new masters as well. "Directions to a Butler," originally the man servant who was the "bottler," warned that the position required the greatest exactness and entailed the most variety of work:

> In waiting at the sideboard, take particular care to supply each person at the table with a different glass; and when any Person calls for Liquor, obey with all expedition, and let no one call twice. If anyone desires a glass of bottled ale, take care not to shake the Bottle, because it will make it thick. Take care also not to wipe the Mouth of it with the Palm of your Hand, it being a very slovenly Trick. (Anon. 1785: 57–58)

There was also advice on training servants in elite courtesy works. Fenelon advised: "Accustom them [servants] not to suffer any thing nasty or misplaced; but that they mark strictly the least disorder in a House: Make them also to observe, that nothing contributes more to Housewifery and Neatness, than to keep constantly every thing in its place" (1707: 220).

With this considerable burden upon them, it was also clear that capable servants were sought after but seldom found. Jonathan Swift's *Instruction to Servants* (1745) resembles *Grobianus* ["King of the Boors"], written by Friederich Dedekin in the late sixteenth century. Although it is not known whether Swift was familiar with this work, a translation of *Grobianus*, which gave humorous examples of bad behavior, by Roger Bull was dedicated to him in 1739 (Mason 1971: 283). In his satirical guide, Swift made it clear that little could be expected from the worst servants and also reveals how artifacts were used in ways modern researchers might not otherwise imagine:

> When you have broken all your earthen drinking vessels below stairs (which is usually done in a week) the copper pot will do as well: it can boil milk, heat porridge, hold small-beer, or in case of necessity serve for a jordan [chamber pot]; therefore apply it indifferently to all these uses; but never wash or scour it, for fear of taking off the tin.... Although you are allowed knives for the servants hall, at meals, yet you ought to spare them, and make use only of your master's.... The servants' candlesticks are generally broken, for nothing can last for ever: but, you may find out many expedients: you may conveniently stick your candle in a bottle, or with a lump of butter against the wainscot, in a powder-horn, or in an old shoe, or in a cleft stick, or in the barrel of a pistol, or upon its own grease on a table, in a coffee cup or a drinking glass, a horn can, a tea pot, a twisted napkin, a mustard pot, an ink-horn, a marrowbone, a piece of dough, or you may cut a hole in a loaf, and stick it there. (Swift 1964: 18, 26–28)

Of course, once servants learned to work unobtrusively in polite situations, they would have been exposed to the sort of learning and nuances of mannerly behavior that was intended to distinguish their masters from the rest of society. Servants who absorbed this information would have been profoundly threatening to elite society and would have compounded the need for subtlety in distinguishing a "gentleman" from a well-trained and observant servant interested in making social capital of his education. As a result of this refinement, as well as that acquired by those involved in working in the luxury trades, prices went down and wages increased, leisure time was becoming a "decency" and not a luxury, and worries on the part of the elite escalated about the "vulgarization of polite society" (Borsay 1989: 300).

The seventeenth-century Turners had indentured servants, some of whom were Irish, who worked around the wharves and warehouses but also in the house. Later, in the eighteenth century, Colonel John Turner owned three enslaved blacks, presumably bought from family connections in Barbados. Rebecca, Titus, and Lewis appeared in the colonel's probate record in 1743 and were apparently freed by 1758, but remained the financial responsibility of the third John Turner after the death of his mother in 1768 (Felt 1849: 416).

The artifacts with which some of these rituals were enacted were also used functionally, as well as symbolically. Sometimes wine taken in company was simply to slake thirst, just as a dinner was meant only to satisfy hunger. Sometimes the presence of a porcelain sherd on a site indicates no more than a "cuppa" tea. The material remains of these activities do not necessarily indicate all of the potential social or ideological meanings that the artifacts might represent, but we must consider these in any case, particularly when they are corroborated by documentary evidence. These occasions represent opportunities for social reproduction and for display. They provided the scripts for whatever social drama might unfold.

In addition to a profusion of new goods, and services, the age itself was perceived as unprecedented in terms of social structure and philosophy. Papers like *The Spectator* recommended courtesy as one method of integrating new social positions and views through polite flexibility (though not slavish formalism or hypocrisy) and a removal of the self in favor of larger society (Klein 1995: 229). Integration did not mean democratization, however, and a variety of subtle methods were employed to maintain distinctions that were growing nicer as time progressed. Simplicity and elegance, restraint, and fashionable (nonspecialized) knowledge of new rituals and arts and sciences were part of these strategies. They could not, however, be used as a substitute for the true hallmark of the elite: patina.

Patina

Whereas novelty was something often found in portable, changeable, and therefore, more often, affordable, forms of material culture, *patina* often showed up in larger, more durable artifacts. Discussed most extensively by Grant McCracken in *Culture and Consumption: New Approaches to the Symbolic Character of Consumer Goods and Activities* (1990), patina verifies status claims through the confirmed longevity of that status. In a world where small artifacts and especially clothing made rapidly changing public statements (subject to fashion), only larger objects, like some furniture, houses, and even some landscapes, could convey a sense of permanence or history.

Apart from its physical manifestations of age, which contributes to its symbolic importance, patina creates distinction between new wealth and pedigree. As a subdued marker of this distinction, this device has great value in pointing out newly gained wealth in opposition to that coming from an old family because unless the status markers have the patina of connection with an old family, or have patina but not that associated with the new owner, then those objects immediately stand out as illegitimate claims to that status. The understated quality of patina as a legitimizer is also useful in that it is often not understood by "pretenders" who have newer, more showy goods and less "in-group" knowledge (McCracken 1990: 35).

Although McCracken (1990: 40–41) follows McKendrick in stating that in the eighteenth century, novelty largely replaced patina as *the* critical status marker for all but the very wealthiest, I believe that there is some adjustment necessary in considering merchants in the American colonies. McCracken argues that patina marked the difference between old and new status, and that, according to Elizabethan standards, about five generations was the required length of time to confer that patina. Newly wealthy merchants might have taken some comfort from Defoe's pronouncement that refined education would wipe away any negative associations with trade in just one generation, but they still were tempted to attempt to create patina of their own. This was manufactured (and perhaps, successfully achieved) through selected styles in architecture, which I discuss below.

Architecture is a highly visible statement of permanence, wealth, and history. There are few references to houses in courtesy literature, I suspect, because in elite families, the ancestral home would have been a given. The only reference I could find was very early by Agnolo Pandolfini in *Il Governo della Famiglia* (The Governing of the Family), written between 1425 and 1430. He advised choosing a house that would last a lifetime, paying particular attention to the locality, making certain that the air was clean and the wine would be good (Pandolfini 1869: 57).

David Hancock, in his important study, *Citizens of the World: London Merchants and the Integration of the British Atlantic Community, 1735–1785*, noted the importance that architecture played for his associates in their quest for social power. As they accumulated wealth and became familiar with polite standards of displaying that wealth, the merchant associates (from 1745–1785) bought huge amounts of land and made improvements in their homes, at first in London, then moving to "fashionable suburbs," moving "up" to purchasing overseas plantations, country villas, and possibly, even going so far as to purchase true country estates (Hancock 1995: 286–287). "Property was associated with power: Power follows property, property was their deity, power was 'the true basis and measure of power'" (Hancock 1995: 287). The homes the merchants constructed expressed neoclassical ideals of uncluttered symmetrical form and republican notions of social order, while embodying the modest restraint that signaled true gentility.

In America, there was a similar process of selection and construction to be found in the architecture. By 1725 New England merchants lived in fashionable town homes, the design of which was based on the height of English architectural styles (Bushman 1993: 113). But Sweeney proposes that a house, as the "traditional aristocratic embodiment of the cult of lineage," could give colonial families the form they needed to express their aspirations. He further argues that mansion houses built in America in the second quarter of the eighteenth century were not copied directly from London design books but rather expressed an American interpretation of those styles, a "high-style vernacular" (1994: 11–13).

These high-style homes were designed with polite entertaining in mind and were compartmentalized to provide different settings for differing levels of acquaintances:

> The formal house was beautifully calculated as an instrument both to express etiquette and to back up negotiation. Since each room in the sequence of an apartment was more exclusive than the last, compliments to or from a visitor could be nicely gauged not only by how far he penetrated along the sequence, but also by how far the occupant of the apartment came along it— and even beyond it—to welcome him. (Girouard 1978: 145)

Although they were but pale versions of the stately homes of England's landed elite, the colonial homes were built with the same goals: restricted access and privacy. Cary Carson points out that the Turner house was remodeled to further increase the number of private and semipublic spaces in a busy building that was an office, shop, storehouse, and meeting place in addition to being a home (Carson 1994: 621).

Even though the Turner house was constructed in 1668, I believe it to be an early example of some of these traits. The architectural style was old fashioned when it was constructed, perhaps in an attempt to suggest historical longevity, permanence, and "traditional" right of position and power. More than a hundred years later, the patina that the house accrued through actual longevity was a source of pride to the Ingersolls, a middle-class family, when they acquired the house in the 1780s. In the meantime, for the powerful Turner family, patina had to be constructed and inferred.

Built at the time of John and Elizabeth Turner's marriage in 1668, Abbott Lowell Cummings described the impressive seventeenth-century hall and parlor plan house as "one of the most ambitious examples of first period architecture in Essex County" (1979: 73) (Figure 18). The original plan of the house was that of a two-story East Anglian hall and parlor typical of the postmedieval period with a central chimney stack and entry hallway (Figure 19).

Probably about 1678, approximately the same time as he constructed the back kitchen ell, Captain Turner built a two-and-one-half-

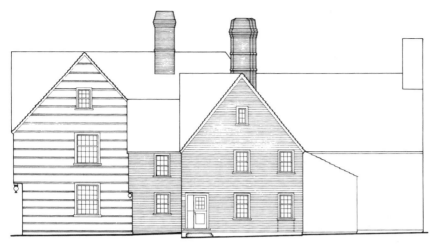

Figure 18. East elevation of the Turner house with a conjectural plan of the seventeenth-century kitchen ell, removed in 1794. Drawing courtesy of Cary Carson.

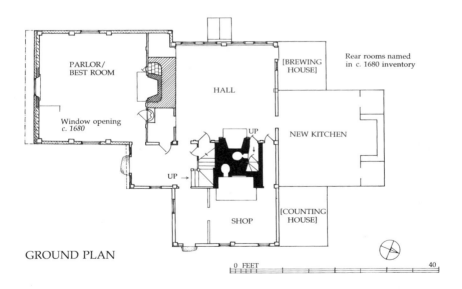

Figure 19. Ground floor plan of the Turner house with a conjectural footprint of the seventeenth-century kitchen ell. Drawing courtesy of Cary Carson.

story parlor addition to the south of the original parlor. This new addition has dimensions that are much more evocative of the classical in their proportions than the original rooms in the house. This ell is approximately one-half the size of the original house plan, running 21.5 feet along the south face of the old house, and being 22 feet north to south.

The ambiance of the room is much more modern than the low ceilings and long rooms of the original part of the house. This is emphasized with the extra high ceilings and what might be the first example in Massachusetts Bay of a hanging plaster ceiling (Cummings 1979: 191). The walls in the house were painted with whitewash and the exposed beams were painted in strongly contrasting shades, first of red, then gray (Cummings 1979: 193). This would have provided attractive, and more important, visible, decor in the otherwise dim rooms, lit only by sunlight, fire, and flickering candlelight in the evenings.

Other adornment on the new front parlor addition included another gable and a second floor jetty or overhang, with finials on the house corners. This represents an example of what Cummings calls the real provincial sumptuousness of the last three decades of the seventeenth century (1979: 39, 112). Unfortunately, in the case of the Turner house, it was also a rare example of unusually poor craftsmanship. Although the overhang was no more than two feet over the south part of the first floor, two of the larger joists were split over the jetty's girt, and therefore do not provide any structural support for that area of the second floor. This weakness was further compounded by the fact that several of the joists do not actually tie in with the overhanging girt, and so the weight of that room itself, the brick from its chimney, and the attic chamber above it were settled on an unstable frame (Cummings 1979: 73). This caused structural problems (that part of the building was near collapse on several occasions) throughout the history of the house, and archaeological evidence of repairs and stabilization in the late eighteenth century was uncovered. Ironically, the restoration process in the early twentieth century undid the eighteenth-century renovations, and the structure again sagged and was in need of similar repair in the 1970s.

The new parlor reflected the reemerging ideals of classical space and proportion. I suggest that it is possible that the Turner house, although it did not have columns or a symmetrical facade, could express the owner's knowledge of classical space, or at least, new fashions in that style coming from England. The Turner house, even with its very subtle differences, would have stood out among other Salem merchants' houses:

> Hall-parlour houses of this sort satisfied virtually all of the upper half of the colonial society in the seventeenth century. Everywhere merchants and planters of means lived in four basic rooms no larger than twenty by twenty, two up and two down, with additional workrooms attached or set apart from the houses. The social place of the owners required no more. The lineaments of the social structure were doubtless as sharply perceived in the seventeenth century as later, but the material expressions were far less pronounced.... People of wealth and recognized standing contented themselves with single-cell houses to the end of the seventeenth century and beyond. (Bushman 1993: 108–109)

The house with its furnishings would have provided a suitably polite setting for producing and reproducing merchant life, a place for business and entertainment. The furnishings in the new, grander parlor (and its chamber) seem to have been particularly selected for meeting and social display: the large windows (made up of diamond-shaped panes held in place with crisscrossing leads) would have looked over the yard sloping down to the public way and wharves and across Salem harbor to Marblehead. The family's ships and warehouses would have been visible from the room, a framed seascape portrait of the sources of their wealth.

Caroline Emmerton, who was responsible for the restoration of the Turner house in the 1910s, uncovered a concealed staircase leading to the second floor during the reconstruction of a chimney stack. She speculated that the "secret staircase" was constructed by the young John Turner in order to protect his sisters during the anarchic period of the Salem witchcraft trials of 1692 (Emmerton 1985). This is a pretty, romantic notion, but it is probable that the staircase was a servant's stairway, probably constructed with the original chimney stack in the seventeenth century, one more feature of the house that would have facilitated entertaining and also afforded a greater segmentation between the Turners and their servants (Cummings 1979: 125).

The variety of gear in the kitchen (as of 1743) seems to reaffirm the amount of entertaining going on in this high-status household, as well as the specialization in cooking wares that further reflects the elite status of the Turners. Skillets, chafing dishes, kettles, frying pans, spits, hooks, dripping pans, toasters, and other implements were listed in the probate inventory of Colonel Turner, along with other dishes of "hard mettle" and pewter, indicating an extraordinary specialization and knowledge of cookery. The presence of tools, including axes, saws, and hatchets, also indicates that even if activities requiring these items were not taking place in the kitchen, then the kitchen was still considered the organizational center of the house for such tasks. One entry for an "Iron Ratt Spring Trap," probably made to order as its value was listed as ten shillings, reveals one of the nuisances of living close to wharves and storage areas (Goodwin 1993: 81).

Although the noise and the nuisance of living next to the wharves on Salem harbor might have intruded occasionally, the setting would have reminded every visitor of the power and wealth of the Turners. However, the Turners also owned many other parcels of land, some of which were used for entertaining. Baker's Island (in Salem harbor) was the location of some of the Turner warehouses, but was also a pleasure garden. It was remembered by Reverend Bentley as a "delightful" and cultivated garden while the Turners owned it (EIHC 1902: 241).

More important to entertaining was a plot of land at Castle Hill in Salem. Also used for farming, Castle Hill was the site of the "hog barbecue" described by Benjamin Lynde, Jr., whose family owned land adjacent to the Turners' there. Although there was no house on the property, the land, in addition to providing income and produce, would have communicated important ideas about the Turners. Land traditionally represented inherited wealth and in the seventeenth and eighteenth centuries it also denoted the Roman virtues of patriotism and simple, decent country life. Hancock's "associates" bought large amounts of land in the country and used the earth to rub the shine off their mercantile wealth. As discussed in Chapter 3, land ownership and its produce marked the ruling elite in England and was one of the principal arguments made against the gentility of merchants, who were thought to "produce" nothing. In 1711 *The Spectator*, observing the discussion between Sir Andrew Freeport, the created proponent of the merchant class, and Sir Roger de Coverly, a fictional representative of the landed elite, remarked: "And this is always the Case of the landed and trading Interest of *Great Britain*; the Trader is fed by the Product of the Land, and the landed Man cannot be cloathed but by the Skill of the Trader; and yet those Interests are ever Jarring" (Steele and Addison 1988: 447). The essay concludes, not surprisingly, with *The Spectator*, which was sympathetic to the merchant class and Whig policy, arguing that merchants were as worthy as the landed gentlemen and sometimes more so: "Certainly he deserves the Estate a great deal better who has got it by his Industry, than he who has lost it by his Negligence" (Steele and Addison 1988: 450).

Land ownership was invested with patina because of primogeniture and entailment, suggesting a commitment to the community through continued benevolent interest in the tenants. Hancock, describing the decision by one of the merchant associates to run his farm, wrote: "The respect and love of one's laborers, he knows from his treatises and actual experience, was a mark of polite status, in managing his tenants and estates in this manner, he was projecting an image of a latter-day paterfamilias, an hospitable 'Ancient Baron'" (Hancock 1995: 300). Although I do not know whether the land at Castle Hill was rented, I believe that aside from its practical use as a farm, it communicated a symbol of patrician longevity and rural virtue. It added to the Turner family's stature as local leaders and landed elite in America, conferring on them all the patina that might have been found in a titled estate, but with colonial sensibilities and colonial meanings (Figure 20).

Similarly, the Turner house acted as the link between the community and the elite family who built and lived in it. The house has always been the most obvious element of the site's landscape and, with the wharves, bridged the gap between private interests and community interests by denying that there was a difference. At the same time, it also acted as a barrier between the family and their employees or contractors and the rest of the public, by emphasizing social distance and the ultimate inaccessibility of elite culture, at least in terms of mystique, if not actually the material representation of it. The fact that Salem's inventoried wealth owned by the top 10 percent of the population rose from 21 percent before 1661 to more than 60 percent after that time (Greene 1988: 63), emphasizes inaccessibility, as well as the success of the mercantile elite in maintaining their position in Salem (Goodwin 1994b).

Based on the probate inventories of the first two Johns Turner, the house represents, along with the ships, one of the major capital properties owned by the Turners. Not only did the Turner house serve as a dwelling, but it was also used as a shop, a warehouse, a counting house, and a meeting place for commerce as well as civic business. The house, along with other real properties owned by the Turners, was the setting for social gatherings of the upper strata and was modified internally, both structurally and artifactually, to reflect these transactions (Goodwin 1997).

It also represented an investment in the commerce that sustained Salem. By building on the harbor, near their wharf and the rest of the town's maritime activities, the Turners were not only able to keep an eye on their business affairs as they took place, but also were literally placing themselves squarely within the community. This was reinforced by the political and military roles that the first two generations of Turners played and by their Congregationalist and local loyalties. They were symbolically stating that they were actively participating in the business of Salem and were proclaiming their confidence in the structures (material and ideal) that maintained the community there. The

Figure 20. *Governor Benjamin Gerrish* (1714–1752), by John Greenwood. An important merchant who made his fortune in mackerel, Gerrish chose to represent himself in proximity to a pastoral scene, possibly to underscore his land ownership. Merchants in Massachusetts, and elsewhere in America, often had properties outside of town, often farms that provided fresh produce as well as a genteel setting for entertainments. Photograph by Mark Sexton. Courtesy, Peabody Essex Museum, Salem, Massachusetts.

Honorable John Turner, Esquire, by eschewing his trading business, abandoning the Puritan church for Anglicanism, and moving away from the waterfront to the more fashionable center of town immediately after his father's death in 1743 effectively rejected the community to which his father and grandfather belonged and in which they thrived. His movement away from that real place and the ideals attached to it resulted in his economic and social demise, mitigated only by the extent to which his sons were champions of those things and while his father's memory held sway (Goodwin 1997).

As much as they were declaring themselves a part of that trading community with the continued presence of their home, the Turners were by no means suggesting that they were akin to the majority of Salemites who invested their lives in the sea trade. The apparent contradiction between presence within the most active part of the commercial community and the social distance created by the imposing house is similar to that described by Matthew Johnson in his examination of the closure of "polite" housing in Suffolk at a time when discipline by observation was being espoused by the elite (Johnson 1993: 175). In both cases, presence or observation, as Johnson suggests, is required in order to maintain the order (Goodwin 1997).

The traditional style of the house, with its jettied overhangs and pendants, was lavish for the new colonies, but the style was outdated in England. I suggest that the style was meant to create the idea of the Turner family as leaders in the community, with the added reinforcement of a consciously created history, much the same way that Mark Leone described the search for the vindication of authority in the historical and the natural in William Paca's garden in Annapolis (Leone 1984: 27). The Turners and others in Massachusetts were relying on the symbolism of their massive houses to re-create themselves as the indisputable leaders of their communities by right of a constructed "historical" precedent.

The Salem maritime elite communicated to one another and reinforced their social and business ties through formal recreative activities that utilized costly artifacts and exclusive manners. By investing in a public symbol of their commitment to the community—their house and its location amid the busy commercial area by the water—the Turners were, I believe, choosing symbols to demonstrate their belief in the system that sustained every class.

It would be naive, however, to believe that this was the sole intention of the Turners in the construction, refurbishment, and maintenance of the house by the harbor was as part of a community covenant. Richard Bushman's notions about the importance of emulation of the elite classes in the maintenance of power structures must also be considered. He points out that capitalism joined hands with the concept of gentility by providing a source of goods with which the lower classes could emulate the elite (1993: 406). This mechanism at once provided the means for reinforcing the position of the elite, while creating the means for controlling entry into that group, with the rapid flood of status goods, and, more important, the manners associated with their use. The stately house would have remained as an artifact that proclaimed the Turners' status more publicly and more permanently than imported porcelain or expensive wines. "Great mansions were instruments of power—to be paraded before a deferential population whose compliance was necessary for the continuation of authority" (Bushman 1993: 403).

The landscape of the house and the land at Castle Hill ensured the distance between the Turners and the rest of the community socially, even while their physical presence was situated unmistakably in the middle of the busiest parts of town. The imprint of their social power on the landscape was also cemented with the construction of town buildings. In 1712 Colonel Turner, Major Stephen Sewall, and Colonel Samuel Browne, who had married John's sister Eunice, were charged with the construction of a watch house for the town. This was built "nigh the meeting house," and had a "handsome wooden soldier" carved on top with "Anna Regina, 1712" in gold (Perley 1903: 247). Part of the self-aggrandizement of the merchant class described by Borsay, it also had benefits for the community and civic prestige (1989: 253). Historicity, permanence, dynasticism, patriarchy, community, and social reproduction were all thus signaled.

The Spencer-Peirce-Little house provides a similar example. The house, built sometime after 1677 in Newbury, Massachusetts, was constructed of stone in a cruciform plan in the "Artisan Mannerist" style—characterized by the porch entry, asymmetrical window placement, and molded brick detailing (Beaudry n.d.: 14–15). Like the Turner house, the Spencer-Peirce-Little house had been constructed with historic associations in mind:

> Clearly reminiscent of manor houses of old England, the house from the outset carried an aura of association with England's landed gentry. Situated in the midst of some of the best agricultural land in Essex County, this far-from-humble farmhouse was from its earliest days emblematic of the coexistence of traditional agrarian values alongside what was perceived as the profit-oriented arena of mercantile capitalism. (Beaudry n.d.: 15)

Patina was of tremendous consequence for the merchant class in Massachusetts. It was consciously constructed with the goal of shortening the length of time normally required for a "natural" accretion of patina. It was best seen in the largest, most public statements expressed in material culture, houses, and landscapes, and at the same time of maintaining hierarchies, suggesting the interdependence between the merchant elite and the communities in which they resided.

I would also make the argument that patina is also a quality that can be attributed to humans, though more often under the vague and uncomfortably biological description of "breeding." I believe that what courtesy writers in the seventeenth and eighteenth centuries were referring to as elegant ease or the *je ne sais quoi* was for humans what patina was to artifacts, a badge of historical gentility and station. Baltazar Gracian y Morales wrote about "the Secret charm, of the unexpressible somewhat; which the French call *Le Je-ne-sai-quoi*. And the Spaniards *El despejo*":

> [It] is the life of great qualities, the breath of words, the soul of actions, and the lustre of all beauties. Other perfections are the ornament of nature; the unexpressible somewhat, that of perfections. It is observable even in the way of reasoning. It holds much more of privilege than of study; for it is even above all discipline. It is not limited to facility, but reaches the finest Gallantry. It supposes a free and unstinted mind, and to that unstintedness it adds the last strokes of perfection. Without it all beauty is dead, all gracefullness ungracefull. It hath the pre-eminence over valour, discretion, prudence, nay, and majesty it self. It is a politick high way wherein affairs are soon dispatched; and, in fine, the art of coming off gallantly when one is hampered. It adorns the ornaments of perfection on nature. (1685: 117).

CONCLUSION

This charismatic nonchalance is the sort of quality that the courtesy books strove to teach and what many tried to express through their material culture—by the "continuous purchase and display of cultural products" men and women "signalled" their entry into genteel society (Hancock 1995: 281). These consumers had a good idea of what they wanted and, influenced by a number of different factors including price, self-image, aspiration, and interpretation, expressed individual and group identities through these objects. As seen in many examples of research, people have always manipulated material culture to suit their changing identities. Lauren Bresnan (1996) described how the Beekman family, merchants of New York, carefully transformed their identity through the purchase of increasingly more impressive homes and particular, emblematic artifacts, for different "personas." And Janice Radway wrote convincingly about the meanings with which readers imbued mass-marketed romance novels:

> Commodities like mass-produced literary texts are selected, purchased, constructed, and used by real people with previously existing needs, desires, intentions, and interpretive strategies. By reinstating those active individuals and their creative, constructive activities at the heart of our interpretive enterprise, we avoid blinding ourselves to the fact that the essentially human practice of making meaning goes on even in a world increasingly dominated by things and by consumption. (Radway 1984: 221)

Perhaps even the courtesy books were themselves part of this identity marking. Many reprints of earlier works were rebound in fine leather and decorated with gold leaf. Such a volume observed in a library would have been a literal (and literary) symbol of the owner's self-image and pretensions.

One of the challenges of material culture studies (in any period) is that so often there are many meanings of an object that are lost to time. It is equally possible that, sometimes, there is no meaning other than the intrinsic value of the objects. When John Mascarene suffered a nervous breakdown after his first voyage to England, he was accused of having signed over some property to his wife, Margaret, to protect it from his creditors. This accusation hurt the couple deeply, and Margaret wrote in a letter:

> I wish now I had Something Considerable In my hands, for I could deliver it up with all the pleasure in life, to assist in paying any Debt, contracted before, or since, our Marriage. What I can, I will. There is the horse, and Chaise and my Cloths, what My Father gave me, as well as those Mr. Mascarene gave, some rings and Buckles of value, these are all I have, and these I chearfully resign. Indeed I do not know of a better use for these Trinkets. I can truly say I knew no pleasure in wearing them, than that of obliging the Dear Donor—Indeed Sir I never lookt upon poverty as the greatest evill, and even in this near view of it, I am not frighted. (quoted in Shipton 1945: 37)

She disavowed all of the meanings the outside observer might otherwise attribute to the valuable goods in her possession.

Sometimes consumers were successful in negotiating the meanings of their goods, sometimes they were not, but as more were able to purchase goods that had previously only been available to the wealthy, changes were made in elite material culture in order to maintain distinctions of hierarchy. Luxury might have been cheaper to acquire, so more weight was placed on novelty. Patina remained the ultimate expression of genteel wealth, with its implications of longevity and legitimacy. The newly available artifacts, some of them also new in form, and new definitions of gentle status were related, both emphasizing and supporting the other, both the cause of change and the perceived remedy to clarifying the hierarchies that persisted in spite of that change.

A renewed interest in courtesy literature was supported by discussion of polite behavior in *The Spectator* and *The Tatler*, where the role of the merchant was also discussed in relation to the traditional social order. Polite gatherings in single-sex or mixed company, quietly over tea or during more lively occasions (heightened with imported foods), also provided the opportunity to demonstrate this knowledge in moments of group making and allegiance building.

Manners and Women's Roles in Merchant Society | 5

Shall I be one, of those obsequious fools,
That square there lives, by Customs scanty Rules;
Condemn'd for ever, to the puny Curse,
Of Precepts taught, at Boarding-school, or Nurse,
That all the business of my Life must be,
Foolish, dull Trifling, Formality.
Confin'd to a strict Magick complaisance,
And round a Circle, of nice visits Dance,
Nor for my Life beyond the Chalk advance:
The Devil Censure, stands to guard the same,
One step awry, he tears my ventrous Fame.
—*Sarah Fyge, The Liberty*

INTRODUCTION

In the seventeenth and eighteenth centuries, men and women had distinctly different roles prescribed for them by society, promised by the religious and scientific views of the era, and sealed by law, local custom, and courtesy literature. These sources tell us how people were supposed to behave and are particularly useful in understanding the deeper ramifications of social behavior, particularly in "scripted" situations that were steeped in ritual. Despite the difficulty in observing the presence of women in the archaeological record, and frequently in the documentary record, by examining the prescribed mannerly conduct for men and women and comparing that with accounts of women in merchant communities, it is possible to reveal the important roles that women played in merchant society. In order to understand how elite women participated in the creation and reproduction of merchant life, it is also necessary to discuss the legal regulation of women's paid and unpaid work and the secondary research on the circumstances under which women were allowed to work. In this chapter, I outline some of the qualities of men and women as dictated by courtesy literature and underscored in contemporary documents and fiction. With that in mind, I describe what roles I perceive women of the merchant class played in the reproduction of their culture, and the ways in which mannerly behavior facilitated that reproduction for women. Although few of these activities can be directly observed in the archaeological record in terms of assemblage patterns, we can invest recovered artifacts with what we know of the meaning of private or public social occasions.

I take the opportunity in this chapter to focus particularly on women's roles because so much of the actual work of trading or negotiating, in short, of being a merchant, was understood to be "men's" work. Despite the examples of a few extraordinary women who were merchants, this was not the aspect of that life in which women figured prominently. By examining social roles I can better demonstrate how women participated in this society. It should also be understood that the roles that I describe here might also have been assumed by men under certain circumstances (for example, cadet males) and that these roles or some variation thereof probably existed in other social groups in the past as well.

The understanding of manners and mannerly behavior is important here for several reasons, particularly with reference to merchants in Massachusetts. While it can restrict and exclude, mannerly behavior facilitates communication between genders, classes, or other socially defined boundaries by providing ways to negotiate between these groups in a socially sanctioned fashion. This communication was important for social reproduction and long-term connections, sometimes through marriage or the exchange of apprentices between trading families, and sometimes simply through increased intimacy within a group. Manners also provided a way for women in the merchant class to exert power over these communications' directly affecting commerce as well as the recreation of their community.

RESEARCHING WOMEN IN THE PAST

One warm day in 1768, three men carried the earthly remains of Madam Mary (Kitchen) Turner from her final residence in Ipswich, Massachusetts, to her longtime home of Salem a few miles to the south. An acute observer might have noticed some impressive elements in the funeral preparations. According to the statement her son made in claiming expenses from the estate in 1771, the funeral was expensive. He claimed the price of the coffin plates by Samuel Curwen and lettered by Samuel Blyth, money disbursed to servants and friends for the purchase of mourning garb and gloves, and the bills for "keeping" the men and horses that brought the corpse to Salem, the sexton's fee, the estate appraisers, and for the funeral itself. The Honorable John Turner hired a man for 13 shillings 10 pence to "advise the Relations of the Decease of my Mother," and although he eventually took them for his property, along with £80 for their maintenance, he paid for an advertisement to "dispose of the Negro's" (Titus, Rebecca, and Jane) (ECPR, Vol. 346).

Accounts were settled and the rituals and commonplaces of human lives were provided for. The expenses paid out for the legal, religious, and secular undertaking of death came to more than £20. These were not the preparations for the funeral of an unimportant woman.

From church documents we know that Madam Mary Turner outlived her husband Colonel John Turner by 26 years. She had been baptized in 1683 and married in 1701, making her at least 17 or 18 at the time of her marriage to Colonel Turner (Moriarty 1981: 14). She died before November 21, 1768, the date that her probate inventory was taken, and so was at least 85 years old, a veritable ancient, when she died. Mary was traditionally described as one of the most beautiful women in Salem (Emmerton 1985: 20).

Based on her probate inventory, listing property worth about £700, we can make a few assumptions about Mary's adult life. She owned expensive clothing (suitable for the wife of an important merchant and jurist), gold jewelry, buckles, and buttons, and a house furnished with silver plate, porcelain, tin-glazed wares, pictures, books, and an array of expensive furniture. She was literate and possibly numerate, having rented to her son John part of the Turner house and holding debts against her sons-in-law. It her will, she left her estate to be divided equally among her four children, mentioning her daughters each by name: Elizabeth Berry, Mary Bowditch, and Eunice Balston. It was a significant gesture that she left equal shares to her daughters: when her husband John died intestate, the shares went to their sons-in-law. As a widow and *feme sole*, Mary was able to leave her estate as she pleased. This will is one of the only statements we have made by Mary herself.

In all the documents that were written during her life, the only observation we have of Madam Turner herself comes from Benjamin Lynde, Jr., in 1724: "To a charity ball. After, home with mme. Turner" (Lynde 1880: 132). This is not much evidence for a life that must have been filled with all the complexities of socializing, the burdens of housekeeping, child rearing, charity, and the mysteries of religious life.

More solid information about Madam Turner arises from the event of her death than at any other point in her life. As historical archaeologists, we are all too aware that the traces of women who lived centuries ago are often elusive in both the archaeological and historical records, and that to find them, we are exhorted to seek them out in often creative, not always convincing ways. Some of the more successful examples of this endeavor can be seen in work by Seifert (1991), Yentsch (1991), Scott

(1994), Wall (1994), and Beaudry (1995). It seems that where women are segregated, the chances of observing distinguishing features in the archaeological record are better, as seen in the research of De Cunzo (1995b) and the "Sin City" sessions at the 1998 meeting of the Society for Historical Archaeology in Atlanta, where archaeological research on American prostitutes was discussed.

Laurel Thatcher Ulrich (among other historians) makes the point that the "best" women were bound to be the least remarkable and that it was only at the principal points of life—birth, marriage, the birth of children, and death—or through rupture of the social code that a woman might appear in official records—unless one is extraordinarily lucky to have either her diary or letters or remembrances of others about her (1982: 3). The Marchioness of Lambert wrote that one of the "ancients" allowed women "nothing but the single merit of being unknown" and "such as are most praised ... are not always the persons that deserve it best; but rather such as are not talked of at all" (1794: 175). This is a radical thought for a woman living at a time when self-effacement for women was a desirable trait.

In the case of merchant wives (or daughters, sisters, and other dependent females or males), we have the added questions of the roles such women played in British-American elite life in Massachusetts. The mannerly behavior in social roles would enhance the camouflage of "good wives" even more, rendering them less visible for a lack of re-markability. The irony of this is that many of the contemporary sources say that such women should be emulated, so it is frustrating that more has not been recorded about these paragons. Many of the writers stated that for models of virtue were to be found in antiquity. Reverend Colman recalled the mother of Lemuel in Proverbs 31 (1716: 2) in outlining the duties and virtues of a good wife and mother, Brathwait chose examples of virtue from the past, and Fenelon advised looking to the Greek and Roman empires and their mythologies for models (1707: 202).

But people talk or write in detail about how things fail, not about how they succeed. If a journalist writes "all went exactly as I could have wished, not one thing was out of place, the company the genteelest imaginable," it leaves the researcher with a vague, sympathetic satisfaction and room for a good deal of hypothesizing. There is much more to go on if the discontented writer recorded: "Mr. X behaved abominably, tripping over his own large feet and dominating the conversation with recollections of his various stomach illnesses. The only pause in his hymn of self-adoration came when he stuffed the cake (regrettably poor, coarse stuff) into his face. We retired early." Bad manners, like broken laws, tell more about a society than good ones. The behavior dictated by the works of courtesy can help imbue the artifacts with meaning within this social context. To that end, I address the behavior associated with women's roles first.

WOMEN, WORK, AND MANNERS IN THE SEVENTEENTH AND EIGHTEENTH CENTURIES

Courtesy Books and Prescribed Qualities

Elizabeth Bergen Brophy, in comparing Richard Allestree's works *The Ladies Calling* and *The Gentleman's Calling*, observes that the work directed to gentlewomen emphasizes reputation—virtue, modesty, piety—while that directed to gentlemen focuses exclusively on the correct ways of wielding authority (1991: 7). This distinction between the feminine qualities of virtue and masculine traits of authority characterized courtesy literature and social roles in the seventeenth and eighteenth centuries. Although in many instances the recommendations were the same for both men and women, there are gender-specific instructions; but it is clear that women read guides intended for men and vice versa: the copy of *The Gentleman's Calling* that I examined was inscribed "Elisabeth Carleill, her Booke 1692." A brief examination of the qualities prescribed for men and women is important in approaching topics of public behavior.

Gentlemen were cautioned in all things to practice restraint and moderation. By this means, they were able to govern themselves and maintain social distance, a balance between excessive affability and aloofness, which was necessary for maintaining the authority proper to high station.

Hemphill notes that courtesy books stressed courteous behavior to every person of every station, thus creating a polite distance from those both better and worse off than oneself, and avoiding undue familiarity that might smack of sycophancy or brutishness when self-knowledge was crucial (1988: 46). In 1622 Henry Peacham advised "temperance and moderation of the minde" (1968: 185). Latini (ca. thirteenth century) also wrote of the importance of social distance, praising the qualities of circumspection and frugality (1869: 10), and Palmieri in his *Vita Civile* (ca. 1430), espoused temperance (1869: 59).

Honesty, a critical element of honor, was also important and often expressed in advice on dressing and living according to one's proper station. "By gate, laughter, and apparrell, a man is knowne what he is," wrote Peacham (1968: 185). Excessive ornament or expense was as bad as dressing beneath oneself, and honesty of character was equally important in terms of reputation, the emblem of a gentleman. Again, this was strongly associated with representing accurately one's place in society.

Some writers demonstrated crucial masculine qualities by negative comparisons with the feminine. Courage in a man was equivalent to virtuous shame in a woman, for example. "We may well feare least Women too gorgeous in apparrell be without shame, and Men too quaint and effeminate in their dressings, without courage" (Du Bosc 1639: 34) and "[t]he one Sex having advanced into Boldness, as the other have sunk into Effeminacy" (Brown, 1757: 50).

According to Mary Sumner Benson, Locke mentioned only private education for daughters with no further suggestion for training women, while Gervase Markham recommended that a woman could set an example of a religious life for their families, but that they should not by any means consider preaching (Benson 1935: 24–25).

Mary Astell (1666–1731), the author of *Reflections upon Marriage* and *A Serious Proposal to the Ladies* (1694) and who may be the author of *An Essay in Defence of the Female Sex*, wrote fervently in favor of more education for women. She reasoned that because there was no theological distinction between the souls of men and women, that anatomists had found no differences in brain structure, and that "primitive" cultures seemed to make no distinction between the sexes, it must be European men who kept women ignorant by refusing to educate them (Benson 1935: 29–30). Even more remarkably, Astell suggested that usual feminine education was not so defective as might be supposed, because a knowledge of the vernacular and French was a good background for "polite conversation," provided one read widely and carefully (Benson 1935: 32–33).

In general, courtesy manuals directed toward women described personal decorum in public (that is, particularly in the presence of men), in terms of virtue and modesty. Advice that is recommended toward men also had to do with public behavior, but more so with skills (social, business, etc.) and virtues other than chastity. A casual survey of contemporary courtesy books demonstrates the reality of what Samuel Johnson meant when he said, "the chastity of women is of importance, as all property depends on it" (quoted in Porter 1990: 25). From a strictly legal point of view, this was accurate but the notion spilled over into social use to an extravagant degree. Adjectives that describe ideal feminine behavior can be divided into several categories: virtue, honesty, accomplishment, and humility.

Madam Johnson wrote in 1754 that, for women, the "qualities required in order to live with repute are: Virtue, Modesty, Good Sense,

Good Nature, Good Breeding (without the last, none of the rest will avail but little)" (1754: 11). Dr. Gregory (1724–1773) concurred with this point of view, explaining that "modesty isn't dull, but most important" (1794: 10). Brathwait considered virtue the truest expression of gentle birth, claiming that "there is no Ornament like Vertue, to give true beauty to descent.... Honor does not receive its first life from descent" (1631: 55).

The Marchioness of Lambert stressed, however, that women should consider cultivating what she described as "Manly virtues." "I do not confine the merit of women merely to modesty; I give it a much larger extent. A valuable woman exerts the manly virtues of friendship, probity, and honour, in the punctual discharge of her obligations. An amiable woman should not only have the exterior graces, but all the graces of the heart, and fine sentiments of the mind" (1794: 179). This is a bold statement and similar to Castiglione's description of the ideal woman at court, but the statement also reflects the contemporary notion that "friendship, probity, and honour" are inherently masculine in nature, not native to women. It should also be noted that "probity," "honor," and "the punctual discharge of her obligations" are also forms of self-control, as are honesty, modesty, and virtue.

Dress receives a good deal of attention in courtesy literature for women, because it reflects the wearer's attitude. Not only modesty, but thrift and the subjugation of vanity and greed are to be found in resisting the lure of shiny but impermanent baubles, ribbons, buckles, and buttons. There was "no sense tricking out our mortal houses" (Brathwait 1631: 16).

Lack of self-control in this respect also suggested that one was attempting to be something one was not, either in terms of social status, virtue, or other qualities. Affectation was the child of pride and immodesty and suggested a streak of insincerity that would pollute other aspects of life: "Vertuous and descreet Matrons would be loath to weare aught that might give least scandall or offence to their sexe. Forraine fashions are no baits to catch them, nor phantastick, rather phanaticke dressings to delude them.... Decency is their choicest liberty, which sets them forth above all embroidery" (Brathwait 1631: 91). Fenelon wrote "[t]he True Graces depend not on a vain and affected Dress. (1707: 202)" and that "the true Graces always follow, never torture Nature" (1707: 204).

Although some writers valued wit (in terms of the luster of a good mind) as a quality for a woman, many more warned that wit (and its attendant pride) was the antithesis of modesty. Wit corrupted native virtue, convinced women of their superiority, and threatened the natural order of things. A woman's tongue, freed by wit and left uncontrolled by the rational male, was what many writers (male and female) feared would undermine society through gossip at the tea table (discussed in further detail below). Gregory wrote that wit made women prone to vanity and indelicacy, and that while it made them attractive at first, it would eventually repel men by tampering with purity and modesty (1794: 11). He furthermore strongly advised women to hide good sense and education on the grounds that it would either make men jealous or offended because they already know what they need to know (1794: 12). Elizabeth Montagu wrote in 1750 that "wit in women is apt to have bad consequences, like a sword without a scabbard, it wounds the wearer and provokes assailants. I am sorry to say the generality of women who have excelled in wit have failed in chastity" (quoted in Porter 1990: 23).

In Richardson's novels, Pamela wins her aristocratic husband not through her goodness or wit but by tenaciously guarding her virginity, and Clarissa wills herself to death over the loss of her virginity through rape, in spite of the fact that she is not to blame. Although these novels have been condemned for their particularly sentimental middle-classed values, this refrain of the importance of virtue in women is sustained in courtesy literature as well.

One example of how broken rules inform about ideal and reviled behavior comes from the Earle correspondence. Joseph Denham wrote to Mary Earle about her fortunate escape from a most unwelcome guest in the expatriate English merchant community in Leghorn in 1765:

> You are the luckiest woman in the World for you always escape Punishment as if you had never deserved it. Had you been here last Sunday, you would have been persecuted sufficiently for 20 (aye, you may add another cypher) years Penance—Mrs. Strine, Madam! We were hon'd with her delightful company at Dinner: How did you like France Madam? Oh Lord Sir! Don't mention that dear Country. It was certainly the Seat of Paradise, Such Liberty, such Brilliant sprightly conversation, so degage so je ne sçais quoi! Oh dear Charming Country! Better than England Ma'am? England Sir! The most villainous Country under the Sun—why 'tis the P-ss Pot of the Universe Sir. Every thing is so dull & gloomy there, & my Spirits are so depressed in that miserable Country ... Vive la France! Vive la France ...
>
> But I shu'd tell first her Figure—She was dressed quite in the French Taste, & painted an Inch Thick up to the very Eyes, insomuch that when she passed the Main Guard all the officers stood up & busted out a Laughing, imagining it was a Mask. She has a Pair of foolish unmeaning eyes with which she plays the Coquette more than any woman I ever saw. I was in constant fear she wo'd call for a Utensil from the next room a la Mode de France. Her Nostrils are so wide that they appear like the two holes of the Pillory, & being bored in a direct Line, one sees home to the back part of her Skull, for I co'd not perceive the Sight at all interrupted by Brains, so that I suppose she left them in England as a Piece of Furniture quite useless in France. She has an Asthma & Consumption upon her, & is advised to stay here for the Benefit of the Sea Air, & commodore Acton takes her out upon the water every Evening for she loves dearly to be sea-sick she says. She goes to

the Consul's ... every Evening at the conversation where they all ridicule her abominably, so that in short all Leghorn is ... mad about her. (NMGM, D/Earle/3/2/17)

Mrs. Strine is the subject of such ridicule because she flies in the face of prescribed womanly behavior. She is loud, opinionated, forward, coquettish, and affects a makeup, dress, and manners that are not of her own nation. She is not apparently bothered by the fact that people openly laugh at her, as a less "foolish" woman might be. But Mrs. Strine provides an instructive model to the English merchant community in Livorno in her behavior, not only as to what not to do, but the consequences of such behavior—to be universally mocked behind closed doors and, seemingly, to her face as well.

It also must be remarked that however much Denham derides her behavior and pokes cruel fun at her appearance, he betrays some interesting facts about Mrs. Strine that he might not otherwise care to admit. Mrs. Strine has access to the consul's soirées. She has sufficient influence to get the English commodore at Livorno to take her out boating every evening to get "sea-sick." And Denham himself is obliged to invite her to dinner. The expatriate merchant community at Livorno might laugh at Mrs. Strine, be horrified by her appearance and actions, but they still invite her to their gatherings. Power of some sort—economic, social, political—makes her antics tolerable, even if they are a "penance." Power can mitigate (if not excuse) the effects of a good deal of contrary behavior, no matter how much it is ridiculed. As important as mannerly behavior was, it could not compete with sheer social power. The English commodore in Genoa, for all of his might, was subject to similar criticisms as Mrs. Strine for his lack of accomplishments. In 1763 Joseph Denham wrote:

> It is as good as a comedy to see the commodore dance and address himself to the ladies—I believe he never attempted the former before in his life, for he makes a shocking piece of work of it. He goes about to a great number of ladies bowing and making so many Gestures that one would swear he could talk Italian very well, tho' he says nothing at all to them only, Bella! Cara! Si Signora etc for he does not speak even a word of French. (NMGM, Earle 3/2/4)

The weight of his office, however, offset (if did not excuse) whatever shortcomings the commodore might have had in the social graces. He could not dance, showed no restraint in attempting it, and did not speak "even a word of French," the bare minimum for a politely trained gentleman or gentlewoman.

In the face of these bad examples, we have a hard time drawing a picture of what good ones looked like and must rely on inference. Denham describes Mrs. Earle as a "queen of Lilliput," virtuous, a good cook, mother, wife, and neighbor. These bland encomiums do nothing to distinguish personality. The same is true for Elizabeth Turner, Madam Mary Turner, Mrs. Mascarene, or Mrs. Tracy of Newbury, who was described as "dress'd genteelly, sitting at her tea table with her children about her. She is a very handsom accomplished woman, and knows very well how to keep up her dignity" (quoted in Beaudry n.d.: 46). This gives the researcher no picture of them as vivid as the one painted by Denham of Mrs. Strine. She provides a much better example of what not to do than Mrs. Earle does of appropriate behavior to the modern researcher. This is the great problem of researching "good women." With this in mind, the next step to understand what women of the elite merchant class were allowed to contribute to their society is to examine the legal and customary constraints on what work any English women were allowed to do.

Women and Work

Historian Mary Prior has made the point that because of Christian tradition, men have "worked" and were able to define themselves by that work, and by "Adam's curse," women did their "duty," which lacks any identity but a social one (1985: 95). There were also times when a woman was expected to take on some part of her husband's work, because of his absence, illness, or death. Depending on the situation, the law, and the local custom, this was barely tolerated in some instances, but demanded as a responsibility in others. In the seventeenth and eighteenth centuries, it is imperative to recognize the fact that women came to the pinnacle of their social power after marriage, some because they had some security and exercised a limited control over their circumstances in their households, others, as widows, because they might have a degree of wealth and the legal rights as women no longer bound by the constraints of the *feme covert*. Unmarried women often lacked the financial security of married women even though they had the legal rights of a *feme sole*. Lyle Koehler summed up this situation of women in the past by quoting Emily James Putnam in *The Lady*: "In defiance of the axiom that he who works, eats, the lady who works has less to eat than the lady who does not. There is no profession open to her which is nearly as lucrative as marriage" (1980: 108). Susan Amussen reached the same conclusion, agreeing with historian Alice Clark about the inverse correlations between wealth of the family and economic contribution of the wife (1988: 69). With that in mind, it becomes essential to understand when and where women were allowed to work, bearing in mind the importance of unpaid work as discussed by Groneman and Norton

(1987: 4), their legal and customary rights, both as women and members of a particular social group, and therefore, the roles they might have played. By acknowledging these factors, we can begin to comprehend what elite women were permitted to do.

In general, it was believed that:

> The office of the husband is to bring in necessaries: of the wife, well to keep them. The office of the husband is, to go abroad in matters of profit: of the wife, to tarry at home, and see all be well there. The office of the husband is, to provide money, of the wife, not wastefully to spend it. The office of the husband is, to deal, and bargain with all men, of the wife, to meddle or make with no man. (quoted in Amussen 1988: 43)

Accordingly, in England, much research has been focused on rural areas or laboring poor (Clark 1968; Amussen 1988; Hill 1989), but based on them and work on the middle classes, we can see some of the trends that indicate what might also have been acceptable for women of higher status, especially those coming from classes where there was money but no tradition of gentility.

Peter Earle states that "we know virtually nothing about the female labour force in early modern London" (1989a: 329), but in his study of testimony from that city's church court records he has drawn a few general conclusions. He observed that, based on questions asked of female witnesses between 1695 and 1725, *neither* women nor men worked if they did not have to, that women overwhelmingly sought jobs that were in some way related to what they were traditionally taught—cooking or sewing or nursing (which was not considered respectable), and that it was highly unusual for women to pursue "men's" work. Even if widows chose to continue their husbands' trades, they frequently gave it up, most frequently for lack of training or ability (1989a: 338–339). While women consistently earned less than men, the average wage was enough to keep a single woman alive and would have been an important contribution to a family's income if needed (1989a: 343). Although this was somewhat biased in favor of lower middle-class and working-class women, these trends were confirmed by other English research and by observations made of life in colonial America.

Prior confirms these observations about the motivations and restrictions of women's work with her study of working women in Oxford during the seventeenth and eighteenth centuries. She also noted the community's willingness to allow women to work when there was need, finding this preferable to them seeking public relief:

> When women worked, it was from need rather than choice, though some enjoyed it and achieved success. This might be encouraged in wives, and tolerated because of need in the case of widows and sometimes, because of

the business conditions of a far-flung network of kin, rich women might be involved, but the need for spinsters to work outside the shelter of the household received little understanding. (1985: 114)

Outside of domestic service or home-based work, we see these trends in the business world as well. Earle concludes that there was a "definite female presence" in the London business world of the eighteenth century and that perhaps a third of all women of property ran a business of some sort, comprising 5 to 10 percent of all businesses in London (1989b: 173). A more significant role taken by women in business could be seen in investing and loan-making, which allowed women who had capital (again, most frequently widows) to make an income without the problem of competing for other women's work or possibly challenging societal norms by taking on their husbands' former occupations. Earle suggests that while 10–20 percent of London households were run by widows, their livings must not have been very good, based on how few paid more tax than the basic one shilling per quarter (1989b: 167). He states that only a very few would have been independent traders, and that possibly twice that number were investors in London businesses who drew a quarterly profit (Earle 1989b: 168–169). Again, however, only the wealthier women had this opportunity, because according to Koehler (1980: 110), the sum that they received might have increased their purchasing power, but was not enough to offer wider occupational opportunites.

For many years there has been a great deal of discussion over just what women were permitted to do in pre-Revolutionary New England, with one tradition of scholarship describing that period as a golden era of freedoms for women who were able to take advantage of the imbalanced demography that was unparalleled until the twentieth century. More recent research by Norton (1979a, b), Norton and Berkin (1979), and Ulrich (1982) suggests a more restricted view, a delicate balance between local custom, cultural mores, and the law. Women worked outside the home, but most often in trades that were related to traditional "women's work," such as those related to the preparation and service of food and drink, millinery and dress-making, caretaking, and cleaning, and less frequently in trades that were considered "men's work."

In America where the imbalanced demography of a colonial labor force might lead one to expect otherwise, the situation is remarkably similar to that of England. There were general constraints against women working outside the home unless there was financial need, and there were, of course, marked differences between the sorts of work that urban women undertook as opposed to their rural counterparts. Outside work was considered acceptable so long as it helped the family and did not contradict the wishes of her husband. (Ulrich 1982: 37–38).

Did the women of the merchant elite contribute to their families' fortunes, and if so, how? Sylvia Thrupp points out several examples:

> In the merchant class married women's business activities were less often an economic necessity than an outlet for surplus energy or a means of earning additional money to spend. Margery Kempe was the wife of one of the wealthiest merchants at Lynne [in 1405], yet she took up first brewing and then "a new huswyfre," the grinding of corn in a horsemill, because she had time on her hands and because, in her own words, she was envious that any other woman in Lynne "schuld be arrayd so wel as sche." (1992: 170)

Mary Beth Norton has claimed that too often historians have been misled by the lack of lengthy work entries in urban women's diaries, concluding therefrom that city "ladies" contributed little or nothing to the family welfare (1980: 21). Using examples from Nancy Shippen's journal (written in the 1780s), Norton describes wealthy urban women as leisured (1980: 23), but even in the upper classes, girls were "apprenticed" by their mothers at home earlier than boys were generally sent to other families, so that they would have the skills necessary to run a large household later in life. I do not believe that even "pretty gentlewomen" were free from work:

> The management of all domestic affairs is certainly the proper business of a woman; and unfashionably rustic as such an assertion may be thought, it is certainly not beneath the dignity of any lady, however high her rank, to know how to educate her children, to govern her servants, to order an elegant table with economy, and to manage her whole family with prudence, regularity, and method; if in these she is defective, what ever may be her attainments in any other kinds of knowledge, she will act out of character. (Pennington 1794: 123)

Laurel Thatcher Ulrich described the amount of labor dedicated to "service and maintenance," "agriculture," "manufacturing," and "trade" undertaken by Mary Vial Holyoke, sister-in-law to Margaret Mascarene (1982: 70–71). Even though she was married to Edward Augustus Holyoke, a gentleman and physician, Mary was not (or did not choose to be) relieved from doing many of the tasks her less wealthy sisters did. In fact, she also kept the books for Holyoke and thus took the financial well-being of the home on her shoulders in addition to the monumental responsibilities she already had as a wife and mother. Ulrich wrote:

> Pretty gentlewomen simply refined the skills which all good housewives shared. To a knowledge of plain sewing and common cookery they added a concern for grace and style. Mary Holyoke was a gentlewoman not just because she had wine and silver on her table but because she was interested

enough in the fine points of cooking to "dress" a calf's head "turtle fashion" rather than simply dropping it into the pot. Her gentility determined that she would spend at least some of her time updating and remodeling her clothing, that she could afford to send a piece of silk to England to be dyed and "water'd with large water," and that she would know how to monogram as well as construct her husband's scarves. (1982: 71)

The Law and Women's Work

Part of the restrictions on women's active participation in work outside the home came from custom codified into law, particularly those having to do with the rights of property ownership and the legal existence of women. Blackstone in his *Commentaries* (1765–1769) stated that "the very being, or legal existence, of the woman is suspended during marriage" (quoted in Porter 1990: 24). Marylynn Salmon described it as follows:

> The inability of wives to act as individuals at law arose as a corollary to their inability to own property. After marriage, all of the personal property owned by a wife came under the exclusive control of her husband. He could spend her money, including wages, sell her slaves or stocks, and appropriate her clothing and jewelry. With regard to real property his rights were almost as extensive. He made all managerial decisions concerning her lands and tenements and controlled the rents and profits. A conveyance of a woman's real estate was another matter, however. No husband could sell or mortgage real property without the consent of his wife. In one way or another, everything women owned before marriage became their husbands' afterwards. A significant result of this social policy was the inability of femes coverts to contract.... No agreement a woman made could be enforced against her because she owned nothing the court could seize to meet a judgment. Even a woman's contract to provide services was unenforceable. Acceding to common law rules, a woman's services belonged to her husband. They could not be given to another unless he consented. (1986: 15, 41)

The strict observation of these laws could be mitigated, however, by local custom, particularly when it was to benefit the community and within the bounds of social and legal restrictions. Women, even the *feme covert*, exercised a great deal of power, especially when the fate of the family rested on them in terms of survival. "Indeed, the responsibility of the family business, on which the careers of the upwardly mobile sons depended, was very much in the hands of the women, who provided the family with continuity and economic stability" (Prior 1985: 98). Women were constrained by common law in some cases, and by local custom in others, meaning that even though as a *feme sole* a woman had certain legal rights, she could not practically exercise them if they were prohibited by local tradition. Widows in particular were encouraged to find work as a source of income, even when not strictly legal, because their efforts represented less need for support from the community (Prior 1985: 106).

Barbara Todd eloquently described the double bind of the widow in seventeenth- and eighteenth-century English society: although they were expected to remarry, widows would have given up significant legal and economic control that an unmarried woman (particularly one with a little money) had, but at the same time, they were generally depicted in contemporary fiction as silly and scheming in their attempts to remarry (1985: 45–55).

In the case of New England, Ulrich states that local tradition made surrogacy after the husband's death more of an assumption than it might have been in England, again, particularly where the welfare of the family (and cost to the community) was at stake. In these situations, women seem to be released from societal proscriptions regarding wit or retiring behavior and are allowed to bend, if not absolutely break, the common laws regarding women making contracts. "Under the right conditions any wife not only could double as a husband, she had the responsibility to do so. In the probate courts, for example, widows who did not have grown sons were routinely granted administration of their husbands' estates. Gender restrictions were structural rather than psychological" (Ulrich 1982: 38). She states that people characterized the situation not so much in terms of femininity but in roles like "wife" and "neighbor" (1982: 37). This was easier where the workplace was still in the home—"helplessness" emerged when one could not move fluidly between home and workplace to assist in family affairs (Ulrich 1982: 50). Immediate, material concerns overrode ideals.

Elizabeth Turner, widow of Captain John Turner, however, had community and legal sanction to sell rum after her husband's death in 1680, possibly because she needed to care for a large, young family with the wealth of the family tied up in trade. She turned the estate over to her next husband, Major Charles Redford. Mrs. Turner's venture is not so unusual as it has been amply demonstrated by Koehler (1980: 121–122) that the vast majority of women who *were* in business for themselves were widows, probably because they had been left some small nest egg by their husbands for support during widowhood. She might have had some familiarity with the trade before Captain Turner's death, possibly helping him then, and thus was capable of managing the business (see the discussion of the "deputy husband" below). The license for selling "strong waters" was granted only to the most responsible and upstanding citizens, and this suggests that she knew the business and was respected enough to take it over.

On the other hand, Elizabeth's daughter-in-law Mary (Kitchen) Turner was probably in a position to invest and profit from loans after the death of her husband, Colonel Turner. Madam Turner's probate inventory and the subsequent accounts of her funeral expenses reveal that she was engaged, at least in a minor way, in making loans to relatives. Many merchants of the time made loans and lending was a particular source of income for widows, as described by Peter Earle. While she certainly lent out money, possibly even to people outside her family, she was not in the sort of straits that would have made it necessary for her to invest in order to survive; indications from her will, probate inventory, and accounts of Madam Turner's estate suggest that she was more than comfortably well off at the time of her death. It appears as though she was taking advantage of her wealth and her legal state.

ELITE WOMEN'S ROLES IN THE MERCHANT WORLD

Although women were not totally excluded from the world of commerce, most of the secondary sources suggest that there were relatively few women who owned shops or carried on a more intensive sort of commerce. Women were legally restricted from working outside the home, and yet, I propose that elite women did participate in the world of merchant life, to the economic as well as social benefit of their families. Researchers have cited examples of women who worked independently, even a few who took on what was traditionally considered to be "male" work—although this was more often forgiven (or overlooked) when their family had real economic need.

The Feme Sole Merchant

Although women were not allowed by law to own property or enter into contracts (save as the agents or servants of their husbands or fathers) by signing a contract to create a "separate estate," one could maintain her own business or property by having that property conveyed to a friend who held it in trust for the woman. This required the consent of the husband, but could be upheld if the couple were separated (Earle 1989b: 159). Another example of this limited freedom that is pertinent to this study is the legal creation, *feme sole merchant*, that was occasionally found in London. This was a contract, signed by both a freeman husband and his wife, that gave the wife the legal rights of an independent trader, so long as she practiced a different occupation or trade than her husband and did not interfere in any way with his occupation (Earle 1989b: 160).

As merchants (or more properly, as shopkeepers), women understandably tended to exploit their traditionally "feminine" skills and found occupations in millinery, mantua making, lace making, the silk industry, and shop keeping (Earle 1989b: 162). They also tended to take work as tavern keepers, innkeepers, or coffeehouse keepers (Figure 21).

Defoe's writings urged middle-classed girls to learn bookkeeping in order to help their future husbands (and provide against their deaths), and Bernard Mandeville endorsed this skill in *The Virgin Unmask'd* (1709):

> In Holland women sit in their counting houses and do business, or at least are acquainted with everything their husbands do ... the women are as knowing therein as the men, it doth incourage their husbands to hold on in their trades to their dying days, knowing the capacity of their wives to get in their estates, and carry on their trades after their deaths. (quoted in Earle 1989b: 164)

Unlike the Dutch, the English in England and America did not encourage that sort of involvement on the part of women in trade. Koehler notes that in America businesswomen were rare, not appearing in court transcripts, town records, or catalogues of early settlers, and a Boston tax list from 1687 showed that 48 women received incomes from trade or estates, but the list did not specify how many had been active in trade. According to his study, in all of New England throughout the seventeenth century, there were only nine women who worked at a trade other than innkeeping, and only 2.3 percent (N = 23 of 988) of all tradespeople or merchants (not including innkeepers) were women (Koehler 1980: 119).

If wealthier women took an active interest in mercantilism, say by running a shop, investing in a ship, or ordering commodities for their own trade, they potentially invited public censure or ridicule. An exceptional few, like Madam Sarah Knight and Mrs. Elizabeth Murray Campbell Smith Inman of Boston (1726–1785), were directly and successfully involved in trade, though Mrs. Inman herself admitted that others "tended to laugh at her business practices" (Norton 1979a: 50). At the age of 23, Elizabeth Murray brought a stock of dry goods with her from Scotland and opened a shop in Boston, where she sold millinery, sewing supplies, and cloth and taught needlework. Married three times and widowed twice, Inman learned accounting in London and was adamant about arranging the legally binding "antenuptial agreements" with her husbands, which allowed her to maintain her economic independence after marriage. These agreements allowed her to act as if she

Figure 21. *A London Coffee House* (ca. 1668), anonymous watercolor. The coffee house was a place to do business, possibly negotiate closer acquaintances. It is not difficult to imagine the same sort of informal discussions undertaken at a coffee shop today. Courtesy, The British Museum. © Copyright The British Museum.

were a *sole feme*, to keep her own property and make a will and leave her estate to whomever she wished. Her early experiences taught her the value of Defoe's and Mandeville's recommendations: Inman also taught her nieces to sew, read, and do accounts for "how many familys are ruined by the women not understanding accounts?" Mrs. Inman scorned to see "young people being brought up in idleness and entering the world with all its gaieties, triffling away the most active part of the life or marrying imprudently" and encouraged industry even in young women of privilege against times of adversity (Norton 1979a: 52).

Bridenbaugh discovered other examples of women who were active traders and wrote that the "[l]ove of trade extended to merchant's wives and widows" (1938: 340). Though he was convinced that the *feme sole merchant* was more prevalent than perhaps it actually was in the eighteenth century, he does note that the women he studied attempted to use their "influence and affluence" as male merchants did. In a 1733 letter, the "Widows of New York" stated that

> [as] She Merchants ... we in some measure contribute to the Support of Government, we ought to be Intitled to some of the Sweets of it; but we find ourselves intirely neglected, while the Husbands that live in our Neighbourhood are daily invited to dine at Court: we have the Vanity to think we can be full as Entertaining, and make as brave a Defense in case of an Invasion, and perhaps not turn Taile so soon as some of them. (Bridenbaugh 1938: 341)

Perhaps these New York women were more vocal because of the Dutch tolerance of women in trade, but this singular announcement makes several points pertinent to the present discussion. One is that the "She Merchants" recognized the connection between economic influence and political power. Another is that there was a social component associated with the negotiation of political and civil affairs. The notion that being entertaining was a considerable contribution to the commingling of merchant business and political power is critical to my argument, that the bonds formed by members of the elite in social situations were negotiated within the realm of mannerly behavior.

In spite of such examples in the Northeast during the colonial era, Massachusetts, for example, did not enact laws protecting the rights of women in trade until 1787. Necessity, brought on by death, abandonment, or divorce, obviated the need for specific legislation protecting women's rights in trade, but judgment often subjected these to legal contest (Salmon 1985: 45, 46).

Although the *feme sole merchant* was a rarity in New England (even when that role was informally assumed with tacit community approval), there were other ways in which elite women directly participated in the economic aspect of merchant life. I believe that in addition to whatever actual role that women played in mercantile activities, they played other, *noncommercial* roles that contributed directly to their families' fortunes in trade and civil affairs. In examining the fragments that I have uncovered of the lives of the Turner, Mascarene, and Earle women, I have found that they took a fairly limited part in the commercial aspects of their family business but contributed more directly to the family business socially and economically. I describe the three roles that were within the province of elite women of merchant families as *deputy husbands*, *social facilitators*, and *informal advocates*. I cannot say that these roles were the exclusive province of elite women, and they may certainly have been taken by women (or men) of other classes and in other centuries; only further research along these lines will reveal this. Like the true "gentleman," however, these elite women needed to maintain a safe social distance from trade or labor, and this constraint might also alter how these roles were played out in other contexts.

The Deputy Husband

I borrow the term *deputy husband* from Laurel Thatcher Ulrich's *Good Wives: Image and Reality in the Lives of Women in Northern New England (1650–1750)* (1982: 9), to describe a woman who acted as an assistant or even a surrogate to her husband. As discussed above, the deputy husband took on this extra work in addition to her own, generally with the approval of the community.

We see this role very clearly in the letters of John Mascarene to his wife, Margaret, of Cambridge, Massachusetts. While away in London from August 1761 to 1764, John viewed Margaret as his surrogate and wrote to her about maintaining their family business.

> I forgot to mention in my Acc't of Stock the 2 Casks of Pot. Ash[,] one of which is at Mr. Wheelwright's New house and the other is but about ⅓ or ½ full [and] is at Clough's Shop. [I] [s]hould be glad you would get them home[—] they may stand in a dry place in the Shop & if any Persons offer to buy, You may sell for 6/0 Pounds. (Mascarene, September 1, 1761)

In spite of relying on her to look after their livelihood while he was away, John did not expect that Margaret would become in any way self-reliant. In fact, he urged her to seek out the advice and assistance (monetary and otherwise) of their "college friends" from Harvard. He even expected that her friends would help her improve her writing: "provide yourself by means of your friends (who I doubt not will supply you) with good pens as I confess I am sometimes a little at a loss to read some parts of your letter tho so much us'd to your manner of writing" (Mascarene, July 25, 1762). His entrusting business matters to her did not also confer independence.

Another example of the deputy husband can be seen in records relating to the Turner family. There was a shop listed in the 1693 probate inventory of Captain John Turner; it is not known, however, whether Turner's wife Elizabeth kept that shop. What is clear is that Elizabeth obviously knew enough about the trade in molasses and Barbadian rum to ask for (and receive) permission from the Salem Town council to sell "strong liquors" after her husband's death in 1680 (RF-QCEC VIII 1921: 48). This was a license granted only to the most responsible and upstanding citizens, and Elizabeth Turner certainly may have had some knowledge of the business if she undertook this lucrative part of it. Ulrich makes it clear that the widow was more likely to take charge of her husband's estate when there was no son, or in this case, no son of legal majority age (1982: 50).

I agree with Ulrich that women's direct, active participation in the family business tended to be peripheral, with even elite women acting as "servants or agents." As long as it was not intrusive or competed with the husband's work—dares one say dangerous?—it was permissible for a woman either to contribute in a small way to the family business or to keep a modest one of her own. The role of the deputy husband for women in the merchant class could well have been the only introduction that many would have to the world of business and might have become a necessity when the death of a husband made financial survival difficult, in which case the woman was a surrogate acting on behalf of the family and heirs. By understanding the mechanisms of trade as seen in this role, it also informed wives about the business ramifications of social interactions as they played their other roles in the social sphere.

The Social Gatekeeper

In the seventeenth and eighteenth centuries, as now, men and women participated in social gatherings that were more than mere recreation. Meals, dances, teas, charity events, and other gatherings provided occasions to reinforce class solidarity, to add new members or exclude unlikely candidates, and to reproduce the values of the group. These events were a proving ground, an opportunity to demonstrate personal knowledge, social graces, and accomplishments, orchestrated by the mannerly behavior of several individuals for the good of the elite society. Such gatherings provided short-term opportunities in merchant business and long-range processes of group reproduction through marriage and other forms of social connection.

It was in these social situations that mannerly behavior shaped the merchant community, and that, particularly in mixed gatherings, women exercised a quiet influence over those decisions. By forming connections, women of the merchant elite affected the immediate state and future condition of their families' fortunes.

Mary Prior noted that in Oxford, "[i]n the years of prosperity women had an important part to play in the very structure of the trading and political community. Through their marriages immigrants were absorbed into the kinship networks of the community and rose to eminence, and in a time of rapid change they provided stability and continuity. The relationships of the women provided a hidden web of family influence" (1985: 102). This can be seen in a role played by women that was a little removed from the shop and counting house, what I call the *social gatekeeper*. Many researchers have described how social gatherings, such as teas, dances, or dinners are and were opportunities for the display of costly goods and their use as part of social negotiation for marriage, entrée, and allegiance building. We also know about the importance of intermarriage within occupation groups in terms of status from the Stones' research (1984: 19–20) and particularly from McGrath's 1955 work on Bristol merchants in the seventeenth century, so that it is clear these mixed-gender teas and dinners were prodigiously important to the commercial world.

Again, personal deportment was key in these events where potential members of the community could be observed, judged, then included or excluded. The remarkable Mrs. Strine illustrates this, in an example of boorish, antisocial behavior at a dinner, provided for Mrs. Earle through Mr. Denham's letter in 1765: "Mr. Hempson was wishing [Mrs. Strine] might break her neck coming up Stairs. He was out of all Patience Sunday, & took an Opportunity to slip off soon after Dinner, but she staid with us 'till past Six," during which time Mrs. Strine drank too much wine, beer, and punch, flirted outrageously, and belabored the harpsichord (NMGM D/Earle/3/2/17).

Compared with the agreeable musical evening at the Lanes' described by John Mascarene (below), in which all the participants were, quite literally, in harmony, this occasion was ruptured by Mrs. Strine's (reportedly) gluttonous, drunken, and flirtatious behavior in her blatant efforts to show off her fine skin, large jewels, and "ladylike" accomplishments. The ability to play cards, be musical, even eat gracefully demonstrated practiced physical restraint as well as intellectual skills. In this context the knowledge of the appropriate use of a fan, tea cup, or other prop was equally important. Mrs. Strine possessed these skills but negated their value in her reportedly rude attempts to be the center of attention. She showed none of the self-restraint called for in courtesy literature.

Dinners, barbecues, "turtle frolics," dances, and other occasions provided many chances for the social evaluation of men and women. In an apparent parallel to the tradition of grand barbecues in the southern colonies, young Benjamin Lynde wrote about such a party with the Turners on August 26, 1730: "Fair, fine day. Hog barbecued @ Colo's farm [Colonel Turner owned the neighboring property to the Lyndes on Castle Hill], a great frolic; 11 calashes besides horses, etc. After at Mr. Pittmans; Boston Ladies; after at Turner's" (Lynde 1880: 133). In the diary entries of the Lynde family of Salem and the letters of John Mascarene, the writers are very careful to note the presence of women. Benjamin Lynde, Sr. wrote "June 25 [1736], B' fasted with son Benjamin, who then went home; dined at Mr. Anto. Stodd'r with Col. Turner; drank tea with Mrs. Ting, Capt. Ting, etc, club at Wardell's" (Lynde 1880: 75), recording four separate social occasions during a busy day. One wishes that he would have mentioned something of what had transpired during each of them, at breakfast, dinner, tea, and his club, mixed-gender and all-male occasions at home and abroad.

In terms of social display and negotiation, turtle frolics and other such parties required a plethora of social skills, including the preparation and presentation of rare dishes (including punch), holding one's liquor, and dancing (works like Nivelon's 1737 *Rudiments of Genteel Behavior* would have informed the physical bearing and choreography of the participants). Not only was "polish" as important as restraint, but grace and ease were equally valid for social scrutiny. Like the Virginia dances of the 1760s described by Rhys Isaac (1982: 86–87), all of these events were an affirmation of solidarity among the elite. The Salem activities were also opportunities for the young members of the merchant class to observe how their elders behaved and to form connections and alliances of their own. They were allowed in this way to experiment with socialization in a chaperoned environment and to become acculturated into a world that they eventually would inherit.

Some of these activities were more heavily engendered and therefore perhaps more private than others. One example of this is tea drinking, which was strongly engendered as feminine, possibly because of its association with Catherine of Braganza. As early as 1694, 22 years after she reputedly introduced the habit of tea drinking to England, women were characterized as adjourning "to tea and scandal, according to their *ancient* custom" (Kowaleski-Wallace 1994: 132, emphasis hers). This "scandal" or gossip, in addition to the expense, leisure, and pretensions of tea taking, was considered threatening, particularly when indulged in by women of the lower classes who were seen as ruining their families through expense, neglect of housewifely and maternal duties, and slander of their betters (Kowaleski-Wallace 1994: 136–137). *The Spectator* of May 30, 1712, recorded these worries: "It grieves my Heart to see a couple of proud idle Flirts sipping their Tea, for a whole Afternoon, in a Room hung round with the Industry of their great Grandmother" (quoted in Wildeblood and Brinson 1965: 229).

Among the wealthy, a woman taking tea could be considered another form of conspicuous consumption, a man gaining stature by having a wife well versed in the tea ceremony, with the leisure and appropriate dress, setting, and equipage to engage in it. (In fact, in studying elite households, the discussion over who chose the tea wares might be irrelevant if tea service is being used to express a corporate family identity, perhaps through male status.) But where the expense was not seen to emasculate the head of the household, slanderous words still might. The power of women at the tea table was not disputed; the issue was whether it could be harnessed or regulated. This power might have been seen in terms of gossip and idleness or it might have been an indirect recognition of the power women had to shape the community through marriage arrangements.

Rodris Roth's association of tea with "welcoming" is significant, particularly in this respect. The intimacy of teas provided an opportunity for closer examination of manners and personalities, a social device that was a cautious invitation to the outsider to come closer. Depending on who was invited, a tea could either be a family meal or it could be a more formal occasion with the inclusion of guests. If this were the case, then the tea ostensibly would have been the setting in which more permanent alliances could be considered. Long before the point at which teas became an opportunity for chaperoned courting, the guest's deportment and manner could be observed and judged. The invitation to tea was a step away from the outside world, a step closer into the private lives of the host family. Whether it ended in marriage, it certainly proclaimed an intimacy that was immensely important in terms of trust and access. In Richardson's novel, Clarissa Harlowe's parents use the attractiveness and the privacy of family tea to rebuke her, knowing that she cannot resist the quiet ceremony in which she generally plays a principal part (Richardson 1985a: 64).

The same can be said of other gatherings—dinners, charity balls, turtle frolics, and dances—although the increased *public* formality of these was just a half-step toward inclusion. These events were meant for display, for allegiance building, for testing, and, perhaps, for inclusion. The formality of these situations provided the rules that made new acquaintance easier. Considering the use of the term "ease of manner" in the eighteenth century, this would have been one important objective in learning one's manners, paving the way, perhaps, to greater intimacy.

My impression is that where teas and dinners at home were made as a mixed party, they generally were presided over by the hostess (Yentsch 1991: 223–225; Kowaleski-Wallace 1994), and there was some danger in failing to favorably impress her. Gallant politeness was the order of the day, even if some long-term connection was not the goal; if one were socially inept, it might mean one less opportunity to make vital introductions or to talk business (Figure 22). Lord Chesterfield recognized the vital value of this access when he wrote to his son in Paris in 1751:

> I advise you to make yourself domestic. This is to be done by a certain easiness of carriage ... and begets that decent familiarity, which it is both agreeable and useful to establish in good houses, and with people of fashion. Mere formal visits, dinners, and suppers, upon formal invitations, are not the thing; they add to no connection nor information; but it is the easy, careless ingress and egress, at all hours, that forms the pleasing and profitable commerce of life. (Chesterfield 1992: 218)

John Mascarene gleefully wrote to Margaret Mascarene on February 10, 1763, that he was closer than ever to making the political connections that would bring success to his suit.

> I have been [to Mr. Lane's] oftener than before[.] I had a standing invitation indeed to go there when I pleased but as Mr. Lane is entirely a Man of business I was loth to trouble him[.] [B]ut being now more intimate with Mrs. Lane & [her daughter] Sukey I can go there freely ... we spent an Evening there sometime past and were entertain'd by Sukey with a tune on the Harpsichord in which I join'd her with the fiddle ... [and] Mr. Lane has promis'd me I shall not want money for any necessary Expences while I stay here. (Mascarene, February 10, 1763)

By impressing Mrs. Lane, John Mascarene had greater access to Mr. Lane who is willing to take his part in the politics of his suit. I doubt that if he had been less (agree)able as a guest, he would have been granted this entrée. We see how, in contrast to Mrs. Strine's activities as a guest, mannerly behavior, social skills, and personal accomplishments pave the way to intimacy and access so important in merchant society, and how "the tea table is a powerful focal point for gender relations" (Kowaleski-Wallace 1994: 142).

Of course, there is a male counterpart to the role of social gatekeeper found in the largely male domains of political activity, taverns, coffeehouse meetings, and other exclusively male activities. On May 29, 1733, Benjamin Lynde, Sr., wrote that he "came by Moor's [a public

Figure 22. *A Group Portrait, Probably of the Raikes Family* (ca. 1730–1732), by Gawen Hamilton (ca. 1697–1737). This intimate gathering in a rather splendid setting is depicted as informal and familiar, but still subject to the rules of polite behavior. Note the domestic ceremony of the two servants decanting and preparing the drinks on the left. Yale Center for British Art, Paul Mellon Collection.

house in Salem] where (by Col. Turner's example) I also treated the Essex Representatives with a large Sangaree" (Lynde and Lynde 1880: 42). On October 19, 1733, Lynde wrote about the successful conclusion of some political business with other local gentlemen, "all of whom with Col. Turner I treated with wine at Lutwiches" (Lynde and Lynde 1880: 48).

The repeated emulation of Colonel Turner's treating marks the importance of this hospitality outside the home. Whether at coffee-houses, taverns, militia drills, or some other meeting place, these all-male occasions provided an opportunity to gauge potential partners in a somewhat more democratic milieu. If there was sufficient indication that the gentleman in question had the right qualifications, whether political affiliation, business or family connections, or personality, he might be invited to a more formal, more intimate occasion.

The coffeehouse was a setting of particular interest to merchants. Coffeehouses first appeared in Oxford in 1651 and quickly proliferated, established as places where scholars and men of affairs could congregate with like-minded fellows. Those who frequented coffeehouses were not of the nobility but neither were they the laboring poor, but initially a leisured class that shared common interests (Brown 1995: 12). The attraction was in the informal atmosphere that let people meet without distinction of rank, something that would have been particularly attractive to the rising merchant class, not part of the landed elite and certainly wealthier and perhaps better educated than the rest of the middling classes.

Coffeehouses were almost exclusively devoted to a male clientele where, in addition to coffee, tea, chocolate, and other refreshments, business was transacted, information exchanged through papers like *The Spectator* or *The Tatler* and through the mail, and views were freely exchanged: "It is very natural for a Man, who is not turned for Mirthful Meetings of Men, or Assemblies of the fair Sex, to delight in that sort of Conversation which we find in Coffee-houses. Here a Man ... is in his Element; for, if he cannot talk, he can still be more agreeable to his Company, as well as pleased in himself, in being only an Hearer" (Steele and Addison 1988: 286).[1] Figure 21, a watercolor, exemplifies many of the qualities of a coffeehouse. The gentlemen are at ease in this public

---

[1]Views were sometimes expressed so freely that there were occasions when coffeehouses were viewed as hotbeds of sedition. Attempts to close them were generally very quickly overturned, however; Charles II banned coffeehouses in England in 1675 but was forced to rescind the order after just 11 days. It is interesting to note that the threat of the coffeehouse as a politically dangerous meeting place transcended national boundaries, for they were closed periodically for the same reasons by the sultan in the sixteenth-century Ottoman empire, with equal lack of effect (Baram 1998: 2).

place, smoking, drinking coffee, reading, and talking. The only woman present may be the owner, ensconced as the genius loci of the establishment. The atmosphere suggests a polite gathering with rational discourse, orderly busyness. The papers on the tables are reminiscent of the literate middle-classed culture of *The Spectator* and *The Tatler*.

The only instance where John Mascarene mentions coffee outside a coffeehouse (usually the New England Coffee House), is at Ranelagh, another highly public place restricted to those who could afford it. It is compelling to note that Joseph Denham only wrote of coffeehouses in his letters to *Thomas* Earle, an indication of how masculine an environment they were. In 1764 Denham wrote separate letters to both Mr. and Mrs. Earle describing a scandal in which the English consul of Genoa was convinced that his house was haunted, but reports to Mr. Earle that "all Genoa is full of it & nothing else is talked of at the Coffee Houses" (NMGM D/Earle/3/2/14). On another occasion in 1765 he wrote that "Martin has thumped Jaime in the Coffee House & is confined to his house by order of the Governor" (NMGM D/Earle/3/2/19).

John Mascarene wrote nearly all of his letters to his wife from the New England Coffee House in London and posted all of them there. He met with his friends there virtually every day and indicates that coffeehouses were also places where personal appearance was scrutinized; coffeehouses were also where new fashions were introduced (Turberville 1926: 88). Mascarene was concerned with what first impression he would make on his arrival among his friends in London: "My first care [on arriving in London] was to provide a Taylor, Barber, Hatter &c in order to equip myself properly for seeing my Friends & had determin'd not to come into the City till that was accomplished … but finding this afternoon a Letter from Cap'tn Partridge advising me that he was to leave London for Boston this Evening & should be at the N E'd Coffee House[,] I immediately took a coach thither" (Mascarene October 17, 1761).

In addition to buying rounds of drink and treating, the quality of *loyalty*, like amiability, civility, and generosity, was also esteemed in gentlemen. John Mascarene wrote of the solidarity of the New England merchants in London and their frustration with their English brethren in November of 1761:

> Our custom is to meet generally once a day if the Weather permits at the New England Coffee house and make a party to dine together at an ordinarye, the Manner of the Merchants in the City and such as we have Recommendations too or acquaintance with being only to invite [(]& that but seldom[)] such as they think they shall get something by [(]that being their only drift & aim and you may read Self Interest in all their Countenances[).] As to those in higher life it is difficult as well as expensive forming an acquaintance with

them so that were it not for a few of our own Countrymen being here[,] each of us would live as if were in Solitude in this populous City. (Mascarene November 21, 1761)

Here he illustrates not only the difference between English and American merchants, but the problems of trying to make an acquaintance with the upper classes in England. Unfortunately, it seemed as though some of the bustle of London was rubbing off on John Mascarene's friends, for he wrote that "[With] Mr. Lane & the rest of my Friends I am upon very good terms ... tho we do not see one another very often unless it be at the Coffeehouse as the mann'r of the Merchants here is not to concern themselves with those who have not immediate Business with them" (Mascarene July 25, 1762).

Taverns and coffeehouses were considered places for business, but not, perhaps, the best places for intricate or intimate dealings. *The Tatler* observed "that the Gentlemen did not care to enter upon Business till after their Morning-Draught, for which Reason I called for a Bottle of Mum; and finding that had no Effect upon 'em, I ordered a Second, and a Third: After which, Sir Harry reached over to me, and told me in a low Voice, that the Place was too publick for Business; but he would call upon me again to Morrow Morning at my own Lodgings" (Steele and Addison 1988: 122–123).

Another important social phenomenon was clubs, which seem to have emerged from the social atmosphere of coffeehouses and therefore were almost exclusively devoted to a male membership (Figure 23). Clubs were devoted to a wide spectrum of interests, ranging from the scientific and the aesthetic to the absurd. Although many of the social clubs like the Hell-Fire Club or the Mohocks seem to find their pleasures in "a relentless exhibitionism and whose excesses were an affront to the Augustan ideals of moderation and restraint" (Roberts 1996: 59), this was not the sort of club to which John Mascarene made his application. The Society for Encouragement of Arts and Commerce embodied the traits of reason and restraint, not to mention commerce, and John Mascarene was respected for his research into the use of potash as an American commodity. The club had the same advantages of meeting at a particular coffeehouse: the exchange of information and social access that facilitated trade and social reproduction. "In London, the Society for the Encouragement of Arts, Manufactures, and Commerce brought together an impressive array of interested citizens and, in the counties, specifically agricultural societies performed similar services" (Hancock 1995: 283).

Mascarene's interest in joining this organization was not only to find others interested in his theories about economics and commodities,

Figure 23. *A Club of Gentlemen* (ca. 1730), attributed to William Hogarth (1697–1764). Clubs were a popular form of socializing throughout the eighteenth century and members gathered to celebrate topics ranging from scientific subjects to body size. Yale Center for British Art, Paul Mellon Collection.

but also to meet others who might be able to assist him politically. "I was last Wednesday at the Society for Encouragement of Arts & Commerce & was introduc'd by Mr. Hollis to Lord Romney who was then in the Chair as President who welcom'd me as a member & desir'd me to take my Seat upon this I made his Lordship a low Bow (which I was before informed was all that was customarily done) & retir'd to one of the Seats" (Mascarene November 21, 1761). The ritual welcome of a new member was itself steeped in prescribed behavior, something that would have been expected by a gentleman of the time, and the club atmosphere would have "facilitated the ever-rising middle classes, [where] they created a new social hierarchy with all its newly-found freedoms and attendant restrictions" (Roberts 1996: 75). Clubs represented one more example of this close connection between social life and business.

Both the mixed-sex domestic entertainments and the more public, male-dominated meeting places were two sides of the same coin in terms of mixing business with pleasure (or vice versa), but I maintain that while taverns and coffeehouses were places to meet and deal, the home was a place in which to forge more permanent (and theoretically, more lucrative) alliances through marriage. Material improvements also made home more appealing to men, that is, more like outside entertainments in public houses, who were "to some extent, tamed by a private and domestic culture when rises in real wages enabled home and family life to become more of a center and focus for leisure life" (Barker-Benfield 1992: 99). In this respect, impressing the lady of the house (and, indeed, being someone deemed necessary to impress) was imperative. The Marchioness of Lambert warned that "women are born with a violent desire to please; as they find themselves barred from all the ways that lead to glory and authority, they take another road to arrive at them, and make themselves amends by their agreeableness" (1794: 179). This agreeableness was regulated behavior, its mutual suppression of the self embraced for the good of the community and perhaps something that would promote the presence of women in social occasions.

No matter how acquaintances were made or new family members were incorporated, there was a vested interest in maintaining these connections. Part of this, I contend, was achieved through the very tea-table gossip that was considered so dangerous a part of female sociability. By keeping track of friends (or even unfriendly acquaintances), better judgment could be brought to social situations and, as Kathleen Brown argues for Virginian women in the early eighteenth century, identities negotiated for the women themselves (K. M. Brown 1996: 284)—precisely the sort of thing that was going on in male-dominated coffeehouses. "Gossip" might have been construed as disruptive and dangerous when it revealed women's individual identities rather than defining group relations.

Social gatherings were used to try the temper of social steel while forging bonds that would extend beyond the home and even the merchant community. "By 1742 the continued exchange between merchants … [was] slowly and surely welding them together into a distinct social group—the only one in the colonies with a common outlook. In each province they were the leading political interest, exerting a far-reaching influence on legislation; in each town they managed municipal affairs" (Bridenbaugh 1938: 340). The social gatekeeper was an integral part of this process.

The Informal Advocate

The final role predominantly played by women that I describe here is that of the *informal advocate*. In this situation, a woman is treated (or is willing to act) as an intermediary between a man with whom she is socially acquainted and her husband (or male relative) about matters of business. This role tends to overlap with the others in terms of social connections—for example, John Mascarene's interest in social visits that would parlay into access for his official affairs—and of course could exist at any social level. In 1749 Chesterfield wrote:

> There is, at all courts, a chain which connects the prince or the minister with the page of the back-stairs or the chambermaid. The king's wife, or mistress, has an influence over him; a lover has an influence over her; the chambermaid, or the *valet de chambre* has an influence over both … you must, therefore, not break a link of that chain, by which you hope to climb up to the Prince. (1992: 144–145)

He later stated, rather cynically, that "pleasing and governing women, may, in time, be of great service to you. They often please and govern others" (Chesterfield 1992: 217).

In the merchant documents I have seen, the gentleman who requested this indirect access attempted either to establish that the matter was so trifling that he did not wish to bother the husband with another formal request *or* hints that the wife herself was in collusion with him, and sought with the suppliant to overcome the husband's distracted memory or busyness. In spite of this diminishment of what might actually be a serious matter, there is tacit recognition of the woman's control of access. This is a rather intimate cooperation between men and women, probably only properly negotiated by equals, near equals, or those associated within a social cluster of sociability and employment (Wrightson 1986: 190–191).

The existing half of the correspondence between Joseph Denham and Mary Earle, the wife of Thomas Earle, Denham's employer, consists of Joseph's letters to Mary while he was working in her husband's trading houses in Genoa, Livorno, and Civita Vecchia in Italy (NMGM D/Earle/3/2/1–32). In his letters, dating from 1763 to 1781, Denham provides Mary (and occasionally her husband Thomas) with court and society gossip, news of their mutual friends (who were also Thomas's partners), and information about the latest styles, as well as criticism of her handwriting and punctuation.

Joseph Denham's tone is often charming, sometimes crossing the line from courtly attention to daring flirtation, and he occasionally used their exchange as an opportunity to ask her to remind Mr. Earle of business arrangements. This was all done under the aegis of the civility owed between them as members of the same "social cluster." Although he had been a guest of the Earles and was well educated, Denham was not quite of their economic status or social stature. He attempted to rationalize his continued correspondence with Mrs. Earle by asserting that he had taken on the role of her instructor, jester, and gossip, jokingly assuming the role of *cicisbeo* (Italian, literally "beautiful chick-pea"), the male champion (*cavalier servente*) of a married woman. The term has its origins in twelfth-century courtly literature and originally implied a chaste relationship (*Oxford English Dictionary*, s.v. cicisbeo). This changes over time, however. Samuel Sharp, in his *Letters from Italy* (1767), wrote with palpable disgust about the Italian habit of taking a *cicisbeo*

> Many people in England imagine the majority of Cicesbeos to be an innocent kind of dangling fribble; but they are utterly mistaken in the character; nor do I find that it is understood here that the Ladies live in greater purity with their Cicesbeos than with their husbands; and, generally speaking, with much less; If only one half of the Ladies practiced this custom, the other half would despise them; but, in fact, very few have any pretence to upbraid the rest with bad conduct.... To give you an idea in one word, how much the mode of inseperableness betwixt them is established, suffice it to say, that if you invited five ladies to dinner, you of course lay ten plates, as each for a certainty brings her Cicesbeo with her. (Sharp 1767: 73–74)

For the English in the eighteenth century, the word had faintly ridiculous connotations, both for the devoted *cicisbeo*, or for the husband foolish enough to allow such a follower, and I believe this gave Denham the license to use the term. By cloaking his epistolary devotion in an apparently innocent, joking reference, Denham is able to flirt, gossip, correct Mrs. Earle's spelling, and, perhaps most important, keep open an avenue to *Mr.* Earle's attention with his letters. The role that Joseph Denham took on for himself as the epistolary companion of Mrs. Earle was not unique, and it is possible that he may have had a genuine interest in her, quite apart from her obvious value to him as a conduit to his employer.

A brief discussion of the importance of letter writing in the early modern period is appropriate here. When visits and other forms of socializing were not possible, connections could be maintained over long distances only by letter writing. The Earle-Denham correspondence regularly recorded the health, activities, and business affairs of friends throughout Italy and England, and it is probably no coincidence how many of these friends were also in business with Denham and the Earles. Thus, letter writing, having arisen as an aristocratic art in sixteenth-century Italy, was a skill that had many valuable returns in the seventeenth and eighteenth centuries, socially as well as economically. Later English guides described letter writing as "small literary performances" (Bushman 1993: 90, 92–93). The epistolary novel that characterized eighteenth-century literature underscored this; one particularly important scene in *Pamela* occurs when Mr. B. discovered Pamela's writing skills: "Why, Pamela, you write a pretty hand, and *spell* very well too. You may look into any of my mother's books to improve yourself" (Richardson 1985: 44) (Figure 24). In London, John Mascarene encouraged Margaret Mascarene to improve her penmanship while reminding her of his affection for her.

> [I] should be glad you would be a little more careful of your hand ... as I confess I am sometimes a little at a loss to read some parts of your letter tho so much us'd to your manner of writing[.] I hope however this advise will not have a tendency to discourage you[.] [I]f I thought it would I should not have said it for however desirous I may be of your mending your hand ... if it gives you any trouble and thereby abates the satisfaction you may have in the entertainment you give me I would willingly dispense with them tho' it should cost me a day to fish out a page. (Mascarene July 25, 1762)

Letters were also shared to spread news to friends and family and for entertainment. Joseph Denham expected his letters to be read by Mr. Earle and asked Mrs. Earle to pass messages on to their shared acquaintance. Because he sometimes relayed off-colored jokes or was sexually explicit about the nature of his homesickness, Mascarene warned his wife about being discreet in what she passed on to her friends (especially her unmarried sisters, whom he called "the virgins") by writing "I observe You make pretty free with my letters in reading parts to them to your friends but as I am not over cautious in regard to my diction when

Figure 24. *"Pamela is represented in this piece, writing in her late Lady's dressing room …"* (1745), engraving by Jos. Highmore. Photograph by Jeffrey R. Dykes. Courtesy, Peabody Essex Museum, Salem, Massachusetts.

writing to You being not so necessary, I hope you will be careful not to communicate what may be incorrect" (Mascarene June 11, 1762).

Informal advocacy could have dramatic results. On one occasion, Joseph Denham wrote to Mary Earle about a plan he had proposed to Mr. Earle in 1768 in opening an English trading house near Rome. This was an economically important venture, because theirs would be the first English house there and they could expect to make huge profits from commerce with the pope ("His Holiness has told some English gentlemen, that those of our Nation should have the greatest privileges of any but the subjects of the Church" [Addison 1705: 398]). Joseph Denham wrote: "I wrote Mr. Earle [in January, March, and April] & to this Hour cannot get a single line from him. I doubt not but you know the Subject, & the Time is running on at a great Rate.... If he sho'd not have wrote me by the Time this reaches you I sho'd be much obliged to you to *stuzzicare* [to tease or stir] him a little.... I shall very much esteem your good offices herein" (NMGM D/Earle/3/2/25).

And later in 1779 about the same issue he wrote:

> I heartily wish [Mr. Earle] may imbrace [the plan], for I am sure he wo'd find reason to be pleased with it as he is so great an Enterpriser, & risks his money in Insurance, & the Jamaican Trade & I think he can have no reasonable objection to my Plan. I mention it to you only that you may stimulate him to give me an answer as quickly as possible, that I may know how to regulate myself, otherwise he will cram my Letter into his Pocket & forget it or perhaps light his Pipe with it. (NMGM D/Earle/3/2/30)

Apparently this stratagem of applying through Mrs. Earle worked, because within a short time Denham had been allowed to open a trading house for the Earles in Civita Vecchia, bringing in large sums of money for supplying the Vatican. Despite the fact that her side of the correspondence is lost to time, it is clear that Mrs. Earle had a hand in settling this arrangement.

The informal advocate is a role that was closely related to the social gatekeeper, but this individual worked at a much more intimate, private level. I find this the most interesting of the roles, because here the woman is directly responsible for allowing or denying access that supposedly she alone can grant to a husband, father, or other male connection. I suspect that Mr. Mascarene might also have asked Mrs. Lane, his hostess, for such favors, and one wonders whether Mr. Lynde took the opportunity to importune Madam Turner in the same way on their way home from the charity ball in 1724. If, as De Cunzo (1995a) argues, merchant gentlemen were culture brokers, then equally were their gentlewomen social brokers.

CONCLUSION

Some women, like Mrs. Fyge in *The Liberty* (1703), complained of "Customs scanty Rules" or the "vapid tedium of polite society" (Porter 1990: 22). As formulaic as polite life might have been, and as constricted a role as women were supposed to play, it worked in a number of ways to reproduce society, and perhaps empowered women in subtle but effective ways. It was not always fair, but it worked extraordinarily well, not only reproducing polite society but also, more specifically, the life of the merchant elite. The very predictability of prescribed behavior was useful in regulating entry into that community. It provided the means and opportunities for interaction, critical observation, and judgment, as well as rules for seamless inclusion or graceful exclusion. These rules were particularly important in a time where status distinctions were being blurred, where pedigree remained supreme but was vigorously contested by a newly available and extraordinary wealth.

Law and tradition (sometimes codified as part of courtesy literature) described in general the roles that women and men were expected to play. In some instances, mannerly behavior was used to redefine, redirect, or subvert them in quiet, unobtrusive ways. "Men were intended (so men claimed) to excel in reason, business, action; women's forte lay in being submissive, modest, docile, virtuous, maternal and domestic" wrote Roy Porter, with the instruction that a woman ought "to be ladylike, an ambassadress of grace" (1990: 23, 28). He continues, however, to state that "force of character, charm, inherited wealth or family name gave heiresses or matriarchs enormous bargaining strength and a chance to influence family destinies" (Porter 1990: 25).

Klein argued that the contributors to *The Spectator* sought solutions to the increasing social diversity of the eighteenth century and used "politeness," defined by him as "the submission of the self to the disciplines of social interaction," or manners as a mechanism that would provide people with "a plasticity of self [that] would allow them to see themselves in a context of other selves." Furthermore:

> These disciplines, explored throughout the periodical papers, had already been worked out in numerous courtesy books of the sixteenth and seventeenth centuries. The social disciplines aimed to enhance social interactions, making it more pleasurable and sometimes also more useful and instructive. They constituted an art of pleasing others in conversation and company often in ways that redounded to one's own pleasure or benefit. At its most humanistic, politeness was the means to bring out the best in others and in oneself. Among other capacities that such social discipline demanded was the ability to see oneself in the context of a complex social situation: one had to grasp

one's own desires and interests while comprehending the legitimate desires
and interests of others. The frequent exhortations in *The Spectator* to modesty, discretion, decorum, propriety, and politeness were demands that the
moral agent recognize the social context of his or her actions and so integrate
self and others, parts and wholes. (Klein 1995: 228)

Manners allowed a society full of contradictions to function, negotiating solutions that were culturally acceptable even when law or local
tradition might have dictated otherwise. Women who were not socially
sanctioned to "work" nonetheless did so, contributing in significant ways
to the family economy and social reproduction. Elite men, while maintaining social distance, could (at carefully selected times) bridge that
distance in order to reinforce bonds with the rest of the community, the
segregation of social distinction mitigated by the mask of polite interaction. Merchants could acquire the trappings (in addition to the real
power) of community leadership where otherwise they might have been
barred from the elite by accident of birth. It is a nice but significant
distinction that the rules of *mannerly behavior* are not as explicit as
those contained in *etiquette*. The notions of propriety and social interaction remained generally the same, but judicious use of the flexibility of
manners allowed one to circumvent other restrictions.

Courtesy literature has been attacked throughout the ages as a
source of hypocrisy, masking self-interest or even downright deceit with
pretty words and gestures. Ironically, mannerly guides also emphasized
the importance of trust and of being true to one's rank and the dangers of
pretending to be otherwise. Exceeding one's station was reprehensible
and pretentious, failing to live up to it was ridiculed as clownish, coarse,
or unsophisticated.

Brathwait's comment about the inappropriateness of courtiers' behavior to merchants is significant to this study because, at home in
colonial Massachusetts, the merchant class was the equivalent of courtiers. Colonial wealth might muddy the waters of class distinction, but it
never eradicated the notion of a need for social hierarchy. In this respect,
mannerly behavior reinforced class or cluster boundaries. But because
entrée into this group was predicated not so exclusively by birth as by
wealth and connections, the flexibility that the culture of mannerly
behavior allowed was utilized as an instrument of inclusion as well.

In the eighteenth century, the world of commerce was at least
nominally restricted to men's activities. If manners are a personally
held, *publicly* made statement of order, then the public displays or
activities that were the province of women, who were ostensibly barred
from many aspects of public life, become increasingly important to

identify and understand. The roles played by elite women as part of that merchant community were of tremendous consequence in the continuous exchange of goods, ideas, and connections. The three broad categories discussed above give some insight into the variety of ways that merchant culture was able to function and thrive only through the combined efforts of men and women. These roles had economic importance, because of the opportunity to make deals, contacts, mutual assurances of class solidarity, and the exchange of children and other family members in marriage or apprenticeship, and also social importance for the merchants as an elite class that had acquired influence in military, civic, religious, and legal affairs.

Polite behavior was also of particular interest to the merchant group as commercial creatures: trade with members of other societies, if not coerced, was carried on through diplomatic means and, on a much more fundamental level, socially acceptable mannerly behavior was an integral part of business. Recommendations, letters of introduction or credit, and advice about potential trading partners were made on faith, based on impressions often made from a social perspective, and sometimes exclusive of business knowledge. Decorum, ease of manner, knowledge of the use of the expensive and exotic goods they imported, and the ability to engage a small but select and judgmental audience in company were important. But, above almost all these other attributes, an individual's ability to communicate that he or she was just as his or her appearance suggested was crucial. Business deals made around the globe were founded on trust, and so one's credit (literally and figuratively) was at stake. John Mascarene wrote: "[A]s I have already experienc'd [my friend's] favour in my Introduction to Mr. Wood[,] I doubt not in the least of his assistance in what I expect of him[.] [H]e seems to be a very friendly[,] goodnatur'd & agreeable Man and not like his Brother[,] being as I have found[,] true to his promise and far from being flashy and insincere" (Mascarene March 26, 1762). It was his opinion based on this man's social behavior that led John to trust him in business.

If these commercial activities were negotiated in a social setting, then how much more important were the rules of courtesy directing those occasions? Not only was it crucial to impress your audience with your character and familiarity with their rules of gentle behavior in order to gain acceptance and access, but in New England, where wealth was neither patrician nor many generations old, and where trade caused abrupt changes of fortunes if not status, manners provided the means for negotiating the necessary civil interaction between genders and among people where social mobility made status uncertain. I believe that members of each of the families studied in this work who suffered some sort of social upset were preserved by their participation in the polite society.

By starting with an understanding of publicly prescribed behavior, then examining the surviving documentary record and noticing what was remarked, exalted, or ignored, it is possible to identify two features of merchant culture. The first is how men and women both shared in creating and reproducing that social and economic life. The second is how mannerly behavior was used as a bridge in traversing boundaries that otherwise might be barriers in a changing world. Mrs. Earle's venison pasties were more than thoughtful gifts to her friends and associates, they were a homely reminder of England to the expatriate merchants in Italy and a source of community, with all its pleasures and responsibilities. The same can be said of Mrs. Mascarene's sharing of a specially imported ale with her neighbors or even Madam Turner's funeral, and the archaeologically recovered material remains of these events add yet another dimension to our understanding of these phenomena.

Conclusion | 6

An Archaeology of Manners

> How rude were our manners, how uncouth our Dress, al-
> most naked, how uncomfortable our Habitations, and
> how coarse and homely our most delicate Entertainments,
> 'till astronomical Learning became more universal, and
> brought the art of Navigation to its present Achme and
> Perfection! Then a new Scene of Correspondence open'd
> amongst Mankind, and improv'd the general Union, by
> which Means we imported, not only Commodities of all
> kinds, but whole Arts from distant Nations; and from
> a rude, naked, and savage People, became polite, rich,
> and powerful, and added to all the Necessaries of Life,
> every Convenience that could render the Enjoyment of it
> agreeable.
>
> —Madam Johnson, Madam Johnson's Present:
> Or, the Best Instructions for Young Women ...

INTRODUCTION

Madam Johnson enthusiastically described how the relationship between the development of mercantile commerce and the refinement of
manners reshaped the character of nations and the lives of individuals
in the early modern period. In 1744 Dr. Alexander Hamilton found a
similar situation near Susquehanna, watching an old couple who ate
plain food out of a wooden dish. Not only were the "vittles" unsauced, but
the couple used no cutlery, tablecloth, or napkins, and the fastidious
Hamilton was not inclined to join them. "I looked upon this as a picture
of the primitive simplicity practiced by our forefathers long before the
mechanic arts had supplied them with instruments for the luxury and
elegance of life" (Bridenbaugh 1948: 8).

These new distinctions found in materials and manners communicated many things—intentional and unintentional—in the seventeenth and eighteenth centuries. For the merchant elite, this interest
in mannerly conduct and sociability was a source of incredible wealth.
Participation in polite life furthermore solidified the place of the
wealthy merchant in the large scale of the British social hierarchy and
put him at the apex of smaller communities. Artifacts and manners

were imported with a range of meanings, some quite contradictory, that were nonetheless used simultaneously with a remarkable lack of confusion. In this chapter, I discuss the ways in which manners were employed and how historical archaeologists in turn can use them to make connections between documents, material culture, and social behavior.

MANNERS AS BOUNDARIES

One important use of mannerly behavior is to create and maintain social boundaries. The principal requirement in acquiring effective mannerly behavior is time, which is also the reason that manners can be used as an excluding device. In the short term time is necessary to learn, practice, and master polite conduct with the seamlessness of the *je ne sais quoi*. In the long term time creates the sense of cultural heredity or patina within the group that originated or "owned" manners. Bourdieu recognized this phenomenon as well as the socially structuring and distinguishing nature of mannerly behavior:

> The emphasis on manners, and through them, on mode of acquisition, enables seniority within a class; it also gives the recognized possessors of the legitimate manner an absolute, arbitrary power to recognize or exclude. Manner, by definition, only exists for others, and the recognized holders of the legitimate manner and of the power to define the value of manners—dress, bearing, pronunciation—have the privilege of indifference to their own manner (so they never have to *put on* a manner). (1996: 95)

Mannerly behavior was so long associated with high status that its practitioners were marked either as members of an elite class or as aspirants to such. This was further reinforced by the association of both manners and elite status with arts and learning, so that merchants (and other groups) in England and America fairly scrambled to acquire the material expressions of education and self-improvement for themselves, their homes, and their communities (Klein 1989: 588). Material objects—whether jewelry, church pews, or land—were associated with rank and improvement as well, and they extended the idea of polite conduct and good breeding into objects, which, if not quotidian in themselves, were commonly visible every day, perhaps even strongly invested with the authority of history. The greater the patina of an object, the more likely it was used within elite social boundaries.

The more that the "individual" was valued as a part of society, the more it became necessary to create a means of distinguishing who belonged to what sort of group. When birth and social class were no longer sufficient markers and material culture had largely lost its immediate value in assessing individuals in face-to-face encounters, then polite behavior became the solution for preserving hierarchy. "Exclu-sivity implied a desire to create an artificial social environment, one that could not exist without consciously denying admission to coarse and vulgar people" (Bushman 1993: 51). Because the artificial environment of manners was a social construct, it could be changed as necessary to preserve the value of mannerly behavior as an effective social marker. Like the attempts to enforce sumptuary laws and the gradual adoption by the elite of restrained colors and cuts of clothing, manners (and taste) could be subtly refined to distinguish "legitimate" manners from pre-tenders when manners became too readily accessible. Sometimes this was simply a matter of the correct demeanor, which could only succeed when the actor had enough knowledge of the correct behavior for a particular social context.

> The manner which designates the infallible taste of the "taste-maker" and exposes the uncertain tastes of the possessors of an "ill-gotten" culture is so important, in all markets and especially in the market which decides the value of literary and artistic works, only because choices always owe part of their value to the value of the chooser, and because, to a large extent, this value makes itself known and recognized through the manner of choosing. What is learnt through immersion in a world in which legitimate culture is as natural as the air one breathes is a sense of the legitimate choice so sure of itself that it convinces by the sheer manner of the performance, like a successful bluff. It is not only a sense of the right area to invest in ... [but] ultimately, the self-assurance, confidence, arrogance, which, normally being the monopoly of the individuals most assured of profit from their invest-ments, has every likelihood—in a world in which everything is a matter of belief—of imposing the absolute legitimacy, and therefore the maximum profitability, of their investments. (Bourdieu 1996: 91–92)

While manners preserved social stratification and seemed to pre-serve traditional or conservative ways, they actually created subtle differences in the English social hierarchy in the late seventeenth and eighteenth centuries. Furthermore, although manners definitely con-ferred social power on their practitioners, the very nature of polite behavior carried with it censure for the thoughtless or destructive of manners use against others. Judith Martin, in her persona as Miss Manners, emphasized the notion that manners were not just one more weapon in the arsenal of the socially powerful:

> There is a mistaken notion that etiquette favors the rich or the powerful. No, life favors the rich and powerful; you can have a lot of control you could not otherwise have. If you are required by society to be polite—of course it's a voluntary system policed only by public opinion—you run into having to have equal respect for people who are not as rich and powerful as you. More than that, because of the concept of noblesse oblige, you are required to treat them even better. So etiquette is the greatest friend of the powerless; without it, might makes right. ("Polite Company" 1998: 29)

Although she addressed a modern audience, Martin's statement is historically derived. Manners were and continue to be for communication across polite distance, not for social dueling.

MANNERS AS BRIDGES

Whereas manners in every generation contain strong survivals from previous generations and are, in that respect, conservative, there is an apparent contradiction in the changeability of courteous conduct that reflects present necessities as well as past traditions. Christina Hemphill describes how manners are able to reconcile old and new meanings through ritual. "Rituals cloak cultural conflicts in that they both make the unclear clear and provide ceremonial bridges over the chasms of culture conflict ... rituals accomplish this by performing three functions: Social regulation or control, role creation, and role communication" (Hemphill 1988: 561). She further points out that manners act as social control by reinforcing status when other factors challenge these; they fulfill the creative role by manufacturing the feelings people need to assume new roles; they communicate by allowing people to say one thing and communicate the opposite through their behavior. In this way manners were used in the seventeenth and eighteenth centuries to sustain fluidity in apparently static hierarchies, to reconcile wealth and brand new rank, and to permit gentlewomen to participate in the conduct of business.

From their earliest conception, manners were created to facilitate communication within and between groups. This was of crucial consequence with the embrace of the "individual" that went hand in hand with the broader redefinition of the "gentleman." Works were being addressed to men of wealth or rank (or both) under titles like *The Compleat Gentleman*, *The Gentleman's Calling*, and *The English Gentleman*, indicating a subtle, polite sort of democratization, a loosening of strict social bonds.

With this redefinition, there were simply more people to "talk" to and polite, knowledgeable conversation became an important skill. Guazzo's courtesy work was entitled *La Civile Conversatizione* (*The Civile Conversation*), and Castiglione's *The Courtier* was written as a dialogue to reemphasize this importance of civil conversation. Texts and authors from many centuries underscore this point as well. In 1693 Locke wrote:

> The thing they should endeavour and aim at in Conversation, should be to
> shew Respect, Esteem, and Good-will, by paying to every one that common

Ceremony and Regard which is in civility due to them. To do this, without a
suspicion of Flattery, Dissimulation, or Meanness, is a great Skill, which
good Sense, Reason, and good Company can only teach; but is of so much use
in civil Life, that it is well worth the studying. (Locke 1989: 203)

The first foundation of that communication was *restraint*: "The fact
is that civilization requires some training in restraint so that we can get
along" ("Polite Company" 1998: 27). While that restraint could be restrictive, it also afforded the security of predictability in the social
world. The best kind of polite society—the most convincing sort—
demanded, however, the practitioner move a step beyond personal restraint to the second influential constituent of mannerly communication, *complaisance*. An audience who witnessed a genuine, though
suitably understated, wish to please was more convinced of the practitioner's desire to communicate. The audience in turn was assured of
goodwill and were so prompted to respond in kind, acting according to
the polite script. Writing in *The New-England Weekly Journal* in 1728,
Matthew Adams described the importance of complaisance in civil life:
"The decent Ceremony of a mutual Complaisance, is ... so near of Kin to
Vertue, that I can hardly believe the want of it is reconcileable with
that Religion, which is void of Offense, towards our Maker and Fellow-
creatures" (quoted in Shields 1997: 239–240).

MANNERS AS FRONTIERS

With the boundaries that are created by manners, there are also
frontiers, places to negotiate change politely, that is to say discreetly, so
that it is perhaps unnecessary to openly acknowledge the existing fact
of change. A third quality of manners, then, in addition to restraint and
complaisance, is *flexibility*. Merchants exploited this flexibility. As contributors, in many ways, to the definition of gentleman that was based
more on wealth than the chance of birth, merchants were at the vanguard of eager consumers of mannerly behavior because:

Gentility bestowed concrete social power on its practitioners. It was a resource for impressing and influencing powerful people, frequently a prereq-
uisite for inspiring trust. All who sought worldly advancement were tempted
to use refinement as a bargaining chip in social negotiations. Moreover it
afforded a convenient identity and a definition of position in the confusing
fluidity of democratic society. (Bushman 1993: xix)

Mannerly behavior facilitated communication to factors and partners abroad and with customers at home through trust and sociability,
but it also allowed merchants to take on the aura of a political and

economic elite, by converting their financial and social capital into political power as well. Ritualized socializing provided the means for women to act with authority as social brokers to affect what transpired in the commercial world. Polite conduct also gave merchants a way to remain a part of the wider community, by reinforcing the notion that their fortunes were inextricably linked with that of sailors and farmers and craftsmen. This need to emphasize the mutual reliance while maintaining social distance was facilitated by the comparatively level playing ground of manners. Mather Byles in the *New-England Weekly Journal* (1727) remarked on the phenomenon of business sociability as a democratizing force:

> I have observed in all the Companies I have been in, from the Caravan-Lodge in China, to the Crown-Coffee-House upon the Long-Wharffe, that all Conversation is built upon Equality; Title and Distinction must be laid aside in order to talk and act sociably, and the ungrateful Names of Superiour and Inferiour must loose themselves in that more acceptable and familiar one, the Companion. (quoted in Shields 1997: 237)

Especially in New England, where distance from traditional English society allowed many differences to simmer in the provincial cauldron, ideas of hierarchy were necessarily altered with the colonial frontier life. Manners permitted sociability of individuals for business and pleasure. This new mode of manners in the New England colonies was akin to that noted by "Beau" Nash at Bath: social interaction could only take place where manners bridged other social boundaries such as rank. On many occasions, Dr. Alexander Hamilton recorded the importance and effect of manners in New England's commercial urban centers. Looking back at his experiences at the end of his travels, Hamilton wrote:

> I found but little differences in the manners and character of the people in the different provinces I passed thro', but as to constitutions and complexions, air and government, I found some variety.... As to politeness and humanity, they are much alike except in the great towns where the inhabitants are more civilized, especially at Boston. (Bridenbaugh 1948: 199)

In each of the three merchant-family histories is evidence of the importance of manners in social regulation and construction. John Mascarene was highly sensitive to the manner with which he was received (and with which he presented himself) on visits in London. With the rules of polite conduct, his education, and family connections enabled him to interact freely, though respectfully, with other merchants and with the members of the peerage he encountered socially and in the course of his pursuit of his "memorial." Mascarene's sense of self-presentation in "manner & form" and his concern with notions of mutually accorded respect within the social hierarchy can be seen in the following entry:

> After dressing myself yesterday in manner & form with my Sword, Bag Wig & I went to find out Lord & Lady Ferrer and after walking up & down different parts of the Town before I could hear of them at last found their House near the Park but was still disappointed by their being in the Country and not expected until after Xmas. As soon as I hear they are in Town intend to make them a Visit[.] I am told they are not elevated as some Persons would be on their Promotions (tho instead the manner of their arriving at their Title is a subject of Humiliation), and therefore hope for a better reception. (Mascarene November 27, 1761)

He was also aware that society (and especially that of women) was what polished the manners that made these exchanges possible. In another letter to his wife John wrote of his hopes for a young friend's continued improvement in society: "Mr. Sewall I think was very genteel in his present to Bets[.] I hope by a little of your tuition and that of the other Ladys at Cambridge he will be as remarkable for his politeness as he is for his ingenuity" (Mascarene February 10, 1763).

Because he spent so much time in his rented lodgings yet still wanted to be perceived as a gentleman, the gentility and manners of his landlady and her family, like his oft-stated concern with self-improvement, were very important to Mascarene:

> I spend my time partly in Conversation with my Landlady and her Daughters who are very civil well bred & sensible People[.] my Landlady is very fond of Picquet and we make very often a party together of an Evening & sometimes play at Whiske but never stake any thing not even a Copper[.] the other part of time is spent either in reading or writing with which I endeavor to make the time tolerable and is all I can expect till please God I see you again. (Mascarene December 20, 1761)

Later he used the excuse of a breach of manners to change his quarters: "Mr Lechmere, [Mr.] Barker (a Gentleman from so[uth] Carol[ina]) and myself who all quartered together, finding that our Landlady of late did not behave so genteel to us as before and not being so well attended agreed to shift our Lodgings" (Mascarene October 3, 1766). The landlady's lack of gentility may have been only part of the story or an entirely polite fiction; by this time, John was very worried about his financial straits. Money problems perhaps occasioned the move to a less expensive set of rooms shared with friends. If this were the case then mannerly behavior also allowed him to make this change without any loss of face.

For all of his own failings, Joseph Denham was also conscious and critical of the behavior of those around him, great and base. In a gossipy

1766 letter to Mary Earle, Denham was censorious about the social failings of Mrs. Earle's former maid: "Your Maid Bettina is still with Maria the Washerwoman, but they say is to be married this Month. tho' she lives over Mrs. Ellis, she never had the good Manners to call & see her in her Illness for which I gave her a good Lecture the first Time I saw her afterwards" (NMGM D/Earle/3/2/21). Denham was similarly critical, though less inclined to remonstrate, the Duke of Cumberland, who visited him at Civita Vecchia in April of 1774:

> When I re'ced your kind & very agreeable Letter of the 22d … I was standing behind the Duke of Cumberland's Chair & serving him at Dinner, for HRH had not the good manners to let me sit down, while he was stuffing his mouth with the Wing of a fowl I opened Mr. Earle's Letter, & seeing your hand writing, I gave the Duke the slip & retired into another Room to give you Audience. (NMGM D/Earle/3/2/29)

It does not matter whether Denham was exaggerating this gallant display of his own bad manners; he excused his lack of respect for the duke's rank with his own regard for Mrs. Earle's letters and the duke's lack of equable politeness. Denham's memorable and minute descriptions of Mrs. Strine's poor conduct and the British commodore's gaucheries in Genoa further attest to his concern with polite behavior and the power and impression that it made.

While the Turner family's observations of their social life do not survive, there is ample evidence of their participation in polite society in the observations of their contemporaries and in the material remains of their belongings, house, and landscape. This is particularly true of Colonel John Turner, probably the wealthiest and most influential member of that family. In his private journal, the powerful and respected jurist, Benjamin Lynde, Sr., wrote of emulating Colonel Turner's hospitality. Years later, the Reverend Bentley also recorded what he had learned of the colonel's civic-minded gestures as historical notes he included in his journal. Certainly the clergy had much to gain in the goodwill of wealthy parishioners, as the merchants in Massachusetts were similarly interested in cultivating the clergy and the rest of the community, but the tone of the entries in Bentley's diary is one of awe and respect, even admiration, not what one might expect of a casual remark on the anniversary of an event in a parish history. Something more significant is present in Bentley's notes. The mutual interest of these two groups, indeed, of any several groups in society, may have been discreetly masked in civil behavior, but the successful execution of these gestures also built personal reputations, even personal myths. Their reputations had implications not only for the immediate family but for generations to come.

As formulaic as early modern social life might have been, it worked in a number of ways to reproduce society. It was not always fair, but it was largely effective and sometimes the structure of mannerly life worked better than one deserved. In each of the three historical cases examined, some member of the family caused a tear in the social fabric, but in the end, all of these individuals were either spared repercussions or had the dire results of their situations mitigated because of their (or their families') mannerly participation in their respective communities. The third John Turner broke the social contract of politeness by quite flagrantly adopting a religion, political stance, and demeanor that was opposite to that of his community and forebears and then by using his influence to take a position that had been promised to someone else. But instead of being forced, like so many Loyalists, to flee to London or Nova Scotia or having his house burnt, he was spared because of his father's memory and the role of his sons on the American side of the war.

John Mascarene was also a Loyalist during the Revolutionary War and suffered financially because of it, but his situation was different from that of Turner's. Mascarene was caught between his politics and his good relationship with his community, but was still respected enough to enjoy the intercession of his friends on his and Margaret's behalf after the war.

Joseph Denham's lies were probably the most egregious affronts to mannerly behavior. By changing his name, concealing his first marriage, and not revealing to his employers (and prospective partners) that he had fled debts in England, Denham broke the unspoken rule of this or any social structure by not being what he claimed. Even though he misrepresented his financial state, misled his employers, and tossed aside his marriage vows quite knowingly, Joseph Denham was not completely ostracized by the Earles. That family continued to conduct business with him and looked after his English first wife though they appear to have kept him at arm's length socially.

What allowed these men to be spared—when others might have been banished from polite society—was the solidity of the ranks to which they had been admitted. In these instances, personalities that had been created by mannerly conduct made strong enough impressions on others to cause them to act according to the rules of polite behavior when they might have done otherwise. Perhaps it was also because once having given a convincing enough performance, it would have reflected badly on others within the group to admit to a mistake in character judgment.

The relationship between merchants and their communities was complex and crucial on many levels. As suggested by De Cunzo (1995a), merchants act as brokers of material and ideal culture through their social lives as well as their storefronts, and exist as such only as long as the community can (or is willing to) sustain and support their market ventures. Therefore, it was in the best interest of the merchants to adapt to the community's needs at the same time that they were also shaping those needs through selling imported and manufactured goods.

There is an additional "openness" or social accessibility involved in being a merchant that is associated with having far-ranging contacts in many countries and cultures. Goffman proposed that "[e]very social position can be seen as an arrangement which opens up the incumbent to engagement with certain categories of others.... There are social positions, however, that open up the incumbent to more than mere occupational-others" (1963: 125). These particular cases are police officers or priests, people whose occupations cause them to be approached quite freely for "a wide variety of information and assistance." Merchants, in their roles as traders, salesmen, and bankers to the community, as foreign correspondents, financial negotiators, and controllers of human labor, also would have found it necessary to negotiate with many different sorts of individuals at many levels of society. Even at the very highest levels of the merchant class, where the business of acquiring so much timber or produce to ship to the West Indies and arranging the manufacture of barrels or sacks to carry them would have been handed off to a counting house full of assistants, it still remained that these men were frequently also members of the town or colonial government, active in the military or church, and thus took on an increasingly large mantle of "openness" to the community at large.

Merchants walked a thin line between acquiring and displaying mannerly behavior (and its material components) and creating so much social distance that they alienated the community on which they depended for their wealth and status. Manners made it possible to maintain this balance of relations while maintaining social boundaries. Like rural Maine, urban New England of the seventeenth and eighteenth centuries "was a world neither of free-floating individuals nor of self-contained households" (Ulrich 1987: 33). Merchants were firmly entrenched in a network of mutual obligation and reliance even as they attempted to establish themselves as elite with paternalistic behavior.

> Ultimately, a boss, no matter how exalted ... is dependent for his position on his workers.... One can defy them, scourge them, mock them only to a point ... [but] Miss Manners does not believe that people are ever as pliant out of fear as they are from affection. Whether what one wants them to do is work harder, acknowledge one's near-divinity, or just hand over their money, it is always safest to make them want to do so. (Martin 1990: 312)

Mannerly behavior was the best way to make this apparent contradiction work for the merchant elite. I believe a particularly convincing example of this can be observed in the Turner house itself. As described in Chapter 4, the house's presence in the midst of the urban harborscape in Salem implies ties to (as well as control of) the work and workforce at the same time that its fineness and patina reinforced the notion of social distance between patrician and plebeian. Wharves, the ships, and the house itself were all signs of wealth, but would have been useless without the community needed to support global commerce and provide a market for the goods that were imported (Figure 25). Manners provided social distance and reinforced the importance of close social ties at the same time they reconciled these apparent contradictions.

HISTORICAL ARCHAEOLOGY, MATERIAL CULTURE, AND MANNERS

Manners furnished early modern practitioners with scripts by which individual and group identities could be enacted. But even with these scripts, social anxiety was never completely banished. Personal advancement, social stability, and financial success were at stake, particularly at the more formal occasions, where Bushman remarked that "people did not attend such events to relax, but to present their most beautiful, gracious, and pleasing selves" (1993: 52).

There were accidents of improvisation or worse, the unanticipated changes of fashion that exposed a lack of awareness of mode, novelty, or custom. While visiting Boston, the otherwise poised Dr. Alexander Hamilton noted the discomfiture that unfamiliarity with fashion or local custom could cause:

> I dined with Mr. Fletcher in the company of two Philadelphians, who could not be easy because forsooth they were in their night-caps seeing every body else in full dress with powdered wigs; it not being customary in Boston to go to dine or appear upon Change in caps as they do in other parts of America. What strange creatures we are, and what triffles make us uneasy! It is no mean jest that such worthless things as caps and wigs should disturb our tranqulity [sic] and disorder our thoughts when we imagin they are wore out of season. I was my self much in the same state of uneasiness with these Philadelphians, for I had got a great hole in the lappet of my coat, to hide which employed so much of my thoughts in company that, for want of attention, I could not give a pertinent answer when I was spoke to. (Bridenbaugh 1948: 134)

Manners and the use of material culture in polite company are related as parts of the structure of a culture and both delimit one's social

Figure 25. Certificate of membership for the Salem Marine Society (in the collection of the Peabody Essex Museum). Illustration by Abijah Northey, Jr., and engraved by Samuel Hill (1797). The certificate shows a view of Salem Harbor facing east (*top*) and various scenes of the mercantile community. Photograph by Jeffrey R. Dykes. Courtesy, Peabody Essex Museum, Salem, Massachusetts.

participation. Mere material "triffles," like manners, were used to define the self and one's place in the world; and artifacts, like manners, were carefully selected and imbued with new meaning. By manipulating various legitimizing expressions of luxury, novelty, and patina in clothing, feasts, and landscapes, individuals and groups sought self-expression of their present state and future social aspirations. Both manners and artifacts were emblematic of what the user or practitioner thought about herself, her community, and the rest of the world.

Historical archaeology is often heralded as the study of "everyday life." Cultural meaning shaped daily activities and decisions, and when that meaning is altered, for whatever reason, change of some sort is afoot and deserves attention for what it can tell us about how culture works. While the grubbier aspects of fieldwork may seem to inhabit a different world from the decorous society of the merchant elite in seventeenth- and eighteenth-century England and Massachusetts, it is the ideal means by which we can study not only the roots of colonial polite behavior, but how that behavior assisted in a recognizable (not to say unchanged) translation of English culture adapted to a frontier setting. Archaeologists have the opportunity to observe emic intentions and activities through the examination of contemporary documents while drawing conclusions about what those activities meant from the etic interpretation of archaeological data that allow us to reevaluate previously held notions about power, social structure, and cultural change.

It is imperative for archaeologists to consider the range of meanings of artifacts in social contexts, by which it is possible to view relationships in communities. Understanding the meaning of archaeologically recovered artifacts relies on understanding local social context, and, when possible, considering the subtleties of personal choice as well as public ceremony. In the course of studying these personal interactions and their material remains, it is possible to observe how things can change—can be made to change—without seeming to.

We also see how societies change as they distance themselves from their cultural forebears: regional expressions of this distance appeared almost as soon as the colonists' ships arrived on these shores. New England merchants parlayed historical symbols of authority into community leadership, consciously constructed to resemble that of the landed elite in England. The first generation of colonial merchants was not "to the manner born," but they had brought the trappings as a part of their cultural baggage from England and discovered the utility of mannerly behavior. They did what people always did with manners, adapting old, familiar ones to suit their needs and adopting foreign ones to satisfy new fancies.

Bourdieu commented that the difference between the "legitimate" possessors of manners and those who aspired to that group was found in the ability to imitate those manners:

> The "parvenus" who presume to join the group of legitimate, i.e., hereditary, possessors of the legitimate manner, without being the product of the same social conditions, are trapped, whatever they do, in a choice between anxious hyper-identification and the negativity which admits its defeat in its very revolt; either the conformity of an "assumed" behaviour whose very correctness or hyper-correctness betrays an imitation, or the ostentatious assertion of difference which is bound to appear as an admission of inability to identify. (Bourdieu 1996: 95)

The physical distance of the Atlantic Ocean compounded America's social distance from Britain and imitative "hyper-identification" or "assertions of difference" that clearly were present in British America became markedly more pronounced through the second half of the eighteenth century. These anxieties of identity (either imitative or differentiated) were present all along, but leading up to and after the Revolution, Americans established a separate identity, claiming an "honesty" and "simplicity" in manners that they believed further distanced them from England. Thus, another link was added to the chain of manners: what were pretensions become reality in a new identity.

One tangible example of the importance of correct mannerly behavior was found in the epitaph on a slate headstone in the Charter Street Burial Ground in Salem. It reads:

In Memory of
Capt. Thomas Dean. Merchant
O.B. July 8, 1802
AET. 79
He was a Gentleman of pleasing manners,
and well informed.

Material evidence of the connection between merchants and "pleasing manners" was carved in stone. This connection between civil life and mercantile endeavor also appears in Dr. Alexander Hamilton's description of the night-capped Philadelphians in Boston, where dining and appearing "upon Change" seem to be accorded an equal valence in Hamilton's mind. Both of these incidents echo Lord Chesterfield's observation that "a man who is not well-bred, is full as unfit for business as for company" (1992: 175).

Manners are busy, seemingly contradictory creatures. They evolve or are changed, yet retain recognizable elements of their ancestry. They can rigidly formalize interactions, but by doing so, provide a ready-made script for social exchange, giving comfort to the actors in anticipation rather than reaction. Manners create anxieties in both the untutored and the socially skilled, but they also afford the means by which such anxieties can be ignored or excused in the otherwise worthy practitioner. Manners create complex situations for the use and display of material goods at the same time that they deny the importance of anything but personal character. Mannerly behavior can exclude or include, but with the provision of frontiers also ensure the possibility of negotiation. Manners, like any form of communication, are reassuring and daunting, complex beyond their simple instructions, and finally, a means of continuing old traditions while accommodating cultural change.

References

Addison, J., 1705, *Remarks on Several Parts of Italy, &c. In the Years 1701, 1702, 1703*. Printed for Jacob Tonson, Gray's Inn, London.

Allen, G. W., 1927, *Massachusetts Privateers of the Revolution*. Massachusetts Historical Society Collections, No. 77, Harvard University Press, Cambridge, MA.

Allestree, R., 1682, *The Gentleman's Calling* (Written by the author of The Whole Duty of Man). Printed by R. Norton for Robert Pawlet, London.

Allestree, R., 1673, *The Ladies Calling, By the Author of The Whole Duty of Man*. Oxford, at the Theater.

Allestree, R., 1659, *The Whole Duty of Man, Laid Down in a Plain Way for the Use of the Meanest Reader*. [microform] Printed for T. Garthwait, London.

Amussen, S. D., 1988, *An Ordered Society: Gender and Class in Early Modern England*. Family, Sexuality, and Social Relations in Past Times. Basil Blackwell, Oxford.

Anonymous, 1758, *The Complete Servant Man*, J. Coote, London.

Appleby, J., 1994, Consumption in Early Modern Social Thought. In *Consumption and the World of Goods*, edited by J. Brewer and R. Porter, pp. 162–173. Routledge, London and New York.

Aresty, E. B., 1970, *The Best Behavior: The Course of Good Manners—From Antiquity to the Present—As Seen Through Courtesy and Etiquette Books*. Simon and Schuster, New York.

Bailyn, B., 1986, *The Peopling of British North America: An Introduction*. Vintage Books, New York.

Bailyn, B., 1964, *The New England Merchants in the Seventeenth Century*. Harper and Row, New York.

Baram, U., 1998, An Archaeology of Middle Eastern Pleasures: Coffee and Tobacco in the Ottoman Empire. Paper presented at the Society for Historical Archaeology, Atlanta.

Barker-Benfield, G. J., 1992, *The Culture of Sensibility: Sex and Society in Eighteenth-Century Britain*. University of Chicago Press, Chicago and London.

Beaudry, M. C., 1996, Reinventing Historical Archaeology. In *Historical Archaeology and the Study of American Culture*, edited by L. A. De Cunzo and B. L. Herman, pp. 473–497. Henry Francis du Pont Winterthur Museum, Inc. Winterthur, DE.

Beaudry, M. C., 1995, Scratching the Surface: Seven Seasons at the Spencer-Peirce-Little Farm, Newbury, Massachusetts. *Northeast Historical Archaeology* 24:19–50.

Beaudry, M. C., 1988, Words for Things: Linguistic Analysis of Probate Inventories. In *Documentary Archaeology in the New World*, edited by M. C. Beaudry, pp. 43–50. Cambridge University Press, New York.

Beaudry, M. C., n.d., *"Above Vulgar Economy": Material Culture and Social Positioning Among Newburyport's Merchant Elite*. Unpublished ms. in possession of the author.

Belknap, H. W., 1928, The Grafton Family of Salem. *The Essex Institute Historical Collections* (1):49–64.

Benson, M. S., 1935, *Women in 18th-Century America, A Study of Opinion and Social Usage*. Studies in History, Economics and Public Law, No. 405, Columbia University Press, New York.

Bentley, W., 1907, *The Diary of William Bentley, D.D., Pastor of the East Church, Salem, Massachusetts*, Vols. 1–4. The Essex Institute, Salem, MA.

Borsay, P., 1989, *English Urban Renaissance: Culture and Society in the Provincial Town, 1660–1770*. Oxford Studies in Social History. Clarendon Press, Oxford.

Borsay, P., 1984, "All the Town's a Stage": Urban Ritual and Ceremony 1660–1800. In *The Transformation of English Provincial Towns 1600–1800*, edited by P. Clark, pp. 228–258. Hutchinson & Co., London.

The Boston News-Letter, No. 10, Monday June 19–Monday June 26, 1704. Early American Newspapers, Readex Microprint Company, New York.

Boswell, J., 1986 [1799], *The Life of Samuel Johnson* (edited by C. Hibbert). Penguin Books, London.

Bourdieu, P., 1996, *Distinction: A Social Critique of the Judgement of Taste*. Originally published 1979. Translated by R. Nice, Harvard University Press, Cambridge.

Brathwait, R. E., 1630, *The English Gentleman*. Printed by I. Haviland, London.

Brathwait, R. E., 1631, *The English Gentlewoman*. Printed by B. Alsop and T. Fawcet, for Michaell Sparke, Greene Arbor.

Braudel, F., 1981, *The Structures of Everyday Life: Civilization & Capitalism, 15th–18th Century*. Harper & Row, New York.

Breen, T. H., 1994a, "Baubles of Britain": The American and Consumer Revolutions of the Eighteenth Century. In *Of Consuming Interests: The Style of Life in the Eighteenth Century*, edited by C. Carson, R. Hoffman, and P. J. Albert, pp. 444–482. Perspectives on the American Revolution, R. Hoffman and P. J. Albert, general editors. University Press of Virginia, Charlottesville and London.

Breen, T. H., 1994b, The Meaning of Things: Interpreting the Consumer Economy in the Eighteenth Century. In *Consumption and the World of Goods*, edited by J. Brewer and R. Porter, pp. 249–260. Routledge, London and New York.

Bresnan, L. L., 1996, *The Beekmans of New York: Material Possession and Social Progression*. M.A. thesis, University of Delaware.

Brewer, J. and R. Porter (Eds.), 1994, *Consumption and the World of Goods*. Routledge, London and New York.

Bridenbaugh, C. (Ed.), 1948 [1744], *Gentleman's Progress: The Itinerarium of Dr. Alexander Hamilton, 1744*. University of North Carolina Press, Chapel Hill.

Bridenbaugh, C., 1938, *Cities in the Wilderness: The First Century of Urban Life in America 1625–1742*. Ronald Press Company, New York.

Brophy, E. B., 1991, *Women's Lives and the 18th-Century English Novel*. University of South Florida Press, Tampa, FL.

Brown, J., 1757, *An Estimate of the Manners and Principles of the Times*, L. Davis and C. Reymers, London.

Brown, K. M., 1996, *Good Wives, Nasty Wenches, & Anxious Patriarchs: Gender, Race, and Power in Colonial Virginia*. University of North Carolina Press, Chapel Hill.

Brown, P., 1996, *Come Drink the Bowl Dry: Alcoholic Liquors and Their Place in Eighteenth-Century Society*. Fairfax House, York.

Brown, P., 1995, *In Praise of Hot Liquors: The Study of Chocolate, Coffee, and Tea-Drinking 1600–1850*. Fairfax House, York.

Burke, P., 1994, *Res et Verba*: Conspicuous Consumption in the Early Modern World. In *Consumption and the World of Goods*, edited by J. Brewer and R. Porter, pp. 148–161. Routledge, London and New York.

Bushman, R. L., 1993, *The Refinement of America: Persons, Houses, Cities*. Alfred A. Knopf, New York.

Calvert, K., 1994, The Function of Fashion in Eighteenth-Century America. In *Of Consuming Interests: The Style of Life in the Eighteenth Century*, edited by C. Carson, R. Hoffman, and P. J. Albert, pp. 252–283. Perspectives on the American Revolution, R. Hoffman and P. J. Albert, general editors. University Press of Virginia, Charlottesville and London.

Campbell, C., 1994, Understanding Traditional and Modern Patterns of Consumption in Eighteenth-Century England: A Character-Action Approach. In *Consumption and the World of Goods*, edited by J. Brewer and R. Porter, pp. 40–57. Routledge, London and New York.

Carson, C., 1994, The Consumer Revolution in Colonial British America: Why Demand? In *Of Consuming Interests: The Style of Life in the Eighteenth Century*, edited by C. Carson, R. Hoffman, and P. J. Albert, pp. 483–697. Perspectives on the American Revolution, R. Hoffman and P. J. Albert, general editors. University Press of Virginia, Charlottesville and London.

Carson, C., R. Hoffman, and P. J. Albert (Eds.), 1994, *Of Consuming Interests: The Style of Life in the Eighteenth Century*. University Press of Virginia, Charlottesville and London.

Carson, G., 1966, *The Polite Americans: A Wide-Angle View of Our More or Less Good Manners Over 300 Years*. William Morrow & Company, New York.

Castiglione, B., 1976 [1528], *The Book of the Courtier*. Translated by George Bull. Penguin Books, London.

Centlivre, S., 1718, *A Bold Stroke for a Wife*. 1968 ed. Translated by T. Stathas. University of Nebraska Press, Lincoln, NE.

Chambers, E., 1738, *Cyclopedia: or, an Universal Dictionary of Arts and Sciences*. Vol. II of II, London.

Cheever, G. F., 1859, Some Remarks on the Commerce of Salem. *Essex Institute Historical Collections* 1(3):77–91.

Chesterfield, P. D. S., Earl of, 1992 [1728–1772], *Lord Chesterfield's Letters* (Edited and with an Introduction by David Roberts). Oxford University Press, Oxford and New York.

Clark, A., 1968, *Working Life of Women in the Seventeenth Century*. Reprint of 1919 ed. Reprint of Economic Classics. Augustus M. Kelley, New York.

Clark, P., 1984, The Civic Leaders of Gloucester 1580–1800. In *The Transformation of English Provincial Towns 1600–1800*, edited by P. Clark, pp. 311–345. Hutchinson & Co., London.

Clive, J. and B. Bailyn, 1954, England's Cultural Provinces: Scotland and America. *The William and Mary Quarterly* (Series 3) 11:200–213.

Colman, B., 1716, *The Honour and Happiness of the Vertuous Woman*. Printed by B. Green, Boston.

The Compact Edition of the Oxford English Dictionary, 1988, 2 vols. Oxford University Press, Oxford.

Corfield, P. J., 1982, *The Impact of English Towns 1700–1800*. Oxford University Press, Oxford.

Csikszentmihalyi, M., 1993, Why We Need Things. In *History from Things: Essays on Material Culture*, edited by S. Lubar and W. D. Kingery, pp. 20–29. Smithsonian Institution Press, Washington and London.

Cummings, A. L., 1979, *The Framed Houses of Massachusetts Bay, 1625–1725*. Harvard University Press, Cambridge.

Cummings, A. L. (Ed.), 1964, *Rural Household Inventories: Established by the Names, Uses, and Furnishings of Rooms in the Colonial New England Home 1675–1775.* Society for the Preservation of New England Antiquities, Boston.

Curtin, M., 1985, A Question of Manners: Status and Gender in Etiquette and Courtesy. *Journal of Modern History* 57(3):395–423.

Curtis, L. A. (Ed.), 1979, *The Versatile Defoe: An Anthology of Uncollected Writings by Daniel Defoe.* Rowman & Littlefield, Totowa, NJ.

Da Barberino, F., 1869, Documenti d'Amore. In *Italian Courtesy Books*, edited by W. M. Rossetti, pp. 35–55. London.

Davis, R., 1962, *The Rise of the English Shipping Industry in the Seventeenth and Eighteenth Centuries.* Macmillan & Co., London.

De Beauvoir, S., 1989, *The Second Sex.* Reprint of the 1953 edition. Translated and edited by H. M. Parshley. Vintage Books, New York.

De Cunzo, L. A., 1995a, The Culture Broker Revisited: Historical Archaeological Perspectives on Merchants in Delaware, 1760–1815. *North American Archaeologist* 16(3): 181–222.

De Cunzo, L. A., 1995b, Reform, Respite, Ritual: An Archaeology of Institutions: The Magdalen Society of Philadelphia, 1800–1850. *Historical Archaeology* 29(3).

Deetz, J., 1977, *In Small Things Forgotten: The Archaeology of Early American Life.* Anchor Books, New York.

Defoe, D., 1991 [1724], *Roxana or The Fortunate Mistress* (Edited with an introduction and notes by J. Jack). The World's Classics. Oxford University Press, Oxford and New York.

Defoe, D., 1986 [1724–26], *A Tour Through the Whole Island of Great Britain* (Abridged and edited with an Introduction and Notes by P. Rogers). Penguin Books, London.

Defoe, D., 1967 [1728], *A Plan of the English Commerce, Being a Compleat Prospect of the Trade of this Nation, as well the home trade as the foreign.* Reprints of Economic Classics. Augustus M. Kelley, Publishers, New York.

Della Casa, Giovanni, 1869 [1550], Galateo, or, Concerning Manners: Wherein Is the Character of an Elderly Man Instructing a Youth, Are Set Forth the Things Which Ought to be Observed and Avoided in Ordinary Intercourse. In *Italian Courtesy Books*, edited by W. M. Rossetti, London.

Dennis, W. D., 1903, The Fire Clubs of Salem. *Essex Institute Historical Collections* 39(1): 1–28.

Devine, T. M., 1978, An Eighteenth-Century Business Elite: Glasgow-West India Merchants, ca. 1750–1815. *The Scottish Historical Review* 57, 1(163):40–67.

Douglas, M., 1971, Deciphering a Meal. In *Myth, Symbol, and Culture*, edited by C. Geertz, pp. 61–82. W. W. Norton & Company, Inc., New York.

Douglas, M. and B. Isherwood, 1982, *The World of Goods: Toward an Anthropology of Consumption.* W. W. Norton & Company, New York and London.

Dow, G. F., 1903, Proprietors of Common Lands in Salem. *Essex Institute Historical Collections* 39(1):57–80.

Drabble, M., 1975, *The Realms of Gold.* Ivy Books, New York.

Du Bosc, J., 1639, *The Compleat Woman.* Translated from the French by N. N., London.

Dunn, R. S., 1972, *Sugar and Slaves: The Rise of the Planter Class in the English West Indies, 1624–1713.* University of North Carolina, Chapel Hill.

Earle, A. M., 1924, *Colonial Dames and Good Wives.* Macmillan & Co., New York.

Earle, P., 1989a, The Female Labour Market in London in the Late Seventeenth and Early Eighteenth Centuries. *Economic History Review*, 2nd ser. 42 (3)(1989):328–353.

Earle, P., 1989b, *The Making of the English Middle Class: Business, Society and Family Life in London 1660–1730.* University of California Press, Berkeley and Los Angeles.

Earle, P., 1986, Age and Accumulation. In *Business Life and Public Policy: Essays in*

Honour of D. C. Coleman, edited by N. McKendrick and R. B. Outhwaite, pp. 38–63. Cambridge University Press, Cambridge.

Egan, G., S. Hanna, and B. Knight, 1986, Marks on Milled Window Leads. *Post-Medieval Archaeology* 20:303–309.

Ekholm, E. and J. Deetz, 1971, Wellfleet Tavern. *Natural History* 80(7):48–57.

Elias, N., 1978, *The Civilizing Process. The Development of Manners, Changes in the Code of Conduct and Feeling in Early Modern Times*. Translated by J. Edmund. Urizen Books, New York.

Ellis, J., 1984, "A Dynamic Society": Social Relations in Newcastle-upon-Tyne 1660–1760. In *The Transformation of English Provincial Towns 1600–1800*, edited by P. Clark, pp. 190–227. Hutchinson & Co., London.

Emmerton, C. O., 1985, *The Chronicles of Three Old Houses*. Reprint of 1935 ed. The House of Seven Gables Settlement Association, Salem, MA.

Erasmus, D., 1985 [1530], On Good Manners for Boys/ De civilitate morum puerilium. In *Collected Works of Erasmus*, edited by J. K. Sowards, pp. 269–289. Translated and annotated by B. McGregor. Vol. 25, Literary and Educational Writings 3. University of Toronto Press, Toronto, Buffalo, London.

Essex County (Massachusetts) Probate Records (ECPR in text). Docket 28,367; Vols. 303, 345, and 361. Salem, MA.

Essex Institute, 1916–1925, *Vital Records of Salem, Massachusetts, to the End of the Year 1849*. (6 Vols.) (VRS in text) Essex Institute, Salem, MA.

Essex Institute, 1916–1920, *The Probate Records of Essex County, Massachusetts*. 3 Vols. (1635–1681). Essex Institute, Salem, MA.

Essex Institute Historical Collections (EIHC in text), 1926, Salem Town Records. Town Meetings, Vol. III. *Essex Institute Historical Collections* 62(2):177–192.

Essex Institute Historical Collections, 1913, Diary for the Year 1759 Kept by Samuel Gardner. *Essex Institute Historical Collections* 49(1):1–22.

Essex Institute Historical Collections, 1913, Salem Town Records. Town Meetings, Vol. II. *Essex Institute Historical Collections* 49(1):65–80.

Essex Institute Historical Collections, 1912, Salem Town Records. Town Meetings, Vol. II. 1659–1680. *Essex Institute Historical Collections* 48(1):17–40.

Essex Institute Historical Collections, 1909, Essex County Notarial Records, 1697–1768. *Essex Institute Historical Collections* 45(1):90–96.

Essex Institute Historical Collections, 1907, Salem Town Records. Town Meetings. *Essex Institute Historical Collections* 43(2):33–48.

Essex Institute Historical Collections, 1906, Salem Town Records. Town Meetings, Vol. II. 1659–1680. *Essex Institute Historical Collections* 42(1):41–64.

Essex Institute Historical Collections, 1902, The Misery Islands and What Happened There. *Essex Institute Historical Collections* 38(3):225–256.

Felt, J. B., 1845–1849, *Annals of Salem*, 2 Vols. 2nd ed. Ives, Salem, MA.

Fenelon, F. d. S. d. l. M., 1707, *Instructions for the Education of a Daughter*. Translated by G. Hickes. Printed for M. Cooper and C. Sympson, London.

Fielding, H., 1997 [1749], *Tom Jones*. Bantam Books, New York.

Fielding, H., 1985 [1742], *Joseph Andrews*. Penguin Books, London.

Fowler, S. P., 1870, Diary of the Reverend Joseph Green of Salem Village. *Essex Institute Historical Collections* 10(1):73–103.

Fowler, S. P., 1866, Diary of the Reverend Joseph Green of Salem Village. *Essex Institute Historical Collections* 8(3):91–96.

Friedlander, A., 1991, *Salem Maritime National Historic Site: Historical Research 1626–1990*. Report prepared for National Park Service, Denver Service Center-Eastern Team by the Cultural Resource Group, Louis Berger Associates.

Fyge, S., 1989, The Liberty (1703). In *Kissing the Rod: An Anthology of Seventeenth-*

Century Women's Verse, edited by G. Greer, S. Hastings, J. Medoff, and M. Sansone. Noonday Press, New York.

Gardner, F. A., 1901, Thomas Gardner, Planter, and Some of His Descendants. *Essex Institute Historical Collections* 37(2):201–224.

Garman, J., 1994, At the Edge of the Entrepôt: Production and Social Reproduction in Salem, Massachusetts, 1760–1820. Paper presented at the Society for Historical Archaeology Annual Meeting, Vancouver, B.C.

Gibb, J. G., 1996, *The Archaeology of Wealth: Consumer Behavior in English America.* Interdisciplinary Contributions to Archaeology. Plenum Press, New York and London.

Girouard, M., 1978, *Life in the English Country House: A Social and Architectural History.* Yale University Press, New Haven, CT.

Goffman, E., 1963, *Behavior in Public Places: Notes on the Social Organization of Gatherings.* Free Press, New York and London.

Goffman, E., 1959, *The Presentation of Self in Everyday Life.* Doubleday Anchor Books, Garden City, NY.

Goodwin, L. B. R., 1998, Manners and Gender Roles in 18th-Century (New) English Merchant Society. Paper presented at the The Society for Historical Archaeology Annual Meeting, Atlanta, GA.

Goodwin, L. B. R., 1997, The Turner House and the Harborscape of Salem, Massachusetts, 1668–1996. Paper presented at the American Society for Environmental History, Baltimore.

Goodwin, L. B. R., 1996, Merchants and Manners: Archaeology and Cultural Adaptation in 18th-Century Massachusetts. Paper presented at the Northeastern Anthropological Association Annual Meeting, Plymouth, NH.

Goodwin, L. B. R., 1994a, "A Succession of Kaleidoscopic Pictures": Historical Archaeology at the Turner House, Salem, Massachusetts. *Northeast Historical Archaeology* 23: 8–28.

Goodwin, L. B. R., 1994b, The Turner Family's Role in the Entrepôt of Salem, Massachusetts. Paper presented at the Society for Historical Archaeology Annual Meeting, Vancouver, B.C.

Goodwin, L. B. R., 1993, *"A Stately Roof to Shelter Them": An Historical Archaeological Investigation of the Turner Family of Eighteenth-Century Salem, Massachusetts.* Ph.D. dissertation, University of Pennsylvania. University Microfilms, Ann Arbor.

Goodwin, L. B. R., 1992a, Archaeological Site Examination of the Turner House, Salem, Massachusetts. Report prepared for the Massachusetts Historical Commission.

Goodwin, L. B. R., 1992b, Cultural and Personal Identity at the House of the Seven Gables. Paper presented at the Society for Historical Archaeology Annual Meeting, Kingston, Jamaica.

Gracian y Morales, B., 1685, *The Courtiers Manual Oracle, or, The Art of Prudence*, Printed by M. Flesher for A. Swalle, London.

Greene, J. P., 1988, *Pursuits of Happiness: The Social Development of Early Modern British Colonies and the Formation of American Culture.* University of North Carolina Press, Chapel Hill.

Gregory, J., 1794, Dr. Gregory's Legacy to His Daughters [from *A Father's Legacy to His Daughters*]. In *Angelica's Ladies Library*, By a Lady. J. Hamilton & Co., London.

Groneman, C. and M. B. Norton, 1987, Introduction. In *"To Toil the Livelong Day": America's Women at Work, 1780–1980*, edited by C. Groneman and M. B. Norton, pp. 3–17. Cornell University Press, Ithaca and London.

Guazzo, Stefano, 1967, The Civile Conversation. Trans. by G. Pettie. Reprint of 1581 ed. AMS, New York.

Habakkuk, H. J., 1953, England. In *The European Nobility in the Eighteenth Century:*

Studies of the Nobilities of the Major European States in the Pre-Reform Era, edited by A. Goodwin, pp. 1–21. Adam and Charles Black, London.

Hancock, D., 1995, *Citizens of the World: London Merchants and the Integration of the British Atlantic Community, 1735–1785*. Cambridge University Press, Cambridge.

Harrington, F., 1989, The Emergent Elite in Early Eighteenth-Century Portsmouth Society: The Archaeology of the Joseph Sherburne Houselot. *Historical Archaeology* 23(1):2–18.

Hawthorne, N., 1986 [1851], *The House of the Seven Gables*. Bantam Books, New York.

Hemphill, C. D., 1988, *Manners for Americans: Interaction Ritual and the Social Order, 1620–1860*. Ph.D. dissertation, Brandeis University. University Microfilms, Ann Arbor.

Henry, S. L., 1991, Consumers, Commodities, and Choices: A General Model of Consumer Behavior. *Historical Archaeology* 25(2):3–14.

Herman, B. L., 1984, Multiple Materials, Multiple Meanings: The Fortunes of Thomas Mendenhall. *Winterthur Portfolio* (1):67–86.

Heyrman, C. L., 1984, *Commerce and Culture: The Maritime Communities of Colonial Massachusetts 1690–1750*. W. W. Norton & Company, New York and London.

Hill, B., 1989, *Women, Work, and Sexual Politics in Eighteenth-Century England*. Basil Blackwell, Oxford and New York.

Holyoke, F., 1911, *The Holyoke Diaries, 1709–1856*. The Essex Institute, Salem, MA.

Hood, J. E., 1991, Rural to Urban Transition as Seen at the Ephraim Skerry House Lot, Salem, Massachusetts. Paper presented at the Council for Northeast Historical Archaeology, Newark, DE.

Isaac, R., 1982, *The Transformation of Virginia, 1740–1790*. University of North Carolina Press, Chapel Hill.

Jedry, C., n.d., Unpublished MS on file at the House of the Seven Gables Historic Site.

Madam Johnson, 1754, *Madam Johnson's Present: Or, the Best Instructions for Young Women, in Useful and Universal Knowledge, with a Summary of the Late Marriage Act, and Instructions How to Marry Persuant Thereto*. Printed for M. Cooper and C. Sympson, London.

Johnson, M., 1996, *An Archaeology of Capitalism*. Social Archaeology. Blackwell Publishers, Oxford [UK] and Cambridge, MA.

Johnson, M., 1993, *Housing Culture: Traditional Architecture in an English Landscape*. Smithsonian Institution Press, Washington, DC.

Klein, L. E., 1995, Property and Politeness in the Early Eighteenth-Century Whig Moralists. The Case of the Spectator. In *Early English Conceptions of Property*, edited by J. Brewer and S. Staves, pp. 221–233. Routledge, London and New York.

Klein, L. E., 1989, Liberty, Manners, and Politeness in Early Eighteenth-Century England. *The Historical Journal* 32(3):583–605.

Klein, T. H., 1991, Nineteenth-Century Ceramics and Models of Consumer Behavior. *Historical Archaeology* 25(2):77–91.

Knight, S. K., 1970, *The Journal of Madam Knight*. Reprint of the 1920 edition with introductory notes by George Parker Winship. Boston, Small, Maynard & Company.

Koehler, L., 1980, *A Search for Power: The "Weaker Sex" in Seventeenth-Century New England*. University of Illinois Press, Urbana, Chicago, and London.

Kowaleski-Wallace, B., 1994, Tea, Gender, and Domesticity in Eighteenth-Century England. In *Studies in Eighteenth-Century Culture* (vol. 23), edited by C. H. Hay and S. M. Conger, pp. 131–145. Colleagues Press, East Lansing, MI.

Marchioness of Lambert, 1794, Marchioness of Lambert's Advice to her Daughter. In *Angelica's Ladies Library*, By a Lady, J. Hamilton & Co., London.

Latini, B., 1869, Tesoretto. In *Italian Courtesy Books*, edited by W. M. Rossetti, pp. 8–13. London.

LeeDecker, C. H., 1991, Historical Dimensions of Consumer Research. *Historical Archaeology* 25(2):30–45.

Leone, M. P., 1988, The Georgian Order as the Order of Merchant Capitalism in Annapolis, Maryland. In *The Recovery of Meaning: Historical Archaeology in the Eastern United States*, edited by M. P. Leone and P. B. Potter, Jr., pp. 235–261. Smithsonian Institution Press, Washington, DC and London.

Leone, M., 1984, Interpreting Ideology in Historical Archaeology: Using the Rules of Perspective in the William Paca Garden in Annapolis, Maryland. In *Ideology, Power, and Prehistory*, edited by D. Miller and C. Tilley, pp. 25–35. Cambridge University Press, Cambridge.

Lieberman, D., 1995, Property, Commerce, and the Common Law: Attitudes to Legal Change in the Eighteenth Century. In *Early Modern Conceptions of Property*, edited by J. Brewer and S. Staves, pp. 144–160. Routledge, London, and New York.

Locke, J., 1989 [1693], *Some Thoughts Concerning Education* (Edited by J. W. Yolton and J. S. Yolton). Clarendon Press, Oxford.

Lynde, B., Sr. and Lynde, B., Jr., 1880, *Diaries of Benjamin Lynde and Benjamin Lynde, Jr.* Cambridge Riverside Press, Boston.

Main, J. T., 1965, *The Social Structure of Revolutionary America*. Princeton University Press, Princeton, NJ.

Mandeville, B., 1966, *The Fable of the Bees: or, Private Vices, Publick Benefits*. Third edition of the sixth edition (1732). Commentary by F. B. Kaye. 2 vols. Oxford University Press, London.

Martin, A. S., 1996, Frontier Boys and Country Cousins: The Context for Choice in Eighteenth-Century Consumerism. In *Historical Archaeology and the Study of American Culture*, edited by L. A. De Cunzo and B. L. Herman, pp. 71–102. Henry Francis du Pont Winterthur Museum, Inc., Winterthur, DE.

Martin, J., 1990, *Miss Manners' Guide for the Turn-of-the-Millennium*. Fireside, New York.

Mascarene, 1761–1764, *Mascarene Family Papers: John Mascarene Letterbooks* (MSS 132). Peabody Essex Museum, Salem, MA.

Mason, J. E., 1971, *Gentlefolk in the Making. Studies in the History of English Courtesy Literature and Related Topics from 1531 to 1774*. Octagon Books, New York.

Mather, I., 1953, *Testimony Against Profane Customs, Now Practiced by Some in New England (Namely Health Drinking, Dicing, Cards, Christmas-keeping, New Year's gifts, Cock-scaling, Saints' days, etc)*. Reprinted from the 1687 edition, University of Virginia Press, Charlottesville.

McCracken, G., 1990, *Culture and Consumption: New Approaches to the Symbolic Character of Consumer Goods and Activities*. Indiana University Press, Bloomington.

McGrath, P. (Ed.), 1955, *Merchants and Merchandise in Seventeenth-Century Bristol*. Bristol Record Society, Bristol.

McKendrick, N., 1986, "Gentleman and Players" Revisited: the Gentlemanly Ideal, the Business Ideal and the Professional Ideal in English Literary Culture. In *Business Life and Public Policy: Essays in Honour of D. C. Coleman*, edited by N. McKendrick and R. B. Outhwaite, pp. 98–136. Cambridge University Press, Cambridge.

McKendrick, N., J. Brewer, and J. H. Plumb, 1982, *The Birth of a Consumer Society: The Commercialization of Eighteenth-Century England*. Indiana University Press, Bloomington.

McVeagh, J., 1981, *Tradefull Merchants: The Portrayal of the Capitalist in Literature*. Routledge & Kegan Paul, London, Boston, and Henley.

Miller, D., 1987, *Material Culture and Mass Consumption*. Social Archaeology. Basil Blackwell, Oxford.

Mintz, S. W., 1994, The Changing Roles of Food in the Study of Consumption. In *Consump-*

tion and the World of Goods, edited by J. Brewer and R. Porter, pp. 261–273. Routledge, London and New York.

Mintz, S. W., 1986, *Sweetness and Power: The Place of Sugar in Modern History*. Penguin Books, New York.

Mitchell, I., 1984, The Development of Urban Retailing 1700–1815. In *The Transformation of English Provincial Towns 1600–1800*, edited by P. Clark, pp. 259–283. Hutchinson & Co., London.

Moran, G. P., E. F. Zimmer, and A. E. Yentsch, 1982, *Archaeological Investigations at the Narbonne House, Salem Maritime National Historic Site, Massachusetts*. Cultural Resource Management Study, No. 6, Division of Cultural Resources, North Atlantic Regional Office, Boston, MA.

Morgan, W. J., 1986, *Naval Documents of the American Revolution, 1777*, Vol. 9. Naval Historical Center, Washington, DC.

Moriarty, G. A., 1931, The Turners of New England and Barbados. *The Journal of the Barbados Museum and Historical Society*, pp. 7–14.

Moriarty, G. A., 1913, The Turners of Barbados. *The Essex Institute Historical Collections* 49(4):347–353.

Moriarty, G. A., 1912, The Turner Family of Salem. *Essex Institute Historical Collections* 48(3):263–275.

Morison, S. E., 1921, *The Maritime History of Massachusetts, 1783–1860*. Houghton Mifflin, Boston.

Mrozowski, S. A., L. C. Shaw, M. Holland, and J. M. Zisk, 1988, *Salem, Massachusetts: An Archaeological Survey of the City*. Prepared for the City of Salem, Massachusetts.

National Museums & Galleries on Merseyside, Maritime Archives & Library (NMGM in text), 1995, *The Earle Collection*. Listed by D. Littler, A. Glynn, and K. Garner. National Museums & Galleries on Merseyside, Maritime Archives & Library, Liverpool.

Nivelon, F., 1737, *Rudiments of Genteel Behavior: An Introduction to the Method of attaining a graceful Attitude, an agreeable Motion, an easy air, and a genteel Behavior*. London.

Norton, M. B., 1980, *Liberty's Daughters: The Revolutionary Experience of American Women, 1750–1800*. Little, Brown and Company, Boston and Toronto.

Norton, M. B., 1979b, Myth of the Golden Age. In *Women of America: A History*, edited by C. R. Berkin and M. B. Norton, pp. 37–47. Cornell, University Press, Ithaca and London.

Norton, M. B., 1979a, A Cherished Spirit of Independence: The Life of an Eighteenth-Century Boston Businesswoman. In *Women of America: A History*, edited by C. R. Berkin and M. B. Norton, pp. 48–67. Houghton Mifflin Company, Boston.

Norton, M. B. and C. R. Berkin, 1979, Introduction: Women and American History. In *Women of America: A History*, edited by C. R. Berkin and M. B. Norton, pp. 3–15. Houghton Mifflin Company, Boston.

Oliver, F. E., 1890, *The Diary of William Pynchon of Salem*. Houghton, Mifflin, Boston.

Paine, R., 1971, A Theory of Patronage and Brokerage. In *Patrons and Brokers in the East Arctic*, edited by R. Paine, pp. 8–21. Institute of Economic and Social Research, Memorial University, St. John's, Nfld.

Palmieri, M., 1869, The Vita Civile. In *Italian Courtesy Books*, edited by W. M. Rossetti, pp. 58–59. London.

Pandolfini, A., 1869, Il Governo della Famiglia (the Governing of the Family) (1425–30). In *Italian Courtesy Books*, edited by W. M. Rossetti, p. 57. London.

Patch, I. J., 1861, Abstracts from Wills, Inventories, Etc., on File in the Office of the Clerk or Courts, Salem, Massachusetts. *Essex Institute Historical Collections* 3(2):61–65.

Peacham, H., 1968 [1622], *The Compleat Gentleman*. The English Experience, Number 59, Da Capo Press. Amsterdam.

Lady Pennington, 1794, Lady Pennington's Advice to Her Daughter (Letter of an Unfortunate Lady to Her Daughter). In *Angelica's Ladies Library*, By a Lady, J. Hamilton & Co. London.

Perley, S., 1924, *The History of Salem, Massachusetts*, Vols. I–III, 1626–1716. Sidney Perley, Salem, MA.

Perley, S., 1903, Evidence Relative to the Authenticity of the "First Church" (so-called) in Salem. *Essex Institute Historical Collections* 39(3):229–293.

Phillips, J. D., 1969, *Salem in the Eighteenth Century*. Essex Institute, Salem, MA.

Phillips, J. D., 1933, *Salem in the Seventeenth Century*. Houghton Mifflin, Boston.

Pocock, J. G. A., 1985, *Virtue, Commerce, and History: Essays on Political Thought and History, Chiefly in the Eighteenth Century*. Ideas in Context. Cambridge University Press, Cambridge (UK).

Polite Company: PT Interviews Judith Martin, aka Miss Manners, 1998, In *Psychology Today* 31(March/April):26–29, 86.

Porter, R., 1994, Consumption: Disease of the Consumer Society? In *Consumption and the World of Goods*, edited by J. Brewer and R. Porter, pp. 58–81. Routledge, London and New York.

Porter, R., 1990, *English Society in the Eighteenth Century*. Revised 2nd ed. Penguin Social History of Britain. Penguin Books, London.

Prior, M., 1985, Women and the Urban Economy: Oxford 1500–1800. In *Women in English Society, 1500–1800*, edited by M. Prior, pp. 93–117. Methuen, London and New York.

Radway, J. A., 1984, *Reading the Romance: Women, Patriarchy, and Popular Literature*. University of North Carolina Press, Chapel Hill.

Rameau, P., 1744, *The Dancing Master: or, The Art of Dancing Explained*. Translated by J. Essex, printed and sold by him and J. Brotherton, London.

Raven, J., 1995, Defending Conduct and Property. The London Press and the Luxury Debate. In *Early English Conceptions of Property*, edited by J. Brewer and S. Staves, pp. 301–319. Routledge, London and New York.

Records and Files of the Quarterly Courts of Essex County, Massachusetts (RFQCEC in text), 1911–1975, 9 vols. Salem, MA.

Richardson, S., 1985a [1747–48], *Clarissa: Or the History of a Young Lady*. Penguin Classics, London.

Richardson, S., 1985b [1740], *Pamela*. Penguin Classics, London.

Roberts, M. M., 1996, Pleasures Engendered by Gender: Homosociality and the Club. In *Pleasure in the Eighteenth Century*, edited by R. Porter and M. M. Roberts, pp. 48–76. New York University Press, New York.

Rockman, D. D. and N. A. Rothschild, 1984, City Tavern, Country Tavern: An Analysis of Four Colonial Sites. *Historical Archaeology* 18(2):112–121.

Rolt, M., 1761, *A New Dictionary of Trade and Commerce*. 2nd ed., London.

Rossetti, W. M. (Ed.), 1869, *Italian Courtesy Books*. London.

Roth, R., 1988, Tea Drinking in Eighteenth-Century America: Its Etiquette and Equipage. In *Material Life in America, 1600–1860*, edited by R. B. St. George, pp. 439–462. Northeastern University Press, Boston.

Rutman, D. B., 1965, *Winthrop's Boston: A Portrait of a Puritan Town, 1630–1649*. W. W. Norton, New York.

Salmon, M., 1986, *Women and the Law of Property in Early America*. University of North Carolina Press, Chapel Hill.

Schivelbusch, W., 1993, *Tastes of Paradise: A Social History of Spices, Stimulants, and Intoxicants*. Translated by David Jacobson. Vintage Books, New York.

Schlesinger, A. M., 1968, *Learning How to Behave: A Historical Study of American Etiquette Books*. Cooper Square Publishers, Inc., New York.

Scott, E. M. (Ed.), 1994, *Those of Little Note: Gender, Race, and Class in Historical Archaeology*. University of Arizona Press, Tucson and London.

Seifert, D. J. (Ed.), 1991, Gender in Historical Archaeology. *Historical Archaeology* 25(4).

Sekora, J., 1977, *Luxury: The Concept in Western Thought, Eden to Smollet*. Johns Hopkins University Press, Baltimore and London.

Sewall, S., 1878, *Sewall Papers*, Vol. 1, *1674–1700*. 5th Series. Massachusetts Historical Commission, Boston.

Shackel, P. A., 1993, *Personal Discipline and Material Culture: An Archaeology of Annapolis, Maryland, 1695–1870*. University of Tennessee Press, Knoxville.

Shammas, C., 1994, Changes in English and Anglo-American Consumption from 1550–1800. In *Consumption and the World of Goods*, edited by J. Brewer and R. Porter, pp. 177–205. Routledge, London and New York.

Shammas, C., 1990, *The Pre-industrial Consumer in England and America*. Clarendon Press, Oxford.

Sharp, S., 1767, *Letters from Italy, Describing the Customs and Manners of that Country, In the Years 1765 and 1766*. 2nd ed. R. Cave, London.

Shields, D. S., 1997, *Civil Tongues & Polite Letters in British America*. University Press of North Carolina, Chapel Hill and London.

Shields, D. S., 1990, *Oracles of Empire: Poetry, Politics, and Commerce in British America, 1690–1750*. University of Chicago Press, Chicago and London.

Shipton, C. K., 1960, *Sibley's Harvard Graduates*. Massachusetts Historical Society, Boston.

Smith, W. D., 1992, Complications of the Commonplace: Tea, Sugar, and Imperialism. *Journal of Interdisciplinary History* 23(2):259–278.

Spencer-Wood, S. M. (Ed.), 1987, *Consumer Choice in Historical Archaeology*. Plenum Press, New York and London.

Staves, S., 1989, The Secrets of Genteel Identity in The Man of Mode: Comedy of Manners vs. The Courtesy Book. In *Studies in Eighteenth-Century Culture*, edited by L. E. Brown and P. Craddock, pp. 117–128. Vol. 19. Colleagues Press, East Lansing, MI.

Steele, R. and J. Addison, 1988, *Selections from* The Tatler *and* The Spectator, edited by A. Ross. Penguin Books, London.

Stone, L. and J. C. Stone, 1984, *An Open Elite? England 1540–1880*. Clarendon Press, Oxford.

Styles, J., 1994, Manufacturing, Consumption, and Design in Eighteenth-Century England. In *Consumption and the World of Goods*, edited by J. Brewer and R. Porter, pp. 527–554. Routledge, London and New York.

Sweeney, K. M., 1994, High-Style Vernacular: Lifestyles of the Colonial Elite. In *Of Consuming Interests: The Style of Life in the Eighteenth Century*, edited by C. Carson, R. Hoffman, and P. J. Albert, pp. 1–58. Perspectives on the American Revolution, R. Hoffman and P. J. Albert, general editors. University Press of Virginia, Charlottesville and London.

Swift, J., 1964, *Jonathan Swift's Directions to Servants* (With Drawings by Joseph Low). Pantheon Books, New York.

Thrupp, S. L., 1992, *The Merchant Class of Medieval London [1300–1500]*, With a New Introduction. University of Michigan Press, Ann Arbor.

Todd, B. J., 1985, The Remarrying Widow: A Stereotype Reconsidered. In *Women in English Society*, edited by M. Prior, pp. 54–92. Methuen, London and New York.

Turberville, A. S., 1926, *English Men and Manners in the Eighteenth Century*. Clarendon Press, Oxford.

Ulrich, L. T., 1987, Housewife and Gadder: Themes of Self-Sufficiency and Community in Eighteenth-Century New England. In *To Toil the Livelong Day: America's Women at Work, 1780–1980*, edited by C. Groneman and M. B. Norton, pp. 21–34. Cornell University Press, Ithaca and London.

Ulrich, L. T., 1982, *Good Wives: Image and Reality in the Lives of Women in Northern New England, 1650–1750*. Vintage Books, New York.

Veblen, T., 1994 [1899], *The Theory of the Leisure Class*. 3rd ed. Translated by R. Lekachman. Penguin Books, New York.

Vickery, A., 1994, Women and the World of Goods: A Lancashire Consumer and Her Possessions, 1751–81. In *Consumption and the World of Goods*, edited by J. Brewer and R. Porter, pp. 274–301. Routledge, London and New York.

Villamarin, J. A. and J. E. Villamarin, 1982, The Concept of Nobility in Colonial Santa Fe de Bogata. In *Essays in the Political, Economic, and Social History of Colonial Latin America*, edited by K. Spalding, pp. 125–153. Occasional Papers and Monographs, No. 3, University of Delaware, Latin American Studies Program, Newark.

Vogt, C. C., 1994, *A Toast to the Tavern: An Archaeological Study of a 17th and 18th Century Tavern in Charlestown, Massachusetts*. M.A. thesis, The College of William and Mary.

Wall, D. diZ., 1994, *The Archaeology of Gender: Separating the Spheres in Urban America*. Interdisciplinary Contributions to Archaeology. Plenum Press, New York and London.

Waters, E. S., 1876, The Dean Family in Salem. *Essex Institute Historical Collections* 13(4):263–317.

Weatherill, L., 1996, *Consumer Behaviour & Material Culture in Britain 1660–1760*. 2nd ed. (1988). Routledge, London and New York.

Weatherill, L., 1994, The Meaning of Consumer Behaviour in Late Seventeenth- and Early Eighteenth-Century England. In *Consumption and the World of Goods*, edited by J. Brewer and R. Porter, pp. 206–227. Routledge, London and New York.

Weatherill, L., 1986, A Possession of One's Own: Women and Consumer Behavior in England, 1660–1740. *Journal of British Studies* 25:131–156.

Wertenbaker, T. J., 1949, *The Golden Age of Colonial Culture*. 2nd ed. New York University Press, New York.

Wildeblood, J. and P. Brinson, 1965, *The Polite World: A Guide to Manners and Deportment from the Thirteenth to the Nineteenth Century*. Oxford University Press, London, New York, and Toronto.

Wills, J. E., Jr., 1994, European Consumption and Asian Production in the Seventeenth and Eighteenth Centuries. In *Consumption and the World of Goods*, edited by J. Brewer and R. Porter, pp. 133–147. Routledge, London and New York.

Wrightson, K., 1986, The Social Order of Early Modern England: Three Approaches. In *The World We Have Gained: Histories of Population and Social Structures (Essays Presented to Peter Laslett on his Seventieth Birthday)*, edited by L. Bonfield, R. M. Smith, and K. Wrightson, pp. 177–202. Basil Blackwell, Oxford.

Wurst, L. and R. McGuire, 1998, Immaculate Consumption: A Critique of the "Shop Till You Drop" School of Human Behavior. Paper presented at the Society for Historical Archaeology Annual Meeting, Atlanta, GA.

Wynne-Davies, M. (Ed.), 1990, *The Bloomsbury Guide to English Literature*. Prentice Hall General Reference, New York.

Yentsch, A., 1991, The Symbolic Divisions of Pottery: Sex-Related Attributes of English and Anglo-American Household Pots. In *The Archaeology of Inequality*, edited by R. H. McGuire and R. Paynter, pp. 192–230. Basil Blackwell, Oxford, UK and Cambridge, MA.

Index

References in *italics* refer to illustrative material.

DATE DUE

~~FEB 2 5 2002~~			
~~MAR 2006~~			
			Printed in USA

HIGHSMITH #45230